Uniforms in
Public Schools

A Decade of Research
and Debate

Edited by
David L. Brunsma

Rowman & Littlefield Education
Lanham, Maryland • Toronto • Oxford
2006

Published in the United States of America
by Rowman & Littlefield Education
A Division of Rowman & Littlefield Publishers, Inc.
A wholly owned subsidiary of The Rowman & Littlefield Publishing Group, Inc.
4501 Forbes Boulevard, Suite 200, Lanham, Maryland 20706
www.rowmaneducation.com

PO Box 317
Oxford
OX2 9RU, UK

British Library Cataloguing in Publication Information Available

Library of Congress Cataloging-in-Publication Data

    Uniforms in public schools : a decade of research and debate / [edited by]
David L. Brunsma.
      p. cm.
    Includes bibliographical references and index.
    ISBN 1-57886-306-6 (hardcover : alk. paper)—ISBN 1-57886-307-4 (pbk. :
alk. paper)
      1. Students—United States—Uniforms. 2. Dress codes—United States.
I. Brunsma, David L.
    LB3024.U55   2006
    371.51—dc22   2005017178

For Thomas,
my Jedi Knight in training,

and

Rachel,
my love

Contents

Tables and Figures

TABLES

FIGURES

Acknowledgments

Many dissertations and unpublished manuscripts have been produced in the years since Long Beach Unified School District launched the first district-wide mandatory school uniform policy in the United States. Since that time, I have collected most of these studies for my own research into school uniform policies in American public schools. I started the process of putting together this edited volume of just such work—in an effort to somewhat remedy the presumed "lack" of empirical research so often cited in the *published* literature—almost 2 years ago now. In an effort to secure a variety of pieces, from a variety of locales, with a variety of methodologies, with key variations in context, demographics, and educational circumstances, it was clear that there was more material available than I could possibly include in one volume. Moving from initial letters of inquiry to this final product you now hold in your hands involved many people who deserve acknowledgments and thanks.

First, I would like to give sincerest thanks to the contributors to this volume for their perseverance, patience, and goodwill. For many of them, the chapters they eventually produced for this volume represent work, or extensions of work, done in their dissertations during the pursuit of EdDs or PhDs—work that, for some, had not been on their radar for a while, but for whom coming back to that work has finally allowed the blood, sweat, and tears of dissertation writing to become fruitful in, hopefully, informing policy and future research in this area. I would also like to thank each author's respective mentors and advisors throughout the research process for providing them with guidance and encouraging them to study a phenomenon that has been growing, but that, until very recently, has not received adequate empirical investigation regarding its promises and pitfalls. So, thank you to the following wonderful individuals, for sharing a part of your lives with me on this project, and for adding your work to the body of literature on school uniform policies in public schools: Marilyn DeLong, Linda Abel Fosseen, Eloise Hughes, Yunhee Kim, Sharon S. Pate, Bart A. Reynolds, Viktoria Stamison, and Winston H. Tucker III. A special thanks to one of the above-mentioned contributors, Bart Reynolds, whose outstanding recent dissertation gave me further validation for the need to collect the contributions that appear in this book.

My sincerest thanks goes to the staff at Rowman & Littlefield Education for understanding the need for such a volume and providing me with endless forms of support through what might have seemed at times to be incessant e-mails regarding this project. Cindy Tursman is a brilliant gem of an editor. She has encouraged me for several years now regarding my work on public school uniforms in America; for that I am grateful—thanks, Cindy. Thomas Koerner, the vice president and editorial director of Rowman & Littlefield Education, has been extremely supportive, and I appreciate his e-mails and correspondences, which I consider to be over and above the "call" for him—thanks so much. Wanda Matthews, Rowman & Littlefield's marketing manager, has been there for me in so many more ways than marketing—thanks, Wanda. All at Rowman & Littlefield Education have been blissfully supportive, making this process a fulfilling one.

This project began during my years as an assistant professor at the University of Alabama in Huntsville. My support staff there were crucial in getting this off the ground: Suzanne Nevels with her endless charm and deep spiritual insights; Annie Harris, who has always known virtually everything there is to know about that institution; Elaine, Mary, and all the student assistants along the way. Also, conversations with UAH students and faculty colleagues helped as well. I currently hold a position at the University of Missouri, Columbia, where the support staff have been more than generous and helpful with their time: Stephanie Grimes, Manndi DeBoef, Debbie Friedrich, and Mary Oakes—thanks!!

Finally, none of our work continues without the love and support of family and friends. At the top of the *thank you*s I must place my wife, companion, partner, and best friend, Rachel, who has been there to hear it all, to listen to my groanings and elations, to challenge me and push me to explore the various contours in my work. I love you! Thomas, this book is for you—may you always be full of wonder! Henry and Karina, thanks for being such wonderful children. You all are the center of my universe and make life a joy to live.

Introduction: Evaluating Public School Uniforms—A Decade of Research

David L. Brunsma

Situating the Decade, Situating the Movement

In the fall of 1987, Cherry Hill Elementary School in Baltimore, Maryland, became the first school to receive significant publicity regarding its school uniform policy—whether others were tried, and whether they succeeded or failed, is not readily known. That was the eighties, and the eighties, contrary to popular opinion, was actually the seminal decade for the nascent idea of uniforming *public* school students—largely in reaction to specific incidents of violent and, in some cases, fatal peer competition over designer shoes, jackets, and other items of clothing. However, it was not until the nineties that the idea of implementing mandatory school uniform policies in America's public schools really took flight—the reasons this occurred are exceedingly varied and highly complex (see Brunsma, 2004).

One of key events fueling this flight was the implementation of the first—and now (in)famous—district-wide uniform policy in California's Long Beach Unified School District (LBUSD) in 1994. Even at that early point in the nineties, the public school uniform movement was embryonic. However, in just 10 years since LBUSD, the United States has moved from a handful of public schools using school uniforms as a policy intended to heal not only the original concerns over peer competition related to name-brand clothing, but indeed virtually all the ills ailing public schools to estimates approaching fully one quarter of our (predominantly elementary, predominantly poor, predominantly minority) public schools having and enforcing some form of standardized school uniform policy (Brunsma, 2004; National Center for Educational Statistics [NCES], 2004). The LBUSD case represents one important bookend of uniform evaluation to the "decade of research" covered in this collection—the other bookend has not yet emerged.

The story is quite well known by now. "Well known," but also quite misunderstood. The LBUSD "study" reported results that showed (albeit inconclusively) that the educational facets that one hopes will increase *increased*, while those behavioral and gang-related problems in schools that one desires to decrease *decreased* after uniform implementation. Since the publication of Sue Stanley's research (1996) on the impact of the LBUSD policy and the subsequent barrage of media attention drawn to the LBUSD "results," there appears to have been very little solid, rigorous, methodologically sound empirical research on various uniform policies across the country—or at least this has been the general consensus. This notion—of the lack of scholarly attention to uniform policies and their effectiveness—has led to the misguided impression among educators, administrators, journalists, parents, communities, and even scholars themselves that the LBUSD "study" (i.e., Stanley, 1996) is the only available research to guide communities, parents, educators, and their schools in their decisions to pursue or not to pursue uniform policies. Yet this study has been seriously criticized and is seriously flawed and methodologically vacuous regarding any statements as to the *effectiveness* of LBUSD's foray into uniform policies in the mid nineties (Black, 1998; Brunsma, 2002, 2004; Brunsma and Rockquemore, 1998; Portner, 1998; Posner, 1996; White, 2000; see also Stamison in this volume). Even Clinton, facing reelection in 1996, jumped on the results of the LBUSD study and provided further, presidential impetus to the idea that uniforming public school students is a good idea—because, well, just look at the results in LBUSD.

Despite the belief that LBUSD's "study" represents the only research available to those who desire research-based policy—this is *not* the case. So a bit of clarification is in order: it actually is *not* true that there has been virtually no good, solid empirical research conducted on uniform policies and their effectiveness—there has actually been quite a bit (see Brunsma, 2002, for a critical review of studies at that time and Brunsma, 2004, for an updated version). However, between 1994 and 2004, what *is* true is that the vast majority of this research has *never been published*.

Publication, as one saw in the misinterpreted case of the LBUSD results, is a key first step to the spread of ideas, the availability of research to critique and fuel more solid research, as well as the utility of research to those involved in decision making in our public schools. Much of the empirical research that *has* been conducted over the past 10 years remained largely in dissertation form—the majority of these studies conducted by students of educational administration pursuing their EdD degrees, in partial fulfillment of the requirements of these degrees. What happens is that the majority of these individuals (many whose work is quite outstanding and quite important for us who want to understand the school uniform movement in all its complexities) move quickly from receiving their EdDs into very demanding administrative and other educational positions where they, quite honestly, simply do not have the time or the incentives to publish their work. It is this state of affairs that I seek to remedy with the publication of this collection of studies.

THE PROCESS: COLLECTING THE RECORD
IN ORDER TO SET IT STRAIGHT

The ideas for this volume came during and very shortly after the publication of my critical literature review through Phi Delta Kappan International's From Inquiry to Practice series (Brunsma, 2002). In preparing to write that review, I dug deep into the databases, and while that provided some of what was needed to do a complete review, the results of those searches began to suggest that the common belief in the lack of empirical research on school uniform effectiveness was perhaps not as misguided as I had thought. Then I went deeper and looked at doctoral dissertations across the country (and internationally) to see if perhaps students were pursuing this project for their own doctoral theses—here was the gold mine!

Between 1994 and 2004, some 25 dissertations were produced that looked into the issue of school uniforms (e.g., Bollinger, 2002; Britt, 2001; Davidson-Williams, 1996; Dussel, 2001; Gonzales, 2000; Gregory, 1996; Hughes, 1996; Jones, C. D., 1997; Kim, 1998; Massare, 2004; McCarty, 1999; Murphy, 1997; Murray, 1996; Pate, 1998; Samuels, 2003; Silverio, 2000; Soltner, 1997; VanMater, 2003; Wilson, 1999); however, of these dissertations, to my knowledge, only *two* have been published in any form outside of the dissertation (see Kim, DeLong, and LaBat, 2001; Murray, 1997). This state of affairs warrants a different interpretation regarding seeing the LBUSD study as the "sole empirical source"—it is not.

After reviewing some of these fine dissertations (and some not so fine, with classic problems that have indeed plagued both educational research in general and school uniform research in particular) in the monograph for Phi Delta Kappan International, I decided to embark on *this* project. I contacted (or, in many cases, attempted to contact) the authors of these dissertations primarily throughout the United States. Over a series of months, I eventually had discussions with most of the prospective contributors to this volume and explained to them the project and how important it is for them to publish their results in a more accessible fashion than the dissertation form. Many declined due to the above-mentioned time constraints of their administrative or teaching positions in the K–12 system—declinations that I understood. However, several responded favorably, and we are the beneficiaries here, in this book, of their willingness to do so.

I asked them to contribute to this book, *Uniforms in Public Schools: A Decade of Research and Debate*, in order to offer more varied studies, from various locations, with varying approaches, to the general public, scholars, and educators alike and, in the end, to help remedy a situation where anecdotal papers, news articles, "policy reports," "studies" from clothing companies (i.e., Land's End, Dickies, etc.), and so on, ruled the literature (or I should say, the Internet), not because they represented good, solid research, but simply because they dominated. The authors had studied uniforms in various contexts (i.e., elementary and middle schools in southern New Jersey; a Birmingham, Alabama, or a Boston, Massachusetts, urban school district; Dade County and Polk County in Florida; etc.) and from various time periods of the school uniform movement in the United States. This was both exciting and overwhelming; some of the studies would be quite out of date—or would they?

To try to standardize the contributions I asked each of the authors to consider the following list of questions when revising and updating their dissertations to reflect the situations of the districts and individual schools several years (or more) after their original study. I include these questions for readers' interest, as they represent important questions for anyone interested in studying school uniform policies to consider:

Initial Phases of Policy Formation

- What issues were important for the district/school at the beginning of the discussion period when uniforms were being considered?
- Who were the key actors during these initial conversations?
- What were the key arguments utilized to support or oppose the possibility of adopting a uniform policy?
- Were there any key resistances to the discussion and debate around the uniform policy? If so, what form did they take? If not, why not?
- What, empirically, were the most pressing concerns, issues, etc., in the district/school at this time? For administrators? Teachers? Parents? Students?
- Were these issues also salient in the initial arguments for/against the implementation of the policy?

Moving Forward

- How were the different stakeholders gauged for their interest/support of the policy? Survey? Focus Groups? What were the results of these?
- Was there power sharing in the discussions or was one group primarily overrepresented among the decision makers?
- In the end, in your estimation, from your research on this district/ school, why (or for what group of reasons) was the school uniform policy implemented?
- What were the goals of the policy?
- Were there other reform efforts and policy implementations coinciding with the uniform policy? Were uniforms a solitary effort or part of a larger strategy? A strategy for improving/decreasing what?
- Was there a current dress code policy at the district/school during the time of implementation? Was it enforced?

Involvement and Research

- How did you become involved/interested in the study/evaluation of the uniform policy at the district/school?

- Did the district/school discuss evaluation efforts in regards to this policy? If so, how?
- Was there any resistance to your evaluation/study of the policy at the district/school?
- Fully discuss your methodology for evaluating the effectiveness of the policy at the district/school.
- Discuss the limitations of your methodology for evaluating the effectiveness of the policy at the district/school.
- Fully describe the social, cultural, linguistic, and economic characteristics of the school(s) you studied in your project. [Demographic profile of the school/district]
- What were the key questions motivating your research? Were these your questions? Their (district/school) questions? Both?

Results

- Present results clearly for practitioners, lay persons, community members, etc.
- Did the school(s)/district ever see and/or use your results?

Updates

- What is the current state of the district/school uniform policy?

So What? What Now? Implications

- Beyond the empirical results, what other implications did the policy have for the structure, climate, and operation of the district/school?
- In hindsight, what do you think could've/should've been done differently? In the implementation process? In the methods you used? In your interpretations?
- How, in your estimation, were the different stakeholders affected by this entire process of debating, implementing, and enforcing (and perhaps, repealing) this uniform policy?
- What are the key issues/debates at stake in the pursuit of school uniforms in public schools?

It is my hope that this process has provided a degree of standardization across these contributions and a cement that holds each individual study somewhat together. I think it has.

AN OVERVIEW OF THE BOOK

I have organized this book into three basic parts. The first focuses on the use of school uniforms in public elementary schools (where the practice has been the most prominent). The second focuses on uniform policy implementation and effectiveness in public middle schooling. The third and final part of this book looks at more critical and also comparative approaches to the study of uniforms. Without giving it all away, I do wish to briefly highlight the contributions of each of the chapters in this collection in order to orient the reader who may be looking for specific settings, questions, methodologies, and so on; however, it is my hope that you will indeed peruse all of the contributions, as they each, in their own right, have something to offer as well as something to teach about the actual *study* of uniform policies—methodologically, theoretically, and interpretively.

Part One: School Uniforms in Elementary Schools

The most current estimates of the prevalence of uniform policies in public elementary schools show that in 1998–1999 over 11.5% of all public elementary schools had a standardized uniform policy. By the next year, that had risen to over 15.5% (see Brunsma, 2004), and recent estimates from the 2001–2002 school year show rates of closer to 23% (NCES, 2004). It is clear that the uniform movement has focused predominantly on elementary school children in the public education system of the United States. Two chapters deal with the issues evident in uniform policy formation, implementation, and effectiveness in public elementary school.

In chapter 1, "The Influence of a Mandatory School Uniform Policy in a Rural and an Urban School District," Sharon S. Pate, currently at Illinois State University's Department of Family and Consumer Sciences, takes a descriptive look at the Miami-Dade County, Florida, school district uniform policy adopted in the 1996–1997 school year. Her interest is in describing student crime levels and referrals to juvenile authorities by comparing data before the policy with those after the policy. Like LBUSD, she finds changes over the time periods of study and discusses the need for further replication and more rigorous, in-depth analyses of uniform policies over longer periods of time.

I have also studied uniform policies in a rural elementary school in Pennsylvania. In chapter 2, I present those findings here for the first time. Looking at a whole host of indicators, my chapter discusses the perils and promises of studying uniform effectiveness in instances where one has only *one* school in the "treatment group." This chapter highlights the various concerns with these kinds of limited data, issues of data comparability, and critical reflections of the processes embedded in elementary schools that interrelate with the environmental change that a uniform policy introduces in the schooling experiences of these elementary school children.

Part Two: School Uniforms in Middle Schools

Since 1994, school uniform implementation has also increased in public middle and high schools across this country—though the increases have been much smaller than those for elementary schools. There are no solid estimates of the number of public middle school students who are now attending schools with mandatory uniform policies; however, good guesses would place these numbers at a little less than half the rate for elementary schools (see Brunsma, 2004). The issues involved in middle schooling are quite different from those for elementary schools. Three chapters are devoted to uncovering these differences and evaluating the impact of uniform policies in American public middle schools.

In chapter 3, Eloise Hughes, professor of education and director of field experience at Houston Baptist University, looks at the effects of uniforms on student attendance, discipline referrals, and classroom environment— all key components of advocates' claims of uniform effectiveness—in two middle schools from a large urban/suburban school district in Texas. This district implemented a mandatory uniform policy in the 1995–1996 school year. Using perceptions of teachers, students, and parents, Dr. Hughes takes the reader through a complicated maze of perceptions regarding the uniform policy. Distinguishing between *types* of uniform—a key contribution of her work here—she finds that attendance rates did not change as a result of the policy, but that discipline referrals *did* change, and that they declined differentially depending on the type of uniform utilized. This chapter also provides a rich overview of the literature, court cases, and theoretical underpinning as they relate to uniform usage in public schools.

Also focusing on expanding our conceptualizations of the term "school uniform," Linda Abel Fosseen makes a significant contribution to the literature in chapter 4, "School Uniforms in Middle Schools: Enhancing Identity and Security." Fosseen draws a very different, and theoretically important, conceptual map of the types of uniforms and the *functions* of differing uniform policies. Proposing a complex model of the effects of uniforms on student motivation, affect, and behavior, she tests the model by looking at data from sixth to eighth grade students in 10 economically disadvantaged middle schools in Houston and San Antonio, Texas. She finds that type of uniform is crucial to understanding and evaluating the impact of various policies falling under the fuzzy rubric of "school uniforms." Her findings are broad, and the contribution made in this chapter to the general literature on school uniform policies is clear.

Dr. Winston H. Tucker III takes us to Minnesota in his study of a St. Paul policy implemented between 1995 and 1997. His chapter, "Student Uniforms and School Climate: The Urban Middle School Teachers' Perception," in a unique way, takes us inside the process of moving from the idea of a uniform policy to its implementation and into evaluating perceptions regarding the success of the policy on educational outcomes. Using exploratory research methods, his results present quite a bit to be excited about as well as to be wary of in the process of moving from uniform ideas to uniform outcomes.

Section Three: School Uniforms: Critical and Comparative Processes

The third section of this collection presents two wonderful chapters that bring quite different perspectives to the discussion and debate about school uniforms. While uniforms in public schools may be fairly recent developments in the United States, they have existed in other countries and other societies for quite some time now—we must also look at the comparison of uniform policies in settings other than our own in order to better understand our own situation. In addition, the politics of school uniform policies in public schools are complicated and highly complex. Researchers would do well to attempt to understand the many layers of meanings and political meanderings surrounding the process of uniforming public school students. It is to these critical and comparative dimensions that we turn in this section.

In chapter 6, Yunhee Kim and Marilyn DeLong bring the social and cultural issues involved in adopting and using school uniforms to the fore in a very instructive case study of uniforms in Korea and the United States. Through historical and ideological comparisons between these two societies, as well as through surveying the perceptions of teachers, parents, and students across these societies, Kim and DeLong highlight how it is possible that the underlying values of the United States "may be in opposition to the idea of the school uniform."

Finally, in chapter 7, Viktoria Stamison brings us a long overdue, indepth, and critical look into the Long Beach Unified School District's (in)famous district-wide uniform policy adopted in 1994. This piece, "The Implementation and Impact of Mandatory School Uniforms in Long Beach, California," will, I think, forever change the way we look at what occurred in Long Beach and the aftermath of their bold and vanguard policies. In her own words, "One of the most important lessons learned from this project is that effective public policies must have a clear connection between means and ends." I am proud to bring this slew of fantastic pieces together for the first time in this much-needed volume.

Postscript

It was not until the tail end of putting this volume together that I heard about Bart A. Reynolds's dissertation, *An Analysis of the Evidence Produced by Quantitative Research on the Effects of School Uniforms on Student Discipline and Academic Achievement*, produced in 2004 at Brigham Young University. After reading this dissertation, a meta-analysis of a host of quantitative studies of school uniform policies, with a clear theoretical basis for determining their strengths and weaknesses and discussion concerning where research needed to be headed for us to truly understand and evaluate the effectiveness or failures of such policies, I was convinced that I had found the person to write the postscript for this volume. Dr. Reynolds summarizes the key issues in studying school uniforms, methodologically and interpretively, and provides a very useful synopsis and pressing-ahead in his postscript, "Looking Back, Looking Ahead—On the Future of Educational Research and Training."

CONCLUSION

Contrary to what one reads in the headlines and texts of the nation's most prominent newspapers, contrary to what one hears from the mouths of politicians and educational administrators, and contrary to what one sees on the evening news, there is absolutely nothing simplistic and straightforward about the current movement to uniform public school students in the United States. The debate over whether or not to uniform the students in our public schools (like public schooling itself) is highly controversial, undeniably complex, and, from the analyses and arguments presented in this book, unquestionably rooted deeply in correspondingly multifaceted social, political, legal, cultural, racial, material, and educational structures.

For almost 8 years now I have been studying and writing about the public school uniform movement in the United States. My research has looked, empirically, at the antecedents and effectiveness of school uniform policies on academic achievement and a whole host of other educational, behavioral, and sociopsychological outcomes. Having recently published a book, *The School Uniform Movement and What It Tells Us About American Education: A Symbolic Crusade* (2004, Scarecrow Press), wherein I give an overview of the existing empirical literature and discover that while there is a good deal of it, there is very little that has been published—most of it remains in dissertation and policy brief formats. This state of affairs is in need of a remedy. One aspect of that remedy is the edited volume of empirical studies of uniform policies across the country that you now have in your hands.

This book provides an antidote to the ungrounded, anecdotal components that define the contemporary conversation regarding policies of standardized dress in American K–12 districts and schools. These contributors draw upon years of educational teaching and administrative experience and research directed at objectively and empirically understanding the issue of school uniform policies at two focal levels of schooling: elementary and middle schools. This book is of the utmost importance for those who wish to be informed and insightful participants in the contemporary debate on school uniform policies.

Part 1

SCHOOL UNIFORMS IN ELEMENTARY SCHOOLS

The Influence of a Mandatory School Uniform Policy in a Rural and an Urban School District

Sharon S. Pate

Alarmed by a 1994 report revealing that 40% of Florida teenage males carried a weapon within the previous 30 days, communities began to demand that youth violence and poor discipline in the public school systems be alleviated (Florida Dept. of Juvenile Justice, 2004). Many parents and administrators theorized that mandated uniforms would re-establish school order and safety.

In the early discussions on mandated school uniforms, the key players for school reform included school board members, superintendents, principals, parents, and students. While the school administration presented "awareness sessions," there was no particular group with perceived power. This was truly a joint decision of the people. One of the major topics of discussion during these meetings was the curbing of gang-related clothing. Public school officials, parents, and teachers recognized that student achievement and deviant negative behaviors were affected by the daily peer pressure to dress in fashion or gang attire and tried to eliminate deviant behavior through the implementation of mandatory uniform policies. It was postulated by school administrators and parental supporters of school uniform policies that mandatory uniforms would improve social inequalities (Caruso, 1996). The supporters also believed that mandated uniforms would influence the behavior of those wearing the uniforms and the perception of safety within the school.

The Dade public schools sent surveys to the parents before making a decision on mandated school uniforms. In order to participate, for the urban district, a school needed the approval of at least one family above

50% to implement a mandatory uniform policy. After the parents voted in favor of the uniform, the urban district formed a Uniform Committee at the district level. This committee was directed by the School District Public Relations Department with input from the parents. The Dade County, Florida, mandatory uniform policy was presented to the school board by the Uniform Committee and was approved by the parents of each individual school.

While most parents saw the uniform as a positive change, some parents and students were concerned that a mandatory dress code interfered with their constitutional rights. The response to the constitutional rights argument was quite simply that the courts agreed that the right to a safe school outweighed the individual rights of students to decide what outfit they were wearing. Furthermore, the dress code did not inhibit clothing choice outside of the school environment.

The pressing concerns for the majority of students were related more to where they would purchase the uniform and how they would be disciplined for not conforming—not so much to their constitutional rights. Actually, some students were pleased with the school uniform, citing sociopsychological reason of being able to dress like their classmates without the expense of designer clothing. Though most schools initiated the school uniform as a way to reduce gang influence, there were three additional reasons cited for implementation: to establish a more businesslike atmosphere, reduce absenteeism, and increase academic performance. School administrators and parents who supported a school uniform policy believed that when uniforms were required, students lost their gang or high fashion identity markers and began to base their identity on their school performance.

REVIEW OF LITERATURE

Theorizing about the aspects of social learning, Bandura (1977) states that learning would be extremely difficult if people had to rely solely on the effects of their own actions to inform them about what to do in social learning situations. Empirical research establishes that a person will, upon entering a social context, assess others and assign positions and expectations about their behavior (Stone, 1962; Stryker, 1980). Bandura (1977) believes that aggression or deviant behavior is learned through a process called behavior modeling. He believes that individuals, especially children, learn aggressive responses either personally or through the media from observing others. He states that many individuals believe that aggression will produce reinforcements of additional aggressive group behaviors that are also demonstrated in school settings. Environmental experiences are a second influence on the social learning or violence in children. This is similar to earlier writings by Shaw and McKay in their theory of social disorganization (Shaw and McKay, 1942). They believe that when children are raised in communities where there is a lack of social organization, criminality is likely to occur. Criminality has been addressed in urban school districts by student dress code policies ranging from banning certain types of clothing to the establishment of a mandatory school uniform. In an effort to change both the impressions a person makes on others and resulting competition or criminal interaction patterns, many school districts have mandated a school uniform to improve the school environment.

School dress codes continue to be an essential issue in educational literature in the United States, where clothing, for students, is a part of their hidden curriculum and is thereby a dominant theme for acceptance and social ranking while at school. This peer competition often causes ridicule and rejection of less stylish or less expensive dress by peers. Administrators in districts that have a mandated clothing policy believe that wearing a uniform allows students to model a more positive behavior (Gullatt, 1999). Students, when dressed in the latest gang-related clothing, affect their peer interactions as well as adult perceptions, thus causing a disruption of school classrooms.

School administrators and parents who support school uniform policies believe when uniforms are worn, students lose their gang or high fashion identity and become less violent, thus improving the school environment (White and Beal, 1999). While most schools are initiating the school uniform as a way to reduce gang influence, some are focusing on the uniform as a method of reducing discipline problems. It is important to address gang behavior and related clothing because gang-related incidents are often reflected in the classroom (United States Dept. of Justice [USDOJ], 2000). These gangs begin as early as elementary school for students from neighborhoods where older students perform criminal activities and the younger ones emulate their behavior. Thus, mandatory school uniforms are expected to help students conform more closely to school mores and be accepted by their peers (NCES, 2004).

Students sometimes present themselves in dress where they expect to be reviewed negatively by their elders but positively by their peers, thus causing a societal clash in value systems. Subsequently, in mandatory school uniform dress code settings, students, when not labeled as deviants or nonconformists because of their gang-related clothing, may choose to become higher achievers (Loesch, 1995; Pickles, 2000).

The overwhelming desire to be popular is an ongoing concern for almost every child and intensifies peer pressure to conform (King, 1998). Some school districts have required uniforms when students, though not in gangs, search for identity by emulating gang symbols or styles in an effort to belong. School officials believe students dressed in oversized clothing might be more indicative of success in a local gang. These students are sometimes making more than a fashion statement, because this type of clothing may be used to disguise contraband (NCES, 2004). This style of clothing, popular among children today, arose from the clothing of inner-city gangs, who have worn baggy pants and oversized shirts that could hide weapons and drugs from law enforcement officials. With such clothing shown on television, more children are wearing similar baggy, oversized shirts and pants in the school setting. Such clothing can become a means of transporting weapons to school and thus directly or indirectly increase school violence. When the desire to emulate the clothing in music videos is added to easy access to handguns, the concern for school safety becomes especially essential. Gang-related clothing styles often lead to delinquent behavior since gang clothing statements are quickly absorbed into fashion, even though items that indicate a gang for one area may simply indicate a fashion statement for other areas of the country.

Most anecdotal studies of large metropolitan school districts that have implemented mandatory school uniforms appear to confirm that the schools have greater safety and less disruptive behavior (Adleman, 1996; Burke, 1993). School districts with sufficient reports of disruptive behavior have been granted the legal freedom by the Supreme Court to take the steps required to maintain an effective learning environment. These court cases continue to uphold previous cases stating that the mandatory school uniforms do not violate a student's right to freedom of speech (Dowling-Sendor, 2001).

PROCEDURE

This study compared the secondary data sets of urban elementary schools in the Miami-Dade County School District. This urban public school district was chosen for two reasons: (1) schools with the highest levels of violence tended to be located in urban areas; and (2) the district represented the only urban district in Florida with the mandated school uniform policy adopted for the 1996–1997 school year. The major research objective was to determine if the incidence of crime and violence and the number of referrals of elementary school students to juvenile authorities would decrease after the implementation of the mandatory uniform policy. The data on crimes and violence by students in the selected schools within the school district were compiled for this study. Only schools in the district with a mandatory school uniform policy implemented in 1996 and with data for crimes and violence were included. All data for this study were public domain information obtained through accessing the Miami-Dade County School District website and the Florida Information Resource Network on the World Wide Web. The study included data from 1 year before the implementation and 4 years after implementation. This allowed for study of the same school's discipline data before and after the mandatory dress code policy. These data were analyzed in two ways: (1) students' referrals to juvenile authorities and (2) the incidents of crime and violence in each school. Data used for the mean scores were nominal data on totals of crimes and violence and referrals to juvenile authorities for the students in the schools eligible to participate in this study.

The Miami-Dade County School District at the time of this study had a population in excess of 2,000,000 (United States Census Bureau [USCB], 2000). The Miami-Dade County School District was the fourth largest in the nation and had 300 schools, with over 340,000 students in grades K–12. There are 202 elementary schools in this district, with approximately 177,000 students in grades K–5. The sample for this study included 64 of the 202 elementary schools. Only data for the public schools in this district with the mandatory policy in place for the 1996–1997 school year and 2000–2001 were included in the paired t-test. This research investigated students' crimes and violence and referrals to juvenile authorities of an urban county-wide school district with a mandatory uniform policy in effect for the 1996–1997 school term. Comparison data for this research were on student crimes and violence/referrals to juvenile authorities, represented by the number of crimes committed in schools. This public domain information regarding crimes and violence was collected for the 1995–1996 school year, the 1996–1997 school year, and the 1999–2000 school year. Data consisted of nominal data on the selected areas of student crimes and violence. A paired t-test of pre-policy data included comparing data for the year 1995–1996 with data for the first year after school uniforms were required, and with data from the school year 1999–2000, 4 years later, to investigate the longitudinal effects.

RESULTS

Results within the school district supported a mandated uniform code. This was demonstrated by significant decreases in overall elementary student discipline infractions of crimes and violence. Analysis of the secondary data sets for all the schools where uniforms were required revealed that in the majority of schools, there was a 50% decease in incidences of crimes and violence, and thus fewer referrals to juvenile authorities for the first year after the policy school year, and this trend continued 4 years later. The incidents of crimes and violence and referrals to juvenile authorities had statistically significant ($p < .05$) improvements for the first year and 4 years later, as shown in Tables 1.1 and 1.2.

In Support of Uniforms

Uniforms, as a method of decreasing crimes and violence, are continuing to gain national attention and the support of state courts. School systems are charged to provide a safe and disciplined learning environment for students. When gang behavior, crimes, and violence are prevalent, it destroys the environment and is a distraction from student learning. Violence among students in public schools continues to be of concern to par-

Table 1.1   Paired Numbers of Referrals to Juvenile Authorities in an Urban School District With a Mandated Uniform Dress Code Policy

Comparisons	Mean scores
Prepolicy	1.28
1 year after policy	0.54*
Prepolicy	1.28
4 years after policy	0.39*

Note: N = 64 schools.   * Differences are significant at the .05 level.

ents, students, and administrators as a threat to the overall school well-being. While some parents continue to fight for their children's right to wear the clothing of their choice, there are many news reports of children who have been violently injured or even murdered for their designer clothes, sneakers, or professional sport-team paraphernalia (Suarez, 1997). In their response to increasing school violence, many believe adoption of mandatory school uniform policies will lead to increased school safety and reduce violence. This research indicated that a mandatory school uniform policy is one method of communicating appropriate social learning behavior to improve student behavior. The connection between gang-related clothing and violence in the schools allows administrators to present their case in court, with rulings in favor of schools, when the districts were able to demonstrate evidence of gang behaviors. The importance of a mandated school uniform indicates positive social learning interactions. A mandatory uniform dress code policy was perceived as an educational strategy to reduce juvenile delinquency and provide a structured environment.

Table 1.2   Paired Numbers of Crimes and Violence in an Urban School District With a Mandated Uniform Dress Code Policy

	Mean scores
Prepolicy	88.04
1 year after policy	62.64
2 years after policy	53.84
3 years after policy	48.31
4 years after policy	42.06

Note: N = 64 schools.   * Differences are significant at the .05 level.

In summation, this study adds to the research of mandatory school uni-form dress code policies based on the variables of referrals to juvenile authorities and incidents of crimes and violence. This strategy can im-prove a student's behavior and consequentially the group setting as a re-sult of the individual behavioral changes. Schools today, as well as in the future, will continue to have greater pressure for students to focus on more appropriate social learning behaviors. A mandatory school uniform policy can be one way of improving school systems as their social learning changes from focusing on juvenile delinquency as their peer identity, to focusing on socially acceptable behaviors. Based on the importance of social learning through observing and modeling, the individual messages conveyed by students with a mandatory school dress code can be applied to larger school groups in an effort to improve the school academic set-ting.

FUTURE RESEARCH AND RECOMMENDATIONS

The findings of this study reinforce the need for more research to better understand the importance of a mandatory school uniform policy and its influence on crimes and violence and referrals to juvenile authorities. Replication studies based on referrals to juvenile authorities for other states and school districts are suggested to determine whether they will have similar positive results. Future studies could include psychological profiles of students, student mobility rates, rural districts, additional urban districts, gang clothing, and teacher uniforms. Additional research could take into consideration the effect of uniform progression within a district (e.g., whether the positive aspects can be retained if uniforms are not con-tinued at the high school level).

While the data to support a cause and effect relationship between school uniforms and violence may be, in some cases, a mixed review, the results in school districts that have the policy support the claim that the classroom instructor can have an improved learning environment as a re-sult of spending less time on clothing-related discipline infractions. Lack of data supporting school uniforms does not mean that school uniforms do not work. This research study is one that can assist educators, families, and school officials as they study the effects of limited dress code policies and mandated uniform policies. Many schools in California, Texas, Virginia, Florida, Illinois, Michigan, Tennessee, Kentucky, Mississippi, and Louisiana have initiated a mandatory uniform policy. However, analysis of these schools at a more in-depth level can increase understanding of the obstacles and successes that are related to controlling violence through dress codes.

2

Studying Public Elementary School Uniform Policies With Small Samples: Promises and Perils From Rural Pennsylvania

David L. Brunsma

In the spring of 2001, I was asked to empirically investigate the effectiveness of a school uniform policy at an elementary school in the Mount Carmel Area School District (referred to as "MCASD" from this point forward) located in rural Mount Carmel, Pennsylvania. In a series of reports, I utilized every available option for empirical investigation at my disposal. I was able, through court orders and procedures of discovery in preparation for the imminent trial(s), to demand data from MCASD concerning Mount Carmel Elementary School's (referred to as "MCE" from this point forward) organizational structure, characteristics of their student body, demographic statistics from the surrounding community, test scores, attendance rates, and other relevant educational process and contextual data. The data I eventually received were quite appalling, full of holes, incomplete, and, in some cases, nonexistent when compared to the list of requests I had given MCASD. Nevertheless, through a combination of these data and data secured through my own efforts, I had a set of data that would allow me to begin to understand the impetuses behind MCASD's desire to implement a school uniform policy in the fall of 2000 and the implications of this decision on Mount Carmel education. This experience was also a unique delving into several issues that are key to improving our understanding of uniform policies and their effectiveness: (1) the methodological problems raised by analyzing small samples of schools; (2) the ever-important role of politics, culture, and context in data collection, policy formation, and implementation strategies; and (3) the mismatch between stated goals and consequences of school reform efforts that can be seen only through stringent analyses.

Due to the nature of the data that I received from MCASD, it was necessary to supplement these data with additional information garnered from the Pennsylvania Department of Education (referred to as "PDE" from this point forward) through various means of electronic communication: phone, fax, the Internet, and e-mail.[1] I am grateful to those at PDE, because the PDE data allowed me to compare MCE with other comparable schools in the state of Pennsylvania. These data proved to be crucial for several important reasons. First, having such data allowed me more methodological movement and widened the scope of possible analyses I could perform—given that I had only *one* school (a problem shared by many administrators who do indeed want to understand the impact their policies are having in given schools). Second, the PDE data introduced me to a phenomenon heretofore unknown to me as an educational researcher who is accustomed to working with large, nationally representative data sets collected by the Department of Education's National Center for Education Statistics, which has decades of experience with collecting extremely useful and comprehensive sets of educational data on United States schools. The phenomenon I am referring to here is the extremely regrettable and odious fact that, in certain educational contexts across this country, *school-provided data and state-collected data* (usually reported to the state by the school/district itself) *often do not match.* This finding and realization led me to be wary of the MCASD data I received, and to utilize primarily the PDE data since the variation across Pennsylvania schools should work itself out in the analyses; yet, all the while, I knew fully well that it was highly likely that, for whatever reason, the data reported by MCASD (and MCE) to PDE would be skewed—most likely in their favor. Furthermore, given the context of a recent uniform policy implementation, I was even more wary, since those involved in the administration of the school and the district were standing by their policy "no matter what the data said."[2]

This chapter presents an analysis of the impact of a school uniform policy implemented in Mount Carmel Elementary School in the 2000–2001 school year on a variety of variables of interest to parents, teachers, and educators. These variables include educational processes and outcomes such as student enrollment, teacher:student ratios, attendance rates, aggregate scores on standardized achievement tests (i.e., mathematics, reading, and writing), behavioral incidents, and more serious disciplinary violations (e.g., weapons violations). These analyses were conducted at the school level (versus the individual level) using requested data to be *fully* provided by the schools themselves, in particular, and the Mount Carmel Area School District in general. This chapter presents the results of my investigation into MCE's uniform policy and also more broadly discusses the perils, pitfalls, and potential promises associated with studying school uniform policies with very small samples.

The data I received during the process of discovery included both quantitative data on a variety of the outcomes and processes of importance as well as numerous varieties of qualitative data in the form of letters, reports, depositions, and so on. In this chapter I focus on the quantitative data provided and an assessment of the impact of the 2000–2001 MCE policy on the outcomes of interest. As mentioned above, I received a set of *incomplete* data from Kulpmont Elementary School and MCE (and MCE after Kulpmont merged with MCE for the 1997–1998 school year) from the 1989–1990 through the 1999–2000 school years. I have personally secured data all the way through the 2001–2002 school year from the Pennsylvania Department of Education (i.e., their *School Profiles*, available online). The most recently available data (2001–2002) provide the initial data needed to assess the impact of the uniform policy on a variety of outcomes and processes; yet, one would need an even longer period of time to really understand the impact.

Given the research findings and collection of evidence concerning the impact of uniform policies on educational processes (see Brunsma, 2002), which have yet to provide sufficient evidence to support the effectiveness of school uniform policies on the outcomes of interest to educators and parents (academic achievement, attendance rates, behavioral and disciplinary problems, school climate, and substance use), the data I have at the writing of this chapter do provide some empirical insight into the *relative location* of MCE in comparison to other similar schools on the very variables that cause concern. It is the concern over many of the variables analyzed within this chapter that many believe gives just cause for the implementation of a school uniform policy. The literature, however, *does*

not show evidence that such policies will aid in either reversing problematic trends or securing positive trends in schools.[3]

This chapter does several things. First, it thoroughly describes the data
provided by the schools, their problems, and their limitations, the supple-
mentation of the data with figures from PDE's website, and the quantitative methodologies appropriate for this kind of data, and discusses my
methodology for this chapter in lay terminology. Second, the quantitative
results are presented, interpreted, and discussed. Finally, I conclude and
discuss the findings and limitations as well as implications for other scholars and practitioners in our public schools who wish to evaluate their own
school (or district) uniform policy.

DATA

Requested Data From MCASD

Originally (in 2001), data was requested from MCASD in order to assess
the impact of school uniforms on a variety of outcomes. The original request stipulated a set of data from at least 2 years before the implementation of the policy (in the case of MCASD, and particularly MCE, this was
the 2000–2001 school year) and data for the current school year (2000–
2001). The data I requested were to be *school-level data*, since collecting
data at the student level is limited in that (1) one cannot obtain data from
previous school years, (2) the cost and time factors make such data collection impossible given the time line I was working with, and (3) many of
the variables of interest *are* measured at the school level and are themselves aggregate measures. I requested the following data: (1) school uniform policy (yes or no); (2) grade-level configuration (e.g., K–4, K–6,
etc.); (3) gender composition (percentage male and female); (4) racial
composition (percentage White, Black, Hispanic, etc.); (5) socioeconomic
status of school/student body (i.e., percentage receiving free and/or reduced lunch, any available socioeconomic status data by school, per-pupil
expenditure); (6) type of school (public, Catholic, private); (7) size of
school (enrollment); (8) student–teacher ratio; (9) attendance rate (expressed as a percentage); (10) suspension rates, disciplinary violation
rates, and weapons violations; (11) measures of substance use on campus;

(12) standardized test scores and/or other measures of academic achievement; and (13) PTA participation rates.

The data I received began with the 1989–1990 school year and continued through the 1999–2000 school year. There was understandably very little data from the 2000–2001 school year at that time. There was a significant and concerning mismatch between the data I requested and the data I received from MCASD. The compliance on the part of the schools with the request for data was poor indeed during the years 1989–1996. From 1996 to 2002 the data are more complete; however, they are not 100% complete. When I utilize the incomplete data set that was sent to me by MCASD and the various schools (though critical analyses are conducted only on MCE and Kulpmont), I refer to this data set as the "MCASD data." Having a seriously incomplete set of data made valid results difficult to achieve; however, there was a remedy.

The PDE Data Set

To increase data quality and ensure comparability, in the end, I was able to locate a more complete set of data myself through the Pennsylvania Department of Education's website. PDE's *School Profiles* series contains many (though not all) of the data I requested. However, PDE makes only the years 1996–2002 available to online viewers. Through PDE's *School Profile Archive* and their *Intermediate Unit Violence/Weapons Reports* I was able to produce a data set running from the years 1996–1997 through 2001–2002. When I use the complete data set from PDE (1996–2002), I call this the "PDE data." It is important to note that the data provided by the schools from their files and the data contained in the *School Profiles* and *Violence/Weapons Reports* often *do not match*. Therefore, wherever this occurred I substituted data obtained from PDE. This frustrating state of affairs does not bode well for the compilation of clean, reliable, and valid data in the study of Pennsylvania schools and, possibly, of other school-level data across the country. For most comparisons, the more complete PDE data set is utilized.

The PDE data set contains information on enrollment, grade structure, attendance rates, percentage of students considered low income, class size, number of teachers (therefore one can calculate the teacher:student ratio per school), and math, reading, and writing scores (and percentage in each quartile) (all from the *School Profiles*). The *Intermediate Unit Violence/Weapons Reports* provide data, by school, on the number of disciplinary incidents, the number of offenders, and the number of weapons violations.

Similar Schools

In the *Pennsylvania System of School Assessment Academic Standards Schools Report* series, PDE includes a list of "similar schools," which are identified through the following procedure:

> All schools with the same community type (rural, suburban, or urban as classified by a local school administrator) are grouped together. Then, within a given community type group, the schools with similar socioeconomic characteristics are identified (based on the percent low income figure obtained from PDE Form 4034). (Pennsylvania Dept. of Education, 2000, p. 4)

In order to provide data on schools that were comparable to MCE, I collected data for the 20 schools described as "similar" by PDE[4] from the *School Profiles* and the *Intermediate Unit Violence/Weapons Reports*. These are referred to as "similar schools" throughout this chapter. I also look at schools in the surrounding area for comparison. These "area schools," as they are referred to in this chapter, are Murray Elementary School, Shamokin Area Elementary School, Hartman Elementary Center, Ashland Area Elementary School, Ringtown Elementary School, and Frackville Elementary School. I use these two groups of elementary schools in this chapter to offer close comparison to MCE on the variables of interest: similar schools (to provide demographic comparisons) and area schools (to provide a closer approximation for regional and cultural comparisons—i.e., rural).

METHODOLOGY AND PROCEDURES

Due to the weakness of data collected from MCASD *and* coupled with the methodological difficulties associated with having only one focal school with a uniform policy, the analyses presented in this chapter use descriptive statistical methodologies to illuminate several relevant issues to this case. It is important to note that multivariate analyses (see Brunsma, 2004; Brunsma and Rockquemore, 1998) that allow for more statistical controls simply are not possible with the data furnished by MCASD and PDE's website—and not possible for many who wish to assess effectiveness. There are not enough cases for stringent and robust multivariate analyses (i.e., regression analyses); therefore, a different approach to data analysis was conducted. This revised approach, despite its limitations, does, I think, speak volumes about the past and current state of MCE as an institution of elementary education.

First, I present descriptive statistics using both data sets. Second, I summarize the data graphically using both the MCASD data and the PDE data to provide a longer period of time in order to gain a glimpse into the trends at work in MCE and similar schools. Third, I compare these trend lines to average trends in the similar and area schools in order to place MCE's circumstances and performance in perspective by calculating and graphically representing the variation that exists in schools similar to MCE. This gives us an important contextual perspective on past and present educational procedures at MCE. The similar schools and area schools provide controls for the environmental factors that are associated with academic achievement and school discipline.

RESULTS

This section presents the results of the data analyses. Readers are referred to figures. This section is organized into subsections that deal specifically with particular variables of interest.[5] Throughout the reporting of these results, readers should remember that MCE did not implement a school uniform policy until the fall of 2000—this becomes very important later when the results are discussed in toto.

Enrollment Patterns

Nationally, enrollment in elementary school has been increasing since the mid eighties (NCES, 1995); the trend is based on demographic changes and the increasing numbers of minority children and their enrollments in U.S. schools. Increasing the student body can have dramatic effects on the educational processes within schools—especially elementary schools where teacher:student ratios are of the utmost importance. In the case of MCASD, we see yet another factor that can drastically increase student enrollments: *the combining of two schools into one*. The merging of Kulpmont Elementary School (referred to as "Kulpmont" from this point forward) and MCE in the 1997–1998 school year obviously presented unique educational challenges to elementary education in MCASD.

Looking at Figure 2.1, one can see that before the merger of Kulpmont with MCE, MCE's enrollment ebbed and flowed between 1990–1991 and 1996–1997 (from a low of 474 in 1990–1991 to a high of 530 in 1995–1996), while Kulpmont outgrew its capacities seemingly by the 1994–1995 school year (from a low of 290 in 1990–1991 to hovering just below the 400 mark during the 4 school years before the merger in 1997–1998). Figure 2.1 shows the dramatic increases in enrollments after the merger. The enrollments for MCE between the 1997–1998 and 1999–2000 school years approached 1000 students—decreasing to below 900 in 2001–2002, though still well above the comparison schools. Similar schools (Figure 2.1) also witnessed overall increases in student enrollment (increasing

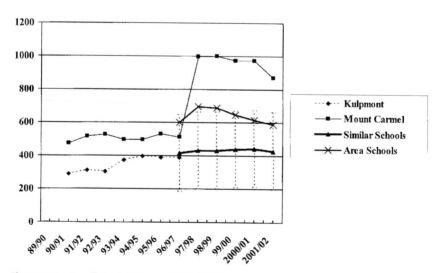

Figure 2.1   Enrollment Patterns 1989–2002

from averages of 417.18 in 1996–1997 to 437.67 by 1999–2000), imitative of national trends in elementary school enrollments. While Kulpmont and MCE were well within 1 standard deviation of elementary enrollments in 1996–1997, MCE, after the merger, was approximately 2.5 standard deviations above the mean for similar schools' average enrollments from 1997–1998 through the 1999–2000 school year!

Though quite significantly different from PDE's similar schools in terms of enrollment, MCE was not all that different from schools in the surrounding *area*. For the school years beginning in 1997–1998 and concluding where the available data ends (2001–2002), MCE remained within 1 standard deviation of area elementary schools in terms of student enrollment in elementary schools. It did have higher enrollments; yet these figures were not drastically higher than those for elementary schools in the surrounding area.

Student–Teacher Ratio and Class Size Patterns

The size of a school's enrollment as well as changes in that enrollment represent a key challenge to schools, a challenge that is rooted in the demographic structure as well as other district dynamics. These changes affect the structural logistics of teaching and educating. One central factor influenced by enrollment is the critical student–teacher ratio and the related size of classes within a school. These factors have been shown in the literature to affect achievement (McGiverin, Gilman, and Tillitski, 1989) and more social equality (Griffith, 1995; Lee, 1995). The merger of Kulpmont and MCE, and the subsequent increase in enrollments, could lead to student–teacher ratios and ensuing class sizes that are less than efficient for effective elementary education. The impact of such changes (particularly in elementary school) could be quite negative.

Early trends in student–teacher ratio and class size in Kulpmont and MCE (i.e., before 1996) are not available, given the data received from MCASD. The only pre-1996 data I have come from the 1990–1991 and 1991–1992 school years at both Kulpmont and MCE. For these two school years, MCE had a student–teacher ratio of 17.24 and 17.83 respectively (calculated by dividing the total enrollment by the number of teachers as given in data received from MCASD and/or the schools themselves), while Kulpmont witnessed a ratio of 16.11 and 18.90 for those

years.[6] It is difficult to assess whether these figures were low or high compared to other schools similar to these since the data are simply not available; however, given later trends, I think these were middling and within
range of similar and area schools.

The data that speak the strongest to the relative position of MCE with
regard to class size and student–teacher ratios come from the PDE data
set (1996–2002). Looking at Figure 2.2, one can see the general trend
over these years. With regard to student–teacher ratios, MCE witnessed
an expected increase during the year of the merger with Kulpmont (20.31
in 1997–1998) and then returned to a bit below its 1996–1997 levels
(18.96) in 1998–1999 (18.30). It went still below that in the following
year (17.22 in 1999–2000) and continued downward from there. This 6-
year trend fell well within the trend for schools similar to PDE, with MCE
falling above yet still well within 1 standard deviation of the similar
schools' average student–teacher ratios. When we compare MCE to area
schools within this same set of years, it is clear that MCE's ratios dipped
below those of elementary schools in the surrounding areas. These data
point to a remarkable feat for MCE and MCASD—maintaining acceptable ratios in the face of increasing enrollments.

It is well documented that class size is crucial to effective academics in

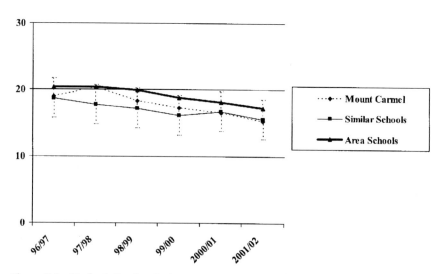

Figure 2.2   Student–Teacher Ratios 1996–2002

elementary schools as well as to classroom (and therefore school-wide) order (Barr and Dreeben, 1983; Boocock, 1980; Coleman et al., 1974). Teacher:student ratios, as an empirical measurement, however, mask one very important feature of schooling: class size. Though the two variables are correlated, the correlation is by no means perfect, and, therefore, it becomes important to look at the percentage of classrooms that fall within the acceptable class size range of 15–20 students. These data tell a *much* different story. While the MCE's student–teacher ratio looked quite stellar, students were not concentrated in classrooms with the optimum 20 students or fewer. Figure 2.3 depicts the fact that from 1996 through 2001,[7] the percentage of MCE's classes that had 20 or fewer students ranged from a low of 9.5 (in 1996–1997) to a high of almost 45 (in 2000–2001). These data fall below the averages for similar schools during these 5 academic years—approximately 1 standard deviation below for the first 3 years of the trend. In 1999–2000, however, MCE managed to increase the percentage of classes of 1–20 enormously, raising its position relative to the similar schools by 0.25 standard deviation—again, applaudable. In comparison to area schools, MCE fared much better, still falling about 0.5 standard deviation below the area schools' averages from 1996–1999, but coming in extremely close to the average in 1999–2000 (-0.03 standard

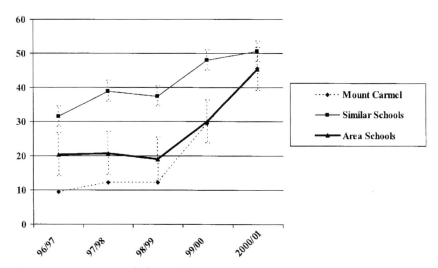

Figure 2.3   Percentage of Classes Size 1–20 1996–2001

deviation), and even closer the following year. Again, it appears that the merging of Kulpmont and MCE caused struggles in achieving acceptable class sizes; however, MCE had turned that around significantly by 1999–2000 and 2000–2001.

While it is not hypothesized that uniforms and policies of standardized dress affect the processes of enrollment and class size, it is these processes (rising enrollments and impending difficulties with managing large student bodies and classes) that could produce irrational fears about factors that *are* hypothesized to be remedied by uniform policies. Again, one must reiterate at this point that hypotheses or not, based on conjecture and anecdote or not, the impact of school uniform policies has not been empirically validated through the growing body of research on the impact of school uniform policies.

Patterns in Attendance Rates

Given the changes outlined above in enrollments and class size, which can fundamentally alter the climate of a school, assessing the attendance rates over time provides insight into whether any impact is observable. Many advocates for school uniform policies assume that a relationship exists between such policies and attendance rates. Though there is no empirical evidence to substantiate such claims, it is clear that waning attendance rates can provide the impetus for school administrators and district policy makers to consider adopting a uniform policy. Is there any evidence that MCE has experienced problematic drops in attendance over the last several years that warrants such a policy (even if based on faulty and evidence-less assumptions)? Did the change from a school with around 500 students to one with close to 1000 students alter the climate significantly enough to affect attendance? Are MCE's attendance trends much different from those for similar and area schools? It is to these questions that I now turn.

The pre-1996 data I received from MCASD are incomplete and seriously questionable, for these data are *district data*—that is, they combine Kulpmont and MCE and report the elementary attendance rate; however, some generalizations can be drawn from looking at the overall trend. In 1992–1993 the attendance rate appears to be approximately 94.69%; in

1993–1994, up somewhat to 95.96%; in 1995–1996, 96.30% (see Figure 2.4). From this point on I use PDE data for comparability to similar and area schools. Figure 2.5 depicts these data. MCE did witness a drop in attendance after the merger with Kulpmont, and this drop continued through the 1999–2000 school year. Similar schools recorded an average increase overall from 1996–2000, but after this their attendance rates began to decline through 2002. After 1999–2000, MCE's attendance rate began to climb ever so slightly to around 94.5% in 2001–2002. When we compare MCE to elementary school attendance rates of schools in the surrounding area, MCE falls within range of these averages and, in fact, area schools have, over the period of this trend line, also witnessed average declines in attendance until 2001–2002, when they climbed to the highest rate among the years documented in Figure 2.5. This is intriguing, because MCE's uniform policy, adopted the previous year, was followed by a mild climb in attendance, but nothing like the climb seen by the area schools (which did not have uniform policies). At any rate, statistically and substantively, MCE does not really stand out with regard to attendance rates. There certainly does not appear to be much cause for alarm.

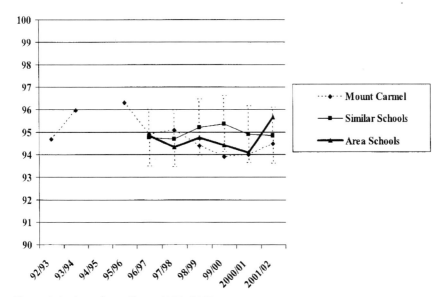

Figure 2.4   Attendance Rates 1992–2002

Chapter 2

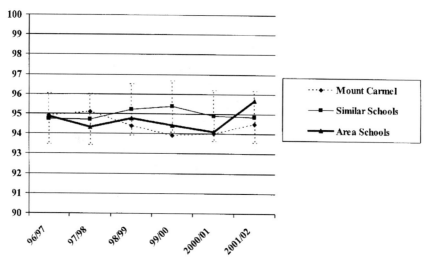

Figure 2.5   Attendance Rates 1996–2002

Patterns in Reading Achievement

Much of the anecdotal literature advocating school uniform policies pre-supposes that standardized dress will increase achievement rates. Again, there is absolutely no research, no theoretical schema, and no data that have provided evidence that would uphold such an assumption. However, it is clear that many administrators, educators, and board members are swayed by this assumption and have sought recourse in such policies when facing falling achievement rates. Since the three "R's" are tested via standardized means toward the end of elementary school, it is prudent to examine whether the achievement rate of elementary students in MCASD has declined or is in a state of concerning flux. Reading, mathematics, and writing are all tested toward the end of the elementary years in Pennsylvania (reading and mathematics in fifth grade, writing in sixth).[8]

The most complete set of data in my possession at the time of this writing is the PDE data set spanning 1996–2002. The data received from MCASD were complete for *only* 2 of the 12 academic years requested; therefore, those data are of little value for the purposes of this project. Thus, I will base my observations on data I collected from PDE's website via the *School Profiles*. These *Profiles* report raw scores as well as the

percentage of students scoring in the top, bottom, and two middle quart-
iles. For our purposes here it is informative to assess the relative place of
MCE compared to similar and area schools on the raw scores, those scoring in the *bottom quartile*, and those scoring in the *top quartile* for each
achievement test.

Figure 2.6 shows the reading scores using all the available data
(MCASD and PDE data). The data for Kulpmont before the merger are
sparse, and little can be derived from them; therefore, I focus on MCE.
One can see that MCE rose from a low of 1220 in 1994–1995 to a high
of 1390 in 1998–1999 and then back down to 1995–1996 levels by 2001–
2002—the year after the uniform policy. Comparing these scores to similar schools, MCE is above the average. The exact numerical results document (not shown here) the extent of this gap: 0.85 standard deviation
above in 1996–1997, 1.62 above in 1997–1998, 0.93 above the following
year, and 1.57 standard deviations above the reading averages of similar
schools in 1999–2000. This puts MCE in approximately the 95th percen-
tile among similar schools in 2 out of the 4 years for which I have adequate data! Also, looking at Figure 2.6 one can observe that MCE is also
consistently above area schools in reading achievement scores. However,
as of 2001–2002, MCE does not stand out any longer as an exemplary

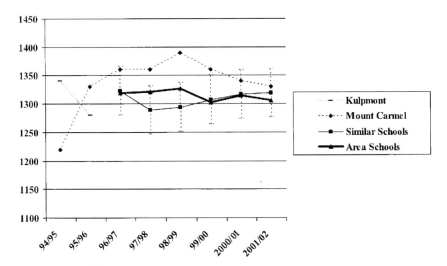

Figure 2.6   Reading Scores 1994–2002

reading/literacy program when compared to similar and area schools—it falls very close to their averages.

Another picture of the reading successes of MCE emerges when we look at the percentage of students achieving in the top reading quartile as well as the number of students failing to move out of the bottom reading quartile. Between 1994 and 1995, and 1998 and 1999, MCE has steadily increased the percentage of students who score in the top quartile in reading (Figure 2.7) with decreases in 1997–1998 (most likely partially caused by the influx of Kulpmont students in that year) as well as another decrease in 1999–2000 (though still more than 20 percentage points above the 1994–1995 levels *and* almost 10 percentage points above 1997–1998 levels). On the other hand, MCE has steadily decreased the percentage of students who fall into the bottom quartile in reading achievement (Figure 2.8). The percentage of MCE students scoring in the bottom reading quartile has increased to 16%; however, this increase is still below the average of similar *and* area schools—which is where a school wants to be when looking at the number of its students failing in any subject.

Looking at Figures 2.7 and 2.8 we see that when we compare MCE to similar schools and area schools, the increases in successful readers and decreases in students requiring more attention, described above, show that

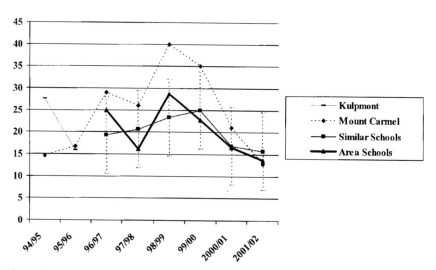

Figure 2.7   **Percentage in Top Reading Quartile 1994–2002**

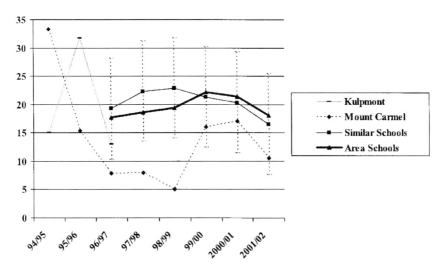

Figure 2.8   Percentage in Bottom Reading Quartile 1994–2002

MCE has done exceptionally well in maintaining reading levels in the face of the other structural changes described earlier in this chapter. From 1996–1997 to 1999–2000, MCE's percentage of top quartile readers has consistently been above the average for similar schools, moving from being 0.5 standard deviation above the mean in 1996–1997 to 1.57 standard deviations above the mean for similar schools in 1999–2000. A similar picture exists for comparisons to area schools. Except in 1997–1998, when MCE fell to almost exactly the mean (-0.01 standard deviation below the mean), MCE has had higher reading scores than area schools. Similarly, MCE has decreased the proportion of students falling into the bottom quartile, and though there was an upturn in this percentage in 1999–2000, MCE has had, even in 1999–2000, significantly lower proportions of students scoring in the bottom quartile in reading when compared to both similar and area schools.

However, after the implementation of the uniform policy in 2000–2001, MCE's reading performance has fallen to levels *below* all comparison schools (though still within range) and, more importantly, below its 1994–1995 levels almost a decade ago! MCE appears to still be quite successful in lowering the number of poor readers, but it is increasingly weak in producing very strong readers through its curriculum. It appears that

changes at MCE in the last 3 school years—including the uniform policy—have influenced its reading performance quite profoundly.

Patterns in Mathematics Achievement

The results documenting patterns in mathematics achievement rates mirror those described above for reading achievement scores, so I do not detail them to the extent that I do above. MCE's mathematics scores (see
Figures 2.9 through 2.11) have ebbed and flowed upward since the 1994–
1995 school year, with slight decreases in aggregate scores in both the
1997–1998 (a decrease of 20 points from the previous year, yet still well
above the average for similar schools) and the 1999–2000 (a 20-point decrease, but still higher [1.31 standard deviations above the mean] than
similar schools) school years. For the years 1996–1997 through 1999–
2000, MCE has consistently moved further away from the average math
scores of similar schools while remaining within range of (but still higher
than) area schools. After the implementation of the uniform policy, it is
clear that MCE's mathematics achievement has dropped significantly. It
has gone from being consistently above all other comparison schools to
actually holding a below-average position by 2001–2002.

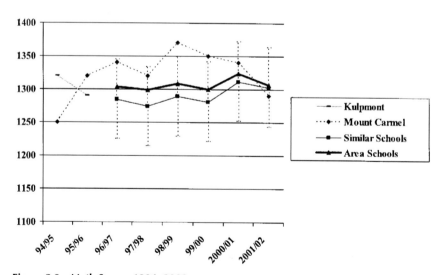

Figure 2.9   Math Scores 1994–2002

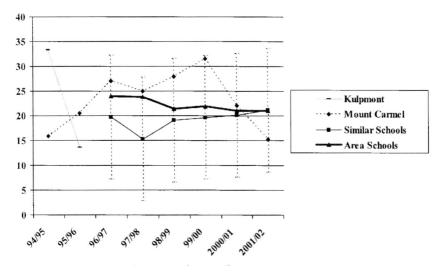

Figure 2.10   Percentage in Top Math Quartile 1994–2002

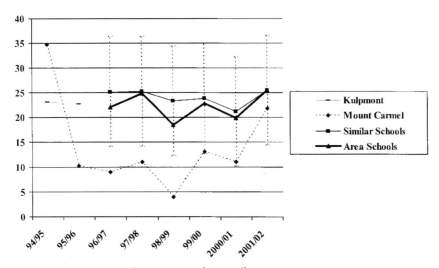

Figure 2.11   Percentage in Bottom Math Quartile 1994–2002

In addition to the raw scores for mathematics, MCE, as with reading, produced more top math students (top quartile) and fewer lower achieving math students (bottom quartile) from 1996 to 2000. However, this situation changed after the 1999–2000 school year when the number of high-scoring math students decreased dramatically and the number of low-achieving mathematics students increased. Whereas before 1999–2000, MCE looked absolutely stellar, after this particular school year, its effectiveness began to wane.

Patterns in Writing Achievement

The data on writing achievement were the most sparse of all the measures of academic achievement. No data were sent from MCASD that were not available through PDE; therefore, I have data from only four points in time: 1996–1997, 1997–1998, 1998–1999, and 2001–2002. Figure 2.12 graphically depicts the MCE trend in writing achievement and the average trend of similar schools. In 1996–1997, before the merger with Kulpmont, MCE's average writing score fell slightly above the average writing scores of the similar schools (0.06 standard deviation above). This fell the following year to 0.77 standard deviation below the average and rose

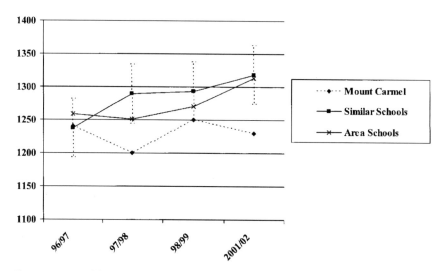

Figure 2.12   Writing Scores 1996–1999, 2001–2002

again to above 1996–1997 levels placing MCE's writing achievement that year at 0.25 standard deviation above the similar schools' average. The story is a bit different when MCE is compared to area elementary schools: MCE's 4-year trend is consistently below the writing average of area schools (ranging from -0.53 to -1.03 standard deviations below the area school averages in those years). It appears that MCE has had the most difficulty in maintaining comparable levels of writing achievement in line with their apparent success in the areas of reading and mathematics, and that the implementation of the uniform policy in 2000–2001 was a possible factor that affected these uncharacteristic downturns in trends for MCE.

From these achievement results, I can infer that, prior to 2000–2001, MCE provided a much better than average academic preparation in reading and mathematics when compared to similar and area schools. Before this time as well, its performance in writing mirrors trends among these comparison schools, and it does not stand significantly above or below the overall patterns of writing achievement among these schools. However, for all three measures of academic achievement at the school level, MCE, after 2000–2001, no longer mirrored the general trends of similar and area schools and began to take a turn for the worse in terms of academic achievement. Whether or not this is due to the implementation of the uniform policy is not certain. However, one thing is certain—environmental changes can and do affect the climate and performance of elementary school students; and that one of these environmental changes at MCE, the uniform policy, altered the terrain of educational processes at MCE is undeniable. However, the *extent* to which it did is uncertain, given this methodology (see Brunsma, 2004, for recent multivariate analyses of public elementary school data).

Substance Use

Reliable data simply are not available to make clear assessments of overall trends in substance use/abuse among elementary students attending MCE, Kulpmont, or any of the other similar and area schools; this is the case across the country (such data tend to be quite unreliable). The only figures I received from MCASD come from reports sponsored by MCASD and prepared by Rocky Mountain Behavioral Science Institute, Inc. (RMSBI).

These reports were entitled *Drug and Alcohol Use Among Mount Carmel Area School District Students* and covered the 1998–1999 and 1999–2000 school years (Rocky Mountain Behavioral Science Institute, Inc., 1999, 2000). The "Executive Summaries" I received documented substance usage among sixth and eighth grade students in MCASD utilizing The American Drug and Alcohol Survey. This researcher applauds MCASD for investigating the level of substance use in their schools; however, as the cover letter from RMBSI indicates, "At this point it is a bit difficult to tell how much of an increase is significant . . . ," reflecting my concerns about utilizing these data to make any generalizations. Substance use is an extremely complicated phenomenon; the complexity is far from re-flected in these brief summaries of reports on MCASD students.

Concern over drug use (particularly on school grounds) among students has emerged as a motive for school boards and administrators to consider standardized dress and uniform policies as possible remedies at most and prevention measures at least. However, there is no empirical evidence to date that has been able to isolate an effect of such policies on reducing substance use. Furthermore, I have been given no suitable data to con-clude whether or not MCASD elementary school students differ signifi-cantly from similar and area elementary school students and therefore can do no more with this issue at this point. Should more reliable and valid data become available, I would be glad to take a look at them—particularly if MCASD is able to obtain a series of longitudinal measures of substance use from 1996 to 2001. At this time these data are not avail-able, and the studies from RMBSI are not useful.

Disciplinary, Behavioral, and Weapons Violations Patterns

Perhaps the primary set of factors prompting individual schools and school districts to consider the implementation of school uniform policies encompasses behavioral problems and disciplinary infractions at the school. It is assumed by many that gang behavior, vandalism, victimiza-tion, student violence, weapons at school, and host of other behavioral/disciplinary infringements can be kept at bay or even decreased by stan-dardized dress such as uniforms. The studies that have looked at the link between uniform policies and these types of activities and actions have found no significant relationship (Brunsma and Rockquemore, 1998; Educational Testing Service, 2000). However, in the current post-Columbine climate, despite the research, schools and districts continue to hold out hope for uniform policies to channel behavior in institutionally acceptable ways and to curb more serious disciplinary violations at the school (e.g., weapons violations). Does MCE radically differ from similar and area schools in terms of discipline issues and weapons violations?

The data received from MCASD were weak indeed. Concerning MCE detentions and suspensions, I was given a hard copy of a word processor document that simply gives 4 school years (1997–1998 through 2000–2001)[9] and the respective number of detentions and suspensions for each year with no explanation or documentation describing the exact nature of these violations. These data are also limited in that I have no control group of schools collecting similar data to use for comparison to MCE. Using the *Annual Reports on School Violence* from PDE, I was able to collect more specific data on the number of incidents at each school as well as the number and type of weapons infractions occurring at MCE and similar and area schools. Aside from the raw numbers, I calculated measures that transform those raw numbers for incidents and weapons violations as a percentage of the student body. This method does allow for more direct comparison with similar and area schools on incidents and violations.

Looking at detentions and suspensions[10] at MCE from 1997 to 2001 (Figure 2.13), we see that the year of the merger with Kulpmont presented MCE with the highest number of detentions (338) for the time period for which I have data. This declined the following year and went back up to 1997–1998 levels in the 1999–2000 school year. Using my method of extrapolation (described in note 9) I projected that MCE was headed for a detention rate of about 301 for 2000–2001 (this is a projection). Concerning suspensions at MCE, the rate has remained quite stable over time (see Figure 2.13), hovering around 60 per year. The projected number of suspensions for 2000–2001 is 37; yet, this number is suspect (see "Conclusion" below). In the end, MCE *appears* to have brought detention and suspension rates down from 1997–1998 levels; however, these data are incomplete, and there is no way to measure whether the uniform policy made an impact on this. In fact, it is possible that *because* of the uniform policy, in the year 2000–2001 there may have been many *more* detentions and suspensions and relocations that are possibly not defined as detentions

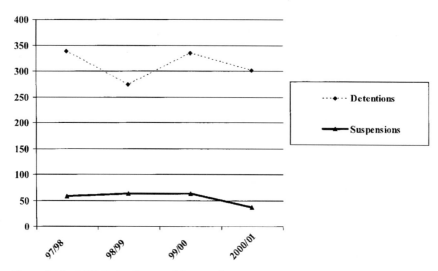

Figure 2.13   MCE Detentions and Suspensions 1997–2001

or suspensions (to Anthracite Behavioral or Behavioral Support or out of the school completely—more on these points below).

Most recently, I have been able to secure more recent data on suspensions, expulsions, and alternative educational assignments for MCE and the similar and area comparison schools. It is to these new data that I now turn. Figure 2.13 graphs the suspension and detention rates among our focal schools. What is first readily apparent is the *wide* discrepancy between the data I was given from MCASD and the data they reported to PDE. For instance, for 1999–2000, Figure 2.18 (using PDE data) reports suspensions at MCE to be at 17; yet, according to Figure 2.13, MCASD had documented almost 60 that same year! I am extremely wary of these data and, quite honestly, have no roadmap that would make me believe either set of data. Records of expulsions, detentions, suspensions, and so on, are extremely volatile and susceptible to terminological tampering, reassigning offenses, and social desirability to present that which looks best. Readers should take Figures 2.13 through 2.23 with quite a bit of skepticism. From my analyses of the data and my experiences with MCASD and PDE and the relationship between the two, it is my opinion that disciplinary infractions have decidedly increased since the implementation of the uniform policy—but have simply been covered up and/or reported as something else (or not reported at all)—more on this below (see Brunsma, 2004).

The *Annual Reports on School Violence* obtained from PDE give raw numbers of incidents "involving acts of violence as defined by the school entity and all *reported* cases involving possession of a weapon on school property" (Pennsylvania Dept. of Education, 1998, p. 1 [emphasis added]). In 1996–1997, MCE had one (1) such incident, and this incident appears to have also been a weapons violation. The weapon involved was a knife. No other information is given as to the nature of this violation— information about the student's intention, as well as interpretations of the violation by school officials may have ranged widely. The following year, 1997–1998, there were *no* incidents and *no* weapons violations. Data from 1998–1999 show 6 incidents of violence, *none* of which were weapon related. Finally, the school year of 1999–2000 saw an increase in the number of incidents (from 6 the previous year to 17), a decrease in 2000–2001, and an off-the-chart increase in 2001–2002. None of these incidents beyond 1996–1997 involved a weapon (according to reported data).

If we compare MCE's trend of incidents to that of similar and area schools from 1996 to 2000 (Figure 2.14), we observe a similar trend of increasing incidents on the school grounds for both similar schools and

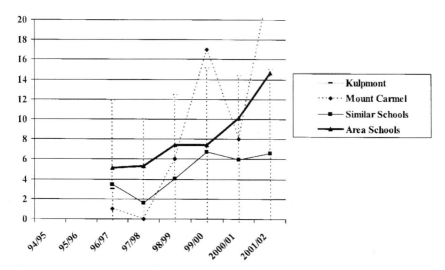

Figure 2.14   Number of Incidents 1994–2002

area schools. MCE's level of violence on the school grounds has not been significantly different from the other schools over these years. The exception to this statement is that in 1999–2000, 17 incidents placed MCE almost 1 (0.94) standard deviation above the average for similar schools and 1.44 standard deviations above the mean for area schools in the number of incidents.[11] Though above the mean on number of incidents, MCE is not exceedingly different from other schools like itself in this aspect. This is especially evident when we look at a more robust measure of incidents: incidents as a percentage of the student body (see Figure 2.15). We can see that MCE is not at all different from similar and area schools in terms of the percentage of its student body involved in violent acts. MCE is below the mean for all years except 1999–2000 and 2001–2002 where, in both instances, it is only 0.61 standard deviation above the mean for area schools. Though violence is concerning in any school at any level, MCE is not significantly different from similar and area schools.

Weapons violations are the most concerning element of disciplinary infractions and are obviously of great concern to educators, parents, teachers, and students. In the years for which I have data available,[12] MCE had one knife violation over this 6-year period. Looking at trends (Figures 2.16 and 2.17), this level of violation is not different from similar schools'

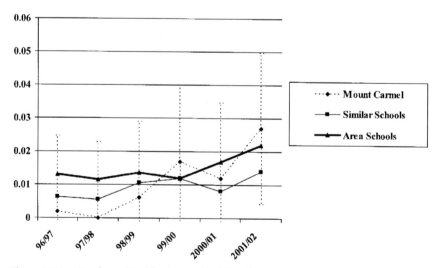

Figure 2.15   Number of Incidents as a % of Enrollment 1996–2002

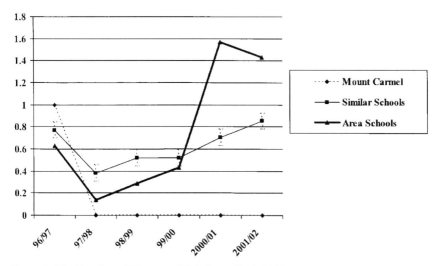

Figure 2.16   Number of Weapons Violations 1996–2002

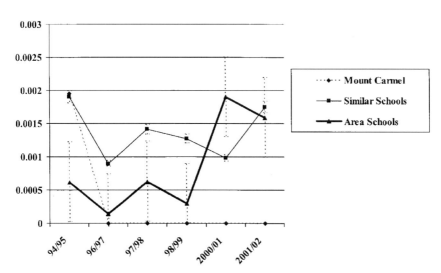

Figure 2.17   Number of Weapons Violations as a % of Enrollment 1994–1995,
1996–1999, 2000–2002

or area schools' levels of weapons violations. MCE's one violation in 1996–1997 placed it 0.21 standard deviation above the mean for similar schools—not a significant gap. Looking at weapons violations as a percentage of enrollment, MCE fares very well. Of course, one cannot say that one weapons violation should not concern a school simply because it is no different from other schools, since one violation can lead to loss of life; however, one does need to look at the trends objectively and, coupled with very little information about the violations themselves, understand that it appears that MCE is a safe place relative to other schools that are similar and other schools in the surrounding area.

One intriguing set of data I did receive is the log for the Mount Carmel Area Elementary School Student Support Room from the beginning of the 2000–2001 school year until December 5, 2000. This document keeps track of the individual students who are sent to this room for a variety of reasons: misbehavior, make-up tests, general behavioral problems, to finish various work assignments, disobedience, and so on. In looking through these logs, a primary reason that students were sent to the Support Room was for *not adhering to the dress code.* No information was given to me to determine whether the Support Room existed before the implementation of the uniform policy at MCE (I have anecdotal evidence that

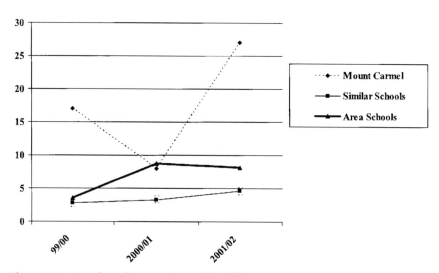

Figure 2.18   Number of Suspensions 1999–2002

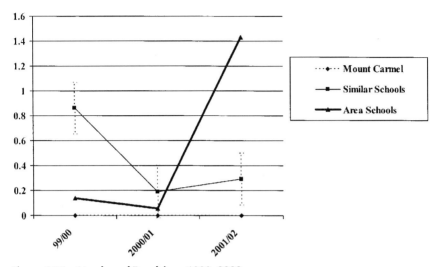

Figure 2.19 Number of Expulsions 1999–2002

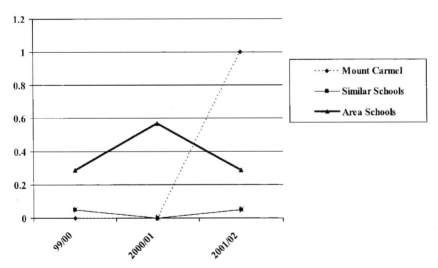

Figure 2.20 Alternative Education Assignments 1999–2002

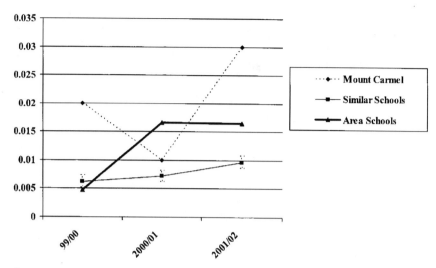

Figure 2.21   Suspensions as a % of Enrollment 1999–2002

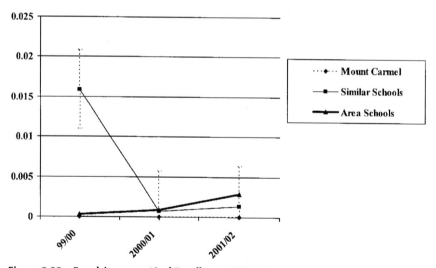

Figure 2.22   Expulsions as a % of Enrollment 1999–2002

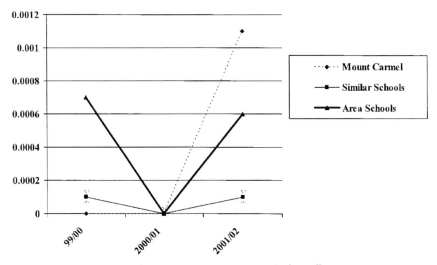

Figure 2.23   Alternative Education Assignments as a % of Enrollment 1999–2002

says it *is* new for 2000–2001); however, the presence of students in the Support Room who are there due to uniform policy infringements does seem to imply that the Support Room *is* something new *and* leads one to several concerns: (1) that the Support Room was a logistical necessity to house all the students who did not comply with the new policy, (2) which seems to indicate that teachers are having to deal with many more individual infractions than previously, and (3) that the policy is responsible for loading teachers with the added role of "fashion police" so often cited in the anecdotal research on the negative impact of uniform policies on teacher workload and disciplinary infractions, thus (4) possibly lending credibility, in this case, to the *creation* of more problems stemming from the uniform policy itself. It is also plausible that, in information sent to PDE, the reasons students must report to the Support Room are not defined in ways that would lead to increases in traditional detention, suspension, and other disciplinary measures, therefore masking the fact that there *are* more policy infractions than may be reflected in the post 2000–2001 data from PDE as well as the MCE data on detentions and suspensions. In fact, if one uses an extrapolation method similar to the one I used to determine number of detentions for 2000–2001, *and* adds the number of those going to the Support Room for uniform policy infringements (about 194 up to December 5), this alone puts the detention rate for 2000–2001 to around 700! This would indicate an unprecedented increase in detentions for MCE—one directly related to the implementation of a uniform policy and the Support Room.

CONCLUSION

This chapter documents the relative position of trends experienced by MCE over the years previous to the implementation of the uniform policy and 1 year subsequent to implementation of the policy. By all conventional measures of schooling processes and outcomes, before the 1999–2000 school year, Mount Carmel Elementary School comes out looking quite effective when compared to similar and area schools. Though its enrollment has undergone significant changes since 1997–1998 with the combining of two schools into one,[13] MCE has managed to (1) maintain acceptable teacher:student ratios (though class sizes are not as effective as they could be), (2) remain effective in educating students in reading and mathematics, (3) reduce the number of students in the bottom quartile on these standardized tests while increasing the number in the top quartile—not simply creating young "average" readers and mathematicians, (4) maintain average writing scores in comparison to similar and area schools, and (5) remain a comparably safe elementary school environment[14] in comparison to other schools.

However, since the 1999–2000 school year, by many indications, MCE is no longer providing the kind of education it once did, not long ago. Though I cannot say through any rigorous statistical analysis (for reasons discussed above) that the uniform policy implementation solely and significantly altered the terrain of education and interaction at MCE to the point of detriment to all involved, it is clear that a downward trend has been occurring for the last 2 school years at MCE in several areas—trends that *do not* mirror the trends of similar and area schools. This is a new state of affairs for MCE.

Some elements of concern raised by my analysis of the data can be identified as well. First, the nature of the data I received and the mismatch with the data that PDE publishes is troubling. In order to effectively assess a school's performance and then compare it to schools similar to itself in terms of socioeconomic level and other dimensions, schools must collect reliable and valid data on the variables of interest to researchers, educators, and parents. Without adequate data, we cannot know where we stand as a school. This is why I utilize PDE data primarily in this chapter, because it allows for more rigorous comparative research.

Second, the existence of the Support Room and the number of children visiting it each day is cause for concern. It is troubling from a research standpoint in that it propels me to question the data on detentions and suspensions. I projected those figures for 2000–2001 and have no information about whether or not MCE defines those visiting the Support Room differently from those falling under the label of "detained." Furthermore, if "detained" and "in the Support Room" are indeed different, one would want to know why they are different. It seems to me that they both are reflective of similar processes (noncompliance, disobedience, etc.) *and* they both change the climate of the school. In fact, the Support Room may alter the climate of the school to a greater extent than detentions and suspensions because of its visible nature.[15] It may be the case that the conclusions I reached above concerning the trend in detentions and suspensions are seriously flawed due to the presence of the Support Room *and* the Behavioral Institutes that house noncompliant students on any given day. Thus, MCE may have witnessed a large increase in the number of detentions and suspensions in 2000–2001 due *solely* to the uniform policy.

This chapter and the analyses of the type shown here direct us away from conjecture, emotion, anecdotes, and assumptions and toward an objective analysis of the extant facts and trends regarding elementary education at Mount Carmel Elementary School and its comparable counterparts across the state of Pennsylvania and in the surrounding areas. I hope readers will take seriously the strengths *and* weaknesses facing elementary education in MCASD and realize that the successes witnessed by MCE pre–uniform policy were ones that were internally and structurally fostered—*without a uniform policy*. Now we are witnessing a new era and a return to a decade before. MCE stands a good chance of regaining the quality of its elementary education if it stays focused on what processes and policies work for their particular set of social and structural conditions according to existing research, and it steers clear of processes and policies that are based on speculation and opinion that have not been shown to be effective.

NOTES

1. The staff at PDE was extremely knowledgeable and helpful—I am indebted to them for their assistance.

2. Herein lies another regrettable and odious fact: the role of scientific research in the policy process and/or as evidence in a court of law. Though space does not allow me to fully discuss these issues, suffice it to say that my experience regarding the issue of school uniform policies in our public schools has indeed been one of swimming against the tide of anecdote and hearsay. My goal as a social scientist studying this educational reform effort has always been simply to understand; however, results that emerge do not always match administrator, parental, or teacher "perceptions" and "assumptions"—my experience (in the courtroom, in the media, in discussions with community members and boards) has evidenced that if results go against the grain of assumption/anecdote, they are likely to be disregarded. In the end, then, our ability to have fruitful dialogue and, more importantly, to achieve understanding on complex policy issues in our public schools declines in such a climate (for more on these issues see Brunsma, 2004).

3. It should be clear that in order to assess the impact of a uniform policy, one needs more than simply one case (in this case MCE) to test statistical models comparing uniformed schools versus nonuniformed schools. One would need several Pennsylvania schools with similar social and economic characteristics that have uniforms and compare that group to another group of comparable schools that do not have uniform policies in order to use multivariate statistical modeling procedures appropriately. We do not have these data stipulations in this case. However, instead of multivariate modeling, I am able to look at the relative location of MCE in comparison to similar schools in the area.

4. These schools are A. L. Wilson Elementary School, Highland Elementary School, Elderton Elementary School, Sheshequin-Ulster Elementary School, Canton Area Elementary School, Chestnut Ridge Central Elementary School, Cranberry Elementary School, Carl G. Renn Elementary School, Forbes Road Elementary School, Forest City Regional Elementary School, Keystone Elementary School, Marion Center Area Elementary School, Montandon Elementary School, North Potter Children's School, Salisbury-Elk Lick Elementary School, Sullivan County Elementary School, Wharton School, Tidioute Elementary School, Williams Valley Elementary School, and H. W. Good Elementary School.

5. Readers would do well to look at the legend of each figure first before studying the figure. In general, I wanted to graphically represent the more statistical language of the findings. The bottom axis of each figure represents the school year, while the y-axis delineates the variable under scrutiny and its metric. The trends should be clear, and the dotted lines rising from each data point on the similar schools' line represent approximately 1 standard deviation away from the data point (which is the average for that year of the variable under analysis in the figure). Readers should look for the trend as well as MCE's relative position alongside the trend, *as well as* where MCE's data points fall *within* the dotted lines. If the MCE trend line is within range of the similar schools' trend line, this means MCE is not very different from the similar schools on that variable. It may be higher or lower—but not significantly so.

6. The large leap in teacher:student ratio for Kulpmont appears to indicate that Kulpmont was increasing in size and that the school was unable to match the increase with a parallel increase in full- and part-time teachers to maintain acceptable class sizes; however, it must be pointed out that maintaining ratios below 1:20 is good for elementary education. The closer a school gets to 20, the less efficient it can be in educating its children.

7. As of the writing of this chapter, PDE did *not* include information on class sizes in its usual *School Profile* series for, as far as I can tell, the first time since its inception. This is indeed curious, and unfortunate, given that we cannot see the changes subsequent to the implementation of the school uniform policy at MCE.

8. Due to the grade structure of similar schools and area schools (i.e., K–4, K–6, etc.) some of the writing achievement data are not available—and not relevant.

9. The 2000–2001 report documented the number of detentions and suspensions as of March 27, 2001. I extrapolated these figures to the end of the year using MCE's calendar from their website. The academic calendar runs from August 29 to June 12, and, according to the *Annual Attendance and Membership Reports*, there are 181 days in the school year, and by March 27, 2001, approximately 141 of those days had been completed; therefore, using this information I was able to project roughly how many detentions and suspensions there would be by the end of the 2000–2001 year.

10. The pattern of detentions and suspensions as a percentage of the enrollment for a given year shows the same pattern as the raw numbers, so I deal with the raw numbers here. Also, measuring detentions and suspensions as a percentage of enrollment can be misleading since an individual student could be detained or suspended more than once in a given year, thus creating a less valid measure.

11. I simply do not have enough information regarding these changes. The increase in violence at MCE could be due to the way the school *defines* violence as well as the degree of effort put into catching these events when they occur.

12. These years, 1996–2002, are actually quite important years, for these years represent the beginning of the debate on school uniforms in the United States and, therefore, the beginning of discussions at the local level about whether or not to implement a school uniform policy. Weapons violations cause great concern *and* represent the greatest impetus for schools to seriously discuss these policies. This is the case in the post-Columbine United States and is not due to documented evidence that uniforms have any impact on weapons infractions.

13. There were not many data for Kulpmont, and what data I did have were without comparisons to similar and area schools; however, Kulpmont, as a whole, was not as effective an elementary school as MCE. In fact, what little data I do have suggest that before the merger, Kulpmont students were headed toward achievement problems and certainly did not fare as well on most dimensions as MCE students. This points to an even more remarkable feat by MCE: incorporating Kulpmont's student body and still maintaining comparable levels of teacher:student ratios and attendance, higher than average achievement scores, *and* fewer weapons violations.

14. I originally asked MCASD for data that one could utilize to indicate the nature of the school climate, and I received little from them in this regard. By all indications used in this chapter, MCE appears to be a safe educational environment when compared to similar and area schools.

15. Also unavailable to me was more information concerning the decisions to send students to the two "schools" identified in the Lunch and Breakfast reports as Anthracite Behavioral or Behavioral Support, Inc. It seems that these are places that problem students go after a series of infractions. In line with this, it would be interesting to see the data on the change in the enrollments of these institutions over time, and specifically during 2000–2001, since the Support Room appears to be yet another creation flowing from the logistical problems stemming from the uniform policy. More information will illuminate these issues.

Part 2

SCHOOL UNIFORMS IN MIDDLE SCHOOLS

3

Effects of Mandated School Uniforms on Student Attendance, Discipline Referrals, and Classroom Environment

Eloise Hughes

In his State of the Union address on January 23, 1996, President Bill Clinton issued the following challenge to public schools across the nation:

> I challenge all our schools to teach character education: to teach good values and good citizenship. And if it means that teenagers will stop killing each other over designer jackets, then our public schools should be able to require the students to wear school uniforms. (Clinton, 1996a)

As a follow-up to the speech, President Clinton directed the U.S. Department of Education to issue a *Manual on School Uniforms*, which was mailed to each public school district in the nation. This manual contains a list of potential benefits of school uniforms, a user's guide to adopting a school uniform policy, and a description of state and local districts that had, as of 1996, initiated uniform policies in their schools. The document states that as a result of the many benefits and successes of school uniform policies, many local communities are deciding to adopt such policies in an attempt to create a safer and more disciplined environment (U.S. Dept. of Education, 1996).

President Clinton continued his "uniform" campaign in his travels to California in February, 1996, when he visited Long Beach, California, where uniforms are mandatory in the public schools (Mathis, 1996). In 1996, the district superintendent, Carl A. Cohn, asserted that they had ex-

51

perienced 36% fewer crime incidents district-wide in K–8 schools since the uniform policy was implemented (Cohn, 1996).

Not everyone agrees with the president's involvement in this issue, however. Walter Shapiro in an editorial in *USA Today* made the following comments regarding the State of the Union speech:

> So many of the issues that the president highlighted—such as education and crime, for example, are primarily the responsibility of local and state governments. It was brave for Clinton to come out for such New Democratic nostrums as school choice and charter schools, but exactly what is the most powerful political leader on Earth doing worrying about school uniforms? (Shapiro, 1996, p. 1).

BACKGROUND

The use of uniforms in schools has been common in private and parochial schools for many years; however, now even public schools are implementing policies mandating them as school officials search for the answers to several of the problems associated with today's schools. Reasons often given suggest that the use of uniforms offers a solution to some very common and often quite serious situations. Many educators maintain that stricter dress requirements set a tone that has been missing in some schools in recent years, one of respect and seriousness of purpose. Others, often with parent and student support, argue that students have grown so fashion conscious that they are distracted from their studies and that the popular clothing has become too expensive for most families (Majestic, 1991). The pressure placed on students by their peers to wear expensive designer clothing has escalated dramatically. Clothes have become the pre-eminent status symbol. To some students, expensive and designer clothing is more important than good grades, success in athletics, or other extracurricular activities (Majestic, 1991; Stevenson and Chunn, 1991).

In response to the growing demand for public school uniforms, the state of Texas has incorporated the following statement in its Education Code (1995):

> A school board may adopt rules that require students to wear school uniforms if the board determines that the requirement would improve the learn-

ing environment of the school; the board must designate a funding source for providing uniforms for students who are educationally disadvantaged.

PROBLEM STATEMENT

Although there is a debate among educators, students' rights advocates, and psychologists over the effects of uniforms on student behavior, few if any studies have examined this phenomena. Leslie (1989) reported that she knew of no studies that had analyzed dress as it relates to prevention of drug use, suicide, alcoholism, acting out, or other student behavior of concern. This new use of uniforms in public schools has led many people to wonder about the effect of uniforms on all kinds of student behavior. Most advocates and opponents of dress codes agree that it is still too early to measure the total effectiveness of mandated school uniforms. Within the next few years, however, educational researchers will have a far larger number of cases to study due to the increasing use of uniforms in public schools.

A survey in the Washington, DC, area indicated that respondents thought school climate, student attendance, and student achievement would improve due to the presence of uniforms; however, a review of individual school profiles for identified schools where students were wearing uniforms did not support those assumptions in most instances (Stevenson and Chunn, 1991). Even though parents surmised that the presence of uniforms would positively impact schools, past data did not support this claim. As a result, the report stated that, at best, the establishment of a uniform policy might serve as *one of the factors* that could lead to improved student attendance and achievement (Stevenson and Chunn, 1991).

More studies in this area are warranted due to the increased use of school uniforms in public schools. Policy makers in the U.S. Department of Education currently know of no other research studies in this area and encourage further investigation (Winters, 1996). It is generally agreed that the decision to use means such as mandated dress codes and school uniforms to control student behavior should be made based on and supported by sound research rather than widespread opinions, popular trends, or political expediency.

PURPOSE OF THE STUDY

The purpose of the present study was to examine the differences in the attendance and behavior of students in schools after mandatory school uniform policies were implemented. The study also examined the perceptions of teachers, parents, and students concerning the effects of wearing school uniforms.

The research questions addressed were these:

- Is there a significant change in student attendance after the implementation of mandatory school uniforms?
- Are there differences by type of school uniform (formal or mode of dress) in the attendance patterns of middle school students who attend schools where a mandatory school uniform policy is enforced?
- Is there a significant change in the number of discipline referrals after the implementation of mandatory school uniforms?
- Are there differences by type of school uniform (formal or mode of dress) in the number of discipline referrals among middle school students who attend schools where a mandatory school uniform policy is enforced?
- What is the attitude of students, teachers, and parents toward the wearing of school uniforms?
- Are there differences by type of school uniform (formal or mode of dress) in the perceptions of students, teachers, and parents toward the wearing of school uniforms?
- What perceptions exist among middle school teachers concerning the effects of wearing school uniforms on the classroom learning environment?
- Are there differences by type of school uniform (formal or mode of dress) in the perceptions among middle school teachers of the effects of wearing school uniforms on the classroom learning environment?

This project was a collaborative research study with the involved school district personnel to collect data that were needed to measure the effectiveness of the school uniform policies and to determine whether or not it should be adopted by all the schools in the district. Policies of wearing school uniforms in public schools should be given a closer examination.

Both private and public schools struggle with the problem of dress codes each year. Many opinions have been offered concerning the relationship between students' dress and their behavior. Not enough valid research, however, currently exists that establishes such a relationship. School officials can make more intelligent decisions regarding dress code policies by taking this issue into consideration. This study should make the decision-making process somewhat less complicated by examining the value of a uniform dress code for the purpose of modifying student attendance and behavior in schools.

DEFINITIONS OF TERMS

For the purposes of this study, the key terms are defined as follows:

- *School uniform dress code*: a school policy of limiting students' dress to garments to be purchased by parents based on school policies;
- *Formal school uniform policy*: the mandating of very specific items of clothing (usually to be purchased from one particular uniform supplier) to be worn by students to school;
- *Mode of dress*: a more casual form of school uniform that usually includes a limitation of colors and/or styles of shirts and pants or skirts that may be purchased from a vendor of the parents' choosing;
- *Classroom learning environment*: the environment within a classroom as described by the behaviors of the teachers and students within that class including classroom management;
- *Discipline referral form*: any form used by teachers to refer student discipline problems to the school principal or counselor when it is necessary or desirable to remove the student from the classroom or refer that student for disciplinary action.

REVIEW OF RELATED LITERATURE

This section provides a review of the literature currently available (as of the writing of my dissertation) concerning the use of school uniforms in public schools. The following categories are examined: (a) reasons given for and against the use of school uniforms, (b) types of school uniforms and variations in school uniform policies, (c) court cases regarding school uniforms, (d) reports from schools that have implemented uniform policies, and (e) studies concerning the effects of school uniform policies. A summary of the literature review concludes the chapter.

Reasons Given for and Against the Use of School Uniforms

The first reason given for school uniforms deals with alleviating the competition and expense associated with school clothing. Increasing competitiveness in the classroom as well as on school grounds, rejection, and ridicule of less stylish, less expensive dress by peers have generated a movement among parents, principals, and some school boards to initiate school uniform and/or dress code policies. Within many inner-city schools, parents are interested in uniform policies as a means of alleviating expensive clothes competition that has drained family budgets, lowered the self-esteem of students who could not afford the more expensive clothing, encouraged illicit activities, and removed attention from the real purpose of school (Stevenson and Chunn, 1991). It is also hoped that uniforms and dress code policies will help inner-city children learn how to dress and to have the demeanor needed to enter and stay in the job market (Stevenson and Chunn, 1991).

Traditionalists claim that standard uniforms have social as well as practical value. They ease the economic burden of buying expensive "fashion," and it can be argued that where there is so much competition (schools), there should not be competition in clothes (Baker, 1987; Cocks, 1988). The 1988 student dress code of Mumford High School in Detroit stated, "Many students feel humiliated, intimidated, or alienated if they do not possess appropriate accouterments" (Mumford, 1988, p. 19). Uniforms are perceived as a good idea because they keep students from worrying about designer clothes and the latest styles. The competitiveness of looking good is thus eliminated (McCain, 1988).

Leaders in public schools that have implemented school uniform policies have done so in the belief that there will be a variety of benefits for students. Some of the reasons given are the increase in the students' sense of membership in the school community, improvement in students' self-image, an improved focus on school work, a reduction in crime, improved discipline, and reduced costs for the family (Cohn, 1996; Virginia State Dept. of Education, 1992). This economic benefit of school uniforms has been one of the major reasons given by school officials who have implemented uniform policies. Some parents, who have a number of children in school, feel that the savings realized by buying the uniforms as compared to the cost of "regular" clothes will be considerable. Students, as well, often feel that uniforms are good because they are not as costly as a larger wardrobe, and they put everyone on an equal footing—no competition, no "sticking out" or being odd (Ascher, 1986).

Still another reason given for the use of school uniforms is safety. This pressure on some students to have what other students have has led to a rash of crime associated with wearing expensive clothing and jewelry in schools. In 1989, a high school student from suburban Baltimore was shot and wounded in a fight over a $95.00 pair of sunglasses. As a result of such incidents, educators in Los Angeles and Detroit stated that they were restricting what students could wear in order to keep the crime out of the schools (Leslie, 1989). They felt that stricter dress codes helped produce a safer academic environment. In addition to the problems of theft, gangs have introduced an even greater threat into public schools. Because gang affiliation is often denoted by certain types/colors of clothing, some school officials argue that by restricting gang attire, they can help curb the incidents of violence.

Advocates of uniforms to control behavior state that "It is well known that many well-disciplined students in private and parochial schools do wear uniforms, and apparently many school officials all over the country believe that requiring students to wear uniforms does enforce discipline" (Roberts, 1989, p. 53). Some school officials claim that they are better advised to concentrate their explanations on observable behavior rather than inner processes. They state that when it is desirable to teach behavior or to train people in skills, appropriate models that exhibit the behavior may greatly reduce trial and error (Blackham and Silberman, 1980).

Another reason cited for the use of school uniforms is that some educators and psychologists feel that self-esteem is enhanced by uniforms. The officials in the growing number of large public schools that have initiated the use of school uniforms say they did so in order to alleviate peer appearance pressure (Dress, Right Dress, 1987). The president of the National Association of School Psychologists states, "Some people may find it odd that students rail at the idea of uniforms. When given the chance to choose their own clothes, the last thing they want is to look different" (Kelly, 1996, p. 1).

Other reasons cited for the use of uniforms in public schools include the opinions of some principals that a uniform policy might impact positively on students' school attendance (Stevenson and Chunn, 1991). Still others note that uniform dress would eliminate some of the inequality in public school education in that students who dress "poorly" may be perceived as being less able to perform the student role and consequently respond to the teachers' expectations and perceptions. Implementation of a school uniform policy could ameliorate some of the detrimental consequences of "tracking" and teacher expectations for learning since all of the students would be dressed alike (Virginia State Dept. of Education, 1992).

In reaction to the strict dress codes now being enforced, advocates for students' rights in schools have voiced strong opinions against the uniform dress codes used in some schools. These students' rights advocates assert that dress codes generally have more to do with the personal preferences of a school administrator than with education. *Personal Appearance. The Rights of Students Handbook* of the American Civil Liberties Union states, for example, that a reasonable dress rule is as follows: "Students have the right to determine their own dress, except where such dress is clearly dangerous, or so inappropriate as to interfere with the learning and teaching process" (ACLU, 1988, p. 38). Behavior problems themselves should be addressed, according to these groups, instead of the banning of certain types of clothing. The ACLU contends that by mandating uniforms, we are treating the symptoms—we are making a "costume" change, not creating a cure-all—and that many poor families cannot afford the required uniform (Portner, 1996). Kohn (1996) agrees that uniforms seem to be a way of circumventing, rather than solving, a problem, and he claims that coercion is never the best solution to problem student behavior.

Reflecting on the movement to stricter dress codes, a spokeswoman for the American Civil Liberties Union observed, "It's really a desperate reaction on the part of school officials frustrated with the lack of solutions to their problems" (Majestic, 1991, p. 5). To some, however, these solutions may seem overbearing. There is a risk that unnecessarily strict dress codes or uniform policies will engender cynicism and controversy and divert energies away from education. Some teachers predict that even in schools where uniforms are mandatory, there will be dissenters who may tie a tie differently or use some other slight difference in dress to rebel against the policy (Crader, 1988).

The basic argument made by students' rights advocates is that students should have freedom of expression when it comes to dress. This idea is also supported by psychologists who are alarmed at the growing attempt by schools to "uniform" their students (Baker, 1987). They argue that regulations like these for dress "douse" the simple joy of dressing, not for success or status, but just as self-expression (Cocks, 1988). Still other psychologists cite students' need to have some leeway. One Washington clinical psychologist claims that teenagers are at a stage where they are trying to separate individually and become independent and that they need to be able to make some decisions (Leslie, 1989). Ronald Crader, a teacher of seventh grade language arts in Madison, Illinois, stated, "It seems ironic that a country that has thrived because of individual differences would use its largest and most important forum, the public schools, to stifle creativity, imagination and individuality" (Crader, 1988, p. 4).

Clothing experts agree with the dissenters against school uniforms. They state that each person needs to bring out his or her own uniqueness, enhance individual strengths, and express specialness through physical appearance (Sass, 1988). By being able to emphasize positive aspects of oneself through dress, confidence in abilities and judgment can be inspired. The opinion of others is important, and each person wants people to see only his or her best side. This feeling is especially important to teenagers, whose insecurities can lead to behavior problems and poor learning habits (Cho and Grover, 1978).

Some psychologists argue that such strict rules are too superficial to affect troublesome behavior, and in some cases may even stimulate youthful rebellion (Leslie, 1989). In addition, some educators claim that the policy of uniforms to control behavior is just another militaristic, punitive way of making kids behave, used by teachers who have not come up with workable solutions for disciplinary or learning problems on their own (Baker, 1987). Gathercoal (1993) argues that school administrators should concentrate on maintaining a safe school environment instead of restricting items of clothing.

Roberts (1989) says that while uniformed children are often perceived to be more organized and respectful of authority, this is not really true. Roberts continues to assert that if any behavior improvements do occur, they will have nothing to do with the uniforms themselves, but the phenomena would be due rather to the Hawthorne effect, giving the children and staff a much needed sense of pride and self-awareness, making them try harder to succeed. "The reason will have nothing to do with uniforms, any more than anyone really believes that uniforms are the reason for good behavior in a successful parochial school" (Roberts, 1989, p. 55). These psychologists contend that students must be free to live in the real world, not an artificial school structure. Individuals can be considered truly disciplined only when they can regulate their own actions. Therefore, it does little good to forcibly stifle some activity of an individual when the consequence is, simply, immediate control (Walsh and Cowles, 1982).

In addition, some specific problems about uniform policies have been identified by groups concerned with the rights of minority groups, including disabled persons. When a school system considers the different effects of a school uniform policy on students, it must address cultural and religious factors as well as developmental stages of the various age groups (Virginia State Dept. of Education, 1992). Schools implementing such policies must be aware of the restrictions placed on some physically challenged students to wear certain kinds of uniforms (Camp, 1993). Also, in the opinion of some, African American youth in urban schools where uniforms have been adopted may experience difficulties because of a cultural heritage favoring bold designs and bright colors (LaPoint, 1992).

Types of School Uniforms and Variations in School Uniform Policies

Typically, school uniforms have been simple in style and color to make them economical, and they may not be of the type that must be purchased from a uniform company. For example, navy blue trousers and skirts, white shirts and blouses, and black shoes provide an economical "uniform" (Virginia State Dept. of Education, 1992). School leaders who select these more casual uniform policies may refer to the uniform as a "mode of dress" rather than using the term *uniform.* Other schools have opted to use a more formal approach involving very specific items of clothing that must be purchased from a uniform company.

Options in uniform policy include voluntary compliance and mandatory compliance. Mandatory compliance policies may or may not include an "opt-out" provision whereby parents can choose to exclude their children from participation in the uniform policy (U.S. Dept. of Education, 1996). Proponents of the various programs cite the specific needs of their school or district as the reasoning behind the policy choice.

Court Cases Regarding School Uniforms

Although students' rights advocates argue that the way one looks and dresses is a fundamental form of personal expression and should, therefore, be protected by the Constitution, not all courts have agreed that students are free to dress and groom themselves as they please. Courts have intervened to consider whether the constitutional guarantees of privacy and free speech apply to school dress codes. They have divided roughly evenly on the question. The 5th, 6th, 9th, 10th, and 11th federal circuit courts generally have upheld the authority of school officials to impose reasonable grooming requirements; the 1st, 4th, 7th, and 8th circuits have held to the contrary that grooming regulations were unconstitutional (Majestic, 1991). Even where courts have struck down arbitrary rules, the judges have balanced the rights of the student against the need of the school to make reasonable health and safety regulations (ACLU, 1988; Leslie, 1989). One other court has recently upheld school dress regulations that required students to "dress in conformity with the accepted standards of the community." It held that the school regulations were reasonably related to the valid educational purposes of teaching community values and maintaining school discipline (Majestic, 1991). Courts have determined that students' choice of dress as a means of personal expression can be regulated by school officials (Jahn, 1992). In 1995, the Supreme Court refused to hear a case where a lower court had ruled that a school had the right to ban the wearing "baggy" pants to school (*Bivens and Green v. Albuquerque Public Schools,* 1995, pp. 95–155).

Courts have upheld the right of schools to ban the wearing or displaying of any gang symbol (Majestic, 1991). The federal courts address the safety issue by stating that "officials have the right to demand conduct that is conducive to the fulfillment of its responsibility to educate" (Landen, 1992, p. 2). The law imposes on school authorities a duty to supervise the conduct of children necessary to their protection because of the tendency of students to participate in aggressive and impulsive behavior; therefore, if a student's manner of dress has the potential of causing violence on campus, that type of clothing must be eliminated (Landen, 1992; Ogletree and Garrett, 1981). Because the legality of dress codes is often challenged, officials have found that policies that stress the importance of reducing distractions that inhibit learning are more likely to be declared legal than policies restricting gang communication through limitations on attire (Burke, 1993; Lane and Richardson, 1992).

When the rules relating to student dress have been challenged legally, it has usually been on grounds that they restrict individual liberties, specifically First Amendment rights of freedom of expression (Virginia State Dept. of Education, 1992). As noted above, at times the courts have agreed with the advocates of students' rights. In 1969, the Supreme Court ruled that school officials are "state" actors whose discipline of students is constrained by the federal Constitution (Majestic, 1991). *Tinker v. Des Moines Independent Community School District* (1969), established the right of students to freedom of expression in school unless the exercise of that right would materially and substantially interfere with the requirements of appropriate discipline or collide with the rights of others in the school (ACLU, 1988; Majestic, 1991).

Any restrictions on student dress must have a legitimate educational rationale. Policies must be clearly stated, be issued with reasonable notice to allow students to comply, and allow for minimal due process before students are disciplined for violations (Landen, 1992). It is generally agreed that a dress code policy that calls for reasonable restrictions and is enforced with common sense can create a better school environment, but restrictive measures can lead to costly lawsuits (Stover, 1990). Courts have supported school boards' dress codes that are based on needs rather than opinions. Since *Tinker*, courts have consistently affirmed that minors have constitutional rights. Codes must be carefully written and consistent with the legitimate goals of schools (Sparks, 1983). In the final analysis, the challenge for school officials is to develop dress codes that are responsive to the needs of their school communities without being unnecessarily restrictive. The challenge for the courts is to allow school officials to exercise their best judgments about how to educate youth, even when the courts may disagree as to the wisdom of these efforts (Majestic, 1991).

In 1996, a state court in Arizona ruled that mandatory uniforms were not an infringement on the rights of students to freedom of expression. Superior Court judge Michael D. Jones stated that he did not wish to second-guess the Phoenix school board that had initiated the uniform policy; he asserted that the school is not a public forum for personal expression (Jacobs, 1995). Several other court cases are pending in California and other states; as yet, the Supreme Court has not specifically addressed this issue.

Reports From Schools That Have Implemented Uniform Policies

During the year following the beginning of the strict dress codes in Detroit, only two locker break-ins occurred (Leslie, 1989). In a 1996 report, the schools in Long Beach, California, declared a major decrease in violent crime in their schools since the advent of a school uniform policy (Cohn, 1996; Daily Report Card, 1996).

Besides freeing children from peer pressure, some school officials anticipate that wearing uniforms may lead to higher grades and better behavior. Some schools even go so far as to consider uniforms the cause of higher test scores. Results supporting these opinions are cited from New York's Harlem and Baltimore, Maryland (Baker, 1987).

In most accounts reported by school officials, the use of uniforms has been most successful where school officials have solicited active parent involvement in the decision making (Majestic, 1991; Virginia State Dept. of Education, 1992). It seems that most often uniforms are being introduced in the elementary grades; perhaps because this is the path of least resistance, where the students are less likely to demand to express themselves through clothing or because it is the best place to introduce positive values and attitudes about school. Another ingredient that seems to have contributed to the success of some school uniform programs is voluntariness. Even without requiring that uniforms be worn, some schools have achieved better than a 90% compliance rate due to general community support (Majestic, 1991). In a recent *USA Today* poll based on the results of 1,008 telephone interviews, 64% of the respondents said they favored their local schools establishing a dress code requiring students to wear uniforms (*USA Today Online*, 1996).

In a section of the *Manual on School Uniforms* (1996) entitled "Model School Uniform Policies," the U. S. Department of Education lists the following reported results from schools using a uniform policy: a decrease in violent crime, an increase in school demeanor, improved behavior, an increase in attendance rates, higher student achievement, a sense of calmness, student pride, a decrease in competitiveness, and a greater focus on positive behavior. The manual suggests that these results indicate that school uniform policies can promote school safety, improve discipline, and enhance the learning environment.

Studies Concerning the Effects of School Uniform Policies

While opinions abound concerning the positive effects of the use of school uniforms, few studies have been conducted in this area. The program evaluation division of the District of Columbia Public Schools in Washington, DC, conducted a study in 1989–1990 concerning the school staff and parent perceptions of need and impact regarding a recently implemented uniform policy. The researchers conducted a survey among the district staff as well as parents from schools where a school uniform policy was in place. The results indicated that even though both teachers and parents perceived an increase in attendance level and achievement level due to the uniform policy implementation, actual data did not support this perception. The researchers concluded that uniforms might be one of the factors that contributes to a school's learning environment, but based on their research, no direct relationship between the uniform policy and attendance or achievement was present (Stevenson and Chunn, 1991).

Another study, conducted by Behling (1993), sought to determine the effects of students' clothing on teachers' and students' perceptions. Pictures of students were shown to teachers and students alike. The faces of the students were not visible to the participants, and the only difference in the pictures was in the clothing worn by the students in the pictures. The teachers and students were then asked a series of questions regarding their preferences. Both a formal uniform and a more casual mode of dress uniform as well as "regular" school clothes were included in the pictures shown. Behling concluded that both teachers and students perceived students wearing uniforms as better behaved and more academically successful and that teachers and students alike preferred the students who wore the more formal or "preppy" uniform.

METHODS

Participants

The participants in this study were the teachers, parents, and students in two middle schools from a large urban/suburban school district in Texas that each initiated the mandatory wearing of school uniforms for the 1995–1996 school year. Each school had approximately 1,100 students, and the population remained fairly stable over the 3 years prior to this study. All of the students in each school were included in the data collection for attendance and discipline referrals. The data were supplied by the school district. School A had an average population in 1995–1996 of 1,088. School B's average population for 1995–1996 was 1,196.

All professional staff (including teachers, administration, and educational aides) from each school were asked to participate in a survey both in the 1995–1996 fall and spring semesters; both Schools A and B had 84 professional staff members.

A volunteer sample of parents from each school was also surveyed. A cover letter, parent survey form, and permission form were mailed to all of the parents in each school. Parents were asked to send the parent survey and the permission form allowing their child to participate in the student survey to the school with their child. Students who had parental permission were then asked to sign a consent form before participating in the survey. School A had 422 parents who completed and returned a survey, representing a 38.79% return rate. School B had 268 parents who participated, representing a 22.41% return rate.

Students from each school also participated in the attitude survey. In School A, 187 students responded, representing a 17.5% response rate: 69 sixth graders, 70 seventh graders, and 48 eighth graders answered the student survey. In School B, 62 sixth graders, 50 seventh graders, and 44 eighth graders participated. The 156 total participants represented a 13.1% response rate.

Instruments

A survey set prepared by the author and personnel from the district, *The School Uniform Opinion Survey*, was developed to determine the perceptions of the teachers, parents, and students toward the wearing of school uniforms. Forms of the survey were developed for teachers (both for use prior to the beginning of the school year and after one semester of school uniform policy implementation), parents, and students. The survey development process involved the researcher, the district program evaluator, and the two principals from the schools where the survey set was to be administered. In the initial development meeting, the researcher and the principals indicated what information they wanted to collect from the surveys. Items were then worded by the researcher and edited by the district's program evaluator yielding the final format for the surveys.

Items 1–14 on each survey are statements reflecting perceptions concerning school uniforms based on the results of a literature review by the researcher. Participants were asked to agree or disagree using a 4-point scale. Items 15–21 are statements concerning the specific dress code policy in each school utilizing the same 4-point scale indicating agreement or disagreement with each statement. Items 22–28 (in the faculty surveys only) are descriptive in nature regarding classroom/school environment where participants indicated the percentage of students in their classes who had displayed certain behaviors. In addition, the *spring faculty, parent,* and *student* forms of the survey ask whether or not the participants preferred the school uniform policy over the previous dress code. Demographic areas of information for faculty include sex, level of primary teaching assignment, years of classroom teaching experience, and whether or not their assignment was primarily in or out of the classroom. Parent demographic information about the sex of their child and his or her grade level was reported. Students were asked to include their sex, grade level, and ethnicity.

Procedures

The data from the two middle schools of the district that implemented the mandatory wearing of school uniforms for the 1995–1996 school year were compared to their own previous year's data when a traditional dress code policy was in effect. The data from the two schools were also compared to each other. After the completion of the school year, the attendance figures as well as the number of discipline referrals were compared for differences. For the attendance and discipline referral portions of the study, data were collected by grading period and/or semester from the general attendance and discipline records of the schools. The discipline referral ratio for each semester was determined by dividing the number of referrals in each of three categories (Level 1, minor offenses; Level 2, moderate offenses; and Level 3, severe offenses) by the total school population. The percentage of increase or decrease in the discipline referrals over the last semester and previous years was then calculated.

The *School Uniform Opinion Survey* was administered to teachers from both schools before the beginning of the 1995–1996 school year asking them to reflect on the previous school year. The survey was administered to the teachers again early in the spring semester. This time, the teachers were asked to respond while reflecting on the first semester of school uniform use.

The parent and student forms of the survey were administered in April and May of the spring semester of 1996. These surveys asked the participants what they perceived the wearing of uniforms would be like, what changes they thought would occur, and what their initial attitude had been toward the wearing of a uniform to school. They also addressed their current feelings as to whether or not their initial perceptions were correct and whether or not their attitude toward wearing uniforms had changed since the beginning of the year. Scores were calculated and means determined on this attitude survey for both schools in the study.

Limitations

Reasons for students' problem behavior have long been explored among educators. Many sources of negative behavior in a school classroom have nothing to do with student dress. The personality and discipline methodology of individual teachers and principals are probably the most important factors in controlling student behavior (Roberts, 1989), and these factors are not addressed in this particular study.

The sample of participating parents was voluntary, and the students' responses were limited by the need to have parental permission for their participation. The voluntary nature of participating in the survey may indicate wider support for the policy than actually exists due to the fact that parents more frequently respond to surveys about programs they consider above average (Borg and Gall, 1989).

Items in the survey were limited to those that met the district personnel's approval and may not always have represented the best wording for research survey items. In some cases, the district program evaluator mandated a particular format and/or wording for items such as those asking teachers to give the percentage of their students who engaged in certain behavior. In other cases, the wording was changed to match the individual principal's perspective. For example, the two school principals differed as to the wording of item 16, which describes the school uniform or mode of dress policy. In this instance, the forms for the surveys for each school were altered to match the particular policy of that school. In order to fulfill the needs and expectations of the district, the individual school principals, and the project investigator, some allowances were made in the wording of items, which may have proven to be awkward or ambiguous to the reader.

While in the same district, the two schools that participated in this survey are quite different in demographic makeup. There are differences between the two schools in socioeconomic background as well as in racial mix; however, these two factors were not considered when comparisons were made between the two types of uniforms and their effects on student attendance and behavior.

RESULTS

This section discusses the results of the data analysis to answer the following research questions:

- Do students who attend a school where a mandatory school uniform policy is enforced attend school more regularly than students who attend schools where there is no such policy?
- Are there differences by type of school uniform (formal or mode of dress) in the attendance patterns of middle school students who attend schools where a mandatory school uniform policy is enforced?

- Do students who attend a school where a mandatory school uniform policy is enforced have fewer discipline referrals than do students who attend schools where there is no such policy?
- Are there differences by type of school uniform (formal or mode of dress) in the number of discipline referrals among middle school students who attend schools where a mandatory school uniform policy is enforced?
- What is the attitude of students, teachers, and parents toward the wearing of school uniforms?
- Are there differences by type of school uniform (formal or mode of dress) in the perceptions of students, teachers, and parents toward the wearing of school uniforms?
- What perceptions exist among middle school teachers concerning the effects of wearing school uniforms on the classroom learning environment?
- Are there differences by type of school uniform (formal or mode of dress) in the perceptions among middle school teachers of the effects of wearing school uniforms on the classroom learning environment?

SUMMARY OF RESULTS

The results of this study indicate that student attendance is not affected by a school uniform policy. In the case of School B, the results stayed exactly the same; in the case of School A, the attendance percentage actually dropped somewhat. These results support the earlier study in the District of Columbia schools (Stevenson and Chunn, 1991), which concluded that the wearing of school uniforms did not increase attendance.

Even though the results at School B appeared to be better in that the percentage of attendance remained exactly the same after the mandatory school uniform policy was implemented as it had been before the use of school uniforms, in actual terms, the results were about even in both School B, where the more informal mode of dress uniform policy was utilized, and School A, where the formal school uniform company approach was used. School uniforms did not have any noticeable effect on student attendance in either school.

Table 3.1   Discipline Referrals Before and After Uniforms, Combined School Data

	Fall 1993	*Fall 1994*	*Change*	*Fall 1995*	*Change from fall 1993*	*Change from fall 1994*
Level III (severe)	0.062	0.067	+8%	0.039	−37%	−42%
Level II (moderate)	0.893	0.689	−23%	0.716	−20%	+4%
Level I (minor)	1.020	0.901	−12%	0.527	−48%	−42%
Overall	1.975	1.657	−16%	1.281	−35%	−23%
	Spring 1994	*Spring 1995*	*Change*	*Fall 1996*	*Change from spring 1994*	*Change from spring 1995*
Level III (severe)	0.072	0.074	+3%	0.056	−22%	−24%
Level II (moderate)	1.167	1.099	−6%	1.010	−13%	−8%
Level I (minor)	1.464	0.832	−43%	0.559	−62%	−33%
Overall	2.703	2.005	−26%	1.625	−40%	−30%

Note: Ratios are equal to the number of discipline referrals over student population.

Based on the results of this study, students who wear school uniforms do have fewer discipline referrals than those students who do not. There was an overall 30% decrease in discipline referrals in the two schools after the implementation of the school uniform policy (see Table 3.1). Even when other factors are considered, this result indicates that the school uniforms had a positive effect on student discipline.

The present study indicates that the mode of dress or more informal school uniform may have greater results in the area of discipline referrals than does the formal school uniform policy. The results in School B indicated a 45% drop in discipline referrals; School A had only an 11% drop.

Based on the results of the *School Uniform Opinion Survey*, teachers are very supportive of the school uniforms policy and believe its effects are apparent in their classrooms. Parents supported the policy as well, but not to the degree that the teachers favored the used of school uniforms. Students, on the other hand, did not support the use of uniforms in any category and did not feel that they added to a more positive school environment.

The faculty of both schools favored the uniform policy; however, the teachers in School A, where the formal uniform was used, had significantly stronger support in the areas of students' rights and school uniform utility value. School B (mode of dress) teachers, on the other hand, had significantly higher scores on the behavior scale.

Parents from both schools supported the uniform policy and wanted it to continue. Parents from School A had stronger support in the areas of students' rights and utility value. Parents from School B, however, scored significantly higher on the scale for behavior, once again supporting the idea that the behavior changes in the students of School B were more dramatic than of those in School A.

Neither group of students favored the uniform policy at all. On the scale representing the students' feelings toward the effects of school uniforms on students' rights, School A students scored significantly higher than School B, indicating that the students who wore the formal uniforms felt that uniforms infringed less upon their rights than did the students who wore the less formal mode of dress uniform. School B students, however, indicated a significantly higher rating on the behavior scale than did the students in School A, although both groups indicated failure to support school uniforms for this purpose.

Overall, teachers noticed several improvements in the student's classroom behavior after the implementation of school uniforms. The areas where teachers perceived that improvement had occurred included violations of the dress code, disrespect toward fellow classmates, the amount of teacher time needed to handle disruptions, and the amount of student time off-task.

The results of this study showed that the teachers in School B, where the informal mode of dress was implemented, perceived a greater number of changes in classroom environment than did the teachers in School A, where the formal uniform was used.

DISCUSSION OF RESULTS, IMPLICATIONS, AND SUMMARY

This section includes a discussion of the results reported above as well as implications for theory, implications for practice, and implications for further research. The chapter concludes with a summary of this research study.

School Attendance

The attendance rates at the two middle schools in this study were already higher than average. The Texas Education Agency reports that the average attendance rate for middle schools in Texas in 1994–1995 was 95.1%, while those in these two schools averaged 96%. Based solely on the results of this research study, however, a school uniform policy does not affect school attendance rates in the case of either type of school uniform. Attendance rates in these schools neither increased nor decreased. These findings support those found by Stevenson and Chunn (1991) in the District of Columbia schools. An effect might be found in schools where attendance rates are lower, but at the present time, research data do not exist that support the idea that students attending schools with a school uniform policy do, in fact, have better attendance rates than students who attend school where no such policy exists.

Discipline Referrals

Discipline referrals for both schools declined at least to some degree after the use of school uniforms. In the category of severe or Level III offenses, the results for both semesters indicated a decrease. It should be noted, however, that this ratio was quite small even before the school uniform policy was implemented. If the individual school data are examined for Level III offenses, School A had an increase for the fall semester, even though in the spring, a large decrease in such offenses occurred. School B, which began with much larger discipline referral ratios, showed a significant decrease both semesters in Level III offenses. These results from School B support the claims of Cohn (1996) concerning the effect of school uniforms on violent offenses. Level II or moderate offenses seem to be the least affected by the school uniform policy when the overall combined school data are examined. In the case of School A, however, Level II offenses actually showed a marked increase after the implementation of the school uniform policy. School B, on the other hand, had a steady decline in Level II offenses for both semesters. Level I or minor offenses, which were the most common for both schools, declined in both schools. It should be noted here that dress code violations fall into the Level I category. With a school uniform policy that is strictly enforced in place, it would seem logical that a reduction in this area would occur, especially if dress code violations had proven to be a problem in the past.

An examination of the individual school data would show that the school uniform policy appeared to have a stronger impact on the number of discipline referrals in School B, where the mode of dress uniform policy was implemented. In School A, where the formal uniform policy was used, the overall discipline referrals declined slightly in the fall semester and actually increased in the spring semester. However, in School B, a steady decline is seen in all three levels of discipline referral ratios including the overall results for both semesters. Although School B showed more significant results, it continued to have higher discipline referral ratios than did School A. These results indicate that the type of uniform may have a relationship to the increase or decrease rate in school discipline referrals with the implementation of a school uniform policy. In this study, the mode of dress uniform policy had more positive results with regard to discipline referrals than did the formal uniform policy.

Teacher Perceptions

Teachers had the highest overall mean on all three scales of the *School Uniform Opinion Survey*. Teachers not only supported the continued use of school uniforms, but they also felt that uniforms had made a difference in their individual classrooms. It is interesting to note, however, that male and female teachers scored similarly on all three scales. In levels of experience, however, some differences in opinion occur. The most experienced teachers (over 15 years) were as supportive of the uniform policy before its implementation as any of the other groups. After a semester of uniform use in School B, where the mode of dress policy was in place, however, these most experienced teachers were much more supportive than they had been before and significantly more supportive when compared to the other groups at their same school. It is significant to note that the most experienced teachers at School B felt that the school uniform policy had had a positive effect on their school's overall environment.

Parent Perceptions

Parents from both schools supported the school uniform policy in all three areas measured. They did not, however, support the policy to the same degree as did the teachers from both schools. Parents of male and female students had similar opinions regarding the school uniform policy. Parents of sixth grade students seemed to favor the policy more than parents of seventh or eighth graders. This support could be due to the fact that they had experienced a similar uniform policy the previous year in their child's elementary school or to the fact that, in general, sixth graders were more supportive of the policy themselves. Parents from both schools indicated their preference for the uniform policy over the previous dress code policy.

Student Perceptions

Students from both schools indicated that they did not support the idea of school uniforms in any of the categories measured. Female students had higher regard for the policy than did male students, and Hispanic and Asian students seemed to show more positive regard for uniforms than did the other ethnic groups. Students indicated that they did not prefer school uniforms over the previous dress code; they did believe that their individual rights had been restricted; and they did not feel that uniforms improved behavior or overall school environment. It should be noted here that neither school allowed the students to participate in the planning and implementation of the school uniform policy. These students seemed to feel, as some psychologists have suggested, that uniform policies reflected the preferences of the adults in their lives more than the educational value that they might contribute to the school environment.

Classroom Environment

Teachers from both schools noted improvement in their classroom environment after the implementation of school uniforms, especially in the case of dress code violations and with regard to students showing respect for each other. In School B, teachers perceived even more improvements in their classroom. School A teachers also noted improvement in their class environment with the exception of disrespect shown the teacher, which showed a slight increase. These results support the Behling study, which suggested that teachers perceive uniformed students to be better behaved than those students who do not wear uniforms. Teachers also felt that they spent less time handling disruptions after the implementation of school uniforms and that students spent less time off-task than before. As in the case of the teachers' general perceptions, these data show that the teachers from these two schools felt very positive concerning the effect a school uniform policy had made in their school.

IMPLICATIONS FOR THEORY

The results from this study do support some of the claims made in support of the use of school uniforms. Discipline referrals did decrease in some instances, and the more severe offenses dropped significantly, supporting the claims of Cohn (1996), the United States Department of Education *Manual on School Uniforms* (1996), and others. Teachers did perceive an improved environment in their classrooms and in their schools, support-ing the earlier Behling (1993) study. Parents, also, felt that uniforms were practical and helped children concentrate on the important issues of school rather than on clothing.

In some cases, however, the data supported those who argue that school uniform policies are not a good idea. Data did not show, for example, that attendance is increased by a school uniform policy, a claim also made in the *Manual of School Uniforms*. And perhaps the greatest discrepancy between the ideas of school uniform advocates and the results found here is seen in two claims often made in support of the use of school uniforms: that they increase self-esteem and relieve peer pressure and competition. Students, who so overwhelmingly reject the school uniform policy, as they did in this study, do not feel that their self-esteem has been improved. The students did not agree with this idea of improved self-esteem, and they indicated that the school uniform policy restricted their rights as indi-viduals to choose what they wear. Even though students of this age more often than not dress alike anyway, these students felt that they should have the right to have at least a part in making that decision.

IMPLICATIONS FOR PRACTICE

The results found in this study indicate that a continuation of a school uniform policy would be advisable. Attendance rates consistently contin-ued at a high rate, and discipline referrals decreased in some areas. Teach-ers and parents felt that the school environment was improved, and this feeling alone would probably have a positive impact on the atmosphere of the school. Students, however, should be given the opportunity to have ongoing input into the decision making concerning the school uniform policy. Perhaps if they were allowed to help in making these decisions, their support would increase, and some of the positive effects predicted concerning self-esteem would indeed occur.

For other schools that are considering implementing a school uniform policy, this study indicates that teacher, parent, and student input should be involved in the initial stages of policy implementation. The few research cases should be studied, as well, to determine their significance in each local school situation. Information and help should be sought from schools that have already implemented a school uniform policy. In addition, legal cases regarding dress code and student rights should be studied, and legal counsel should be sought when plans are being made to initiate a school uniform policy. Efforts must be made to make sure that the individual school policy fits in with that of the state and local district policies. Schools should maintain an ongoing evaluation of the program to determine whether or not the results are worth the cost in time, money, and other resources. As with all school programs, decisions should be made at the end of each school year to determine whether or not the policy should continue as is, undergo alteration, or be terminated.

IMPLICATIONS FOR FUTURE RESEARCH

The results of this study indicate that there are several other areas within the topic of school uniforms that should be explored. Further research is indicated in this area to determine whether or not school uniforms have similar effects on differing school populations. In several areas, student ethnicity proved to show significant differences in survey results. More research is warranted to determine whether or not ethnic background plays a part in clothing preference for students. In addition, research should be conducted to determine if students are more supportive of the school uniform policy when they actually have the opportunity to take part in its formation or revision. Long-term uniform use and its effect on students' behavior and self-esteem should also be conducted. Age groups other than middle school students should also be studied.

Each of the specific claims made by proponents and opponents of school uniforms should be examined much more closely before broad claims are made as to their effectiveness.

SUMMARY

One of many proposals to solve the behavior problems prevalent in public schools is the wearing of school uniforms. The use of school uniforms has been endorsed by President Clinton and has received support of the courts when sound educational or safety reasons are cited. School uniform use in public schools is receiving widespread public attention and increasing in application even though relatively few research studies have been performed regarding their effects.

This study involving two large urban/suburban middle schools indicates that while some of the claims for the use of school uniforms appear to be correct, others do not. School uniforms apparently help to decrease the number of discipline referrals in schools where they are used. Uniforms also increase the positive perceptions of teachers toward student behavior in their classrooms. Parents of middle school students support the idea of school uniform policies. School uniform policies do not, however, appear to increase attendance, and they do not have the support of middle school–age students. Further research is warranted in several areas before school uniforms should be considered the "answer" to many of the problems facing our schools.

4

School Uniforms in Middle Schools: Enhancing Identity and Security

Linda Abel Fosseen

The focus of the empirical research study reported in this chapter was to determine whether significant associations could be found between the wearing of group-identifying school uniforms and students' reported perceptions of their school as a community. This investigation represented an attempt to investigate the effectiveness of school-specific uniforms in enhancing belonging, identity, social cohesion, safety, and security in middle school children. The old debate of how to remove distinctions among students to decrease financial pressures, discrimination, and jealously over designer clothes was *not* our focus.

In this study, *uniforms* were defined as common, but distinctive, clothing functioning to identify the wearers as belonging to a specific group. The application of school-specific iconography (logos) to school clothing creates this distinctive uniform and fosters group identity. Nonidentifying restrictive dress (without group-identifying iconography and ordinarily termed *common dress* or *standard dress*) was included in the investigation as a Hawthorne control variable.

During the design phase of this empirical investigation, a review of the existing literature on school dress (including numerous anecdotal accounts, case studies, descriptive studies, and a limited number of empirical investigations) uncovered a great degree of confusion: The term *standard dress*, which is defined in this study as a subset of dress codes, is often called a "uniform" by others. This confusion can be attributed to prevalent but mistaken beliefs—often unarticulated but commonly underlying both practice and the research literature—that the terms *uniform* and *standard (common) dress* are synonyms and thus interchangeable. It appears that many more dress code studies are represented in the literature than true uniform studies.

With other researchers failing to make distinctions between school dress terms, definitional boundaries are fuzzy, and no one can be certain which specific variables are being investigated, making interpretation and generalization of research results extremely difficult, if not impossible. For example, in the National Education Longitudinal Study (National Center for Educational Statistics, 1994) and follow-up study (NAESP, 2000) user's manuals, the introduction to questions indicated the procedure to gather school dress information (to classify which students wore uniforms or were subject to dress code rules) was only to ask school principals to affirm or negate two statements: (a) "Student uniforms are required" and (b) "Certain forms of student dress are prohibited" (NAESP, 2000). Because principals were not required to describe their schools' "uniforms," there is no way to accurately categorize the actual dress type, other than to assume some dress rules were in place. One principal's definition of "school uniform" might not have not coincided with that of another principal: This leads to a general confusion of which dress variables were really being represented by the NELS studies.

The pervasive confusion illustrated in the NELS 88 studies (National Center for Educational Statistics, 1994) is *not just a question of quantity or degree, but of basic function*: The concepts of *uniforms* and *standard dress* (a special form of a dress code) are diametrically opposite in philosophy, purpose, and methodology (how purpose is achieved). Types of school dress, as defined in this study (no restrictions, general dress codes, special dress codes—that is, standard dress—and logo uniforms), work within their own purpose to achieve distinct and different goals.

The philosophy of common student dress is based on homogenizing a student population. There tends to be agreement among school administrators, educators, and parents that dress codes (standard dress) function to minimize differences to meet goals of reducing jealously among students and reducing financial pressures on parents and students' families. Standard dress eliminates status distinctions and decreases clothing competition *within* a specific school. This purpose is achieved through implementation of restrictive dress codes, often as mandated standard dress. Dress code policies are sets of rules or standards limiting clothing choices: *Such codes are employed to minimize group differences*, reducing disparity by minimizing intragroup differences.

In contrast, a true uniform created by the application of iconography to standard dress is not simply an extension of a dress code, but rather represents a totally different goal: to identify and create distinctions (on the school level), rather than remove distinctions (between students, within the school). The philosophy of uniforms stresses the creation and accentuation of intergroup (between-school) differences facilitated through increased intragroup (within-school) identification. Valid uniforms are group specific and actually create an identity *in addition* to eliminating discrimination within the group.

For example, in the military, the basic purpose of using a unit-specific uniform is to enhance uniqueness. This distinctive uniform accentuates differences by visually setting a unit's soldiers apart, rather than making them look like soldiers in other units. Historically, iconography has played a vital role in developing identity: In the Middle Ages a knight's shield displayed his distinct emblem and set him apart from all other knights by communicating his special identity and rank. Today, the goal of military special colors and logos (a special forces green beret, aviator wings, or submariner dolphins, etc.) is not to reduce jealously, but to *identify*. Similarly, wearing a gang "flash"—a special tattoo, colored scarf, or other clothing accessory unique to an individual gang—is not done to reduce tensions, but to *identify* gang members, not only to themselves, but also to outsiders and other gangs.

This purpose of distinctive identification is achieved only through the iconography: The addition of a distinctive school-specific feature such as a motto or badge (logo) to a common dress not only decreases diversity of appearance in a specific school, but also simultaneously highlights that same school's group identity and thus "makes distinctions *among* schools clear" (Synott and Symes, 1995). The perspective of the current study needs to be re-emphasized: The addition of school-specific iconography applied to student apparel creates a distinct and separate format or category of school dress—a true uniform. Uniform logos or badges are *not simply a* further distinction (extension of a process) of standard dress (often mistakenly called a "uniform"). *The distinction between dress codes and uniforms is not predicated on degree* (i.e., uniforms are more specific than dress codes), *but rather on a distinction in function.*

Though true uniforms typically consist of some variation of common dress with applied group-identifying iconography, common dress is not required to create a uniform: The required element is solely the distinctive group-referenced iconography. This is in contrast to the perspective common in the general literature and articulated by Synott and Symes (1995) that the presence of iconography on dress denotes only an additional differentiation rather than being the critical element creating a uniform.

In this report, the terms describing types of student apparel are strictly defined to decrease confounding of terms and to achieve a consistency lacking in previous reports. The term *dress code* here is utilized to define a rule system limiting apparel choice: Dress codes function to minimize differences between students. The term *uniform* refers solely to apparel bearing an iconographic representation that clearly identifies the wearer as belonging to a specific group. These terminology distinctions become crucial to avoiding confusion when citing from and discussing the research literature: *Absent specific statements referring to iconography applied to dress, the default terminology used to describe restricted (but not described as school-identified) student apparel is "dress code."*

THE PROBLEM WITH DRESS CODES
AND SCHOOL UNIFORMS

Since the late 1980s, especially in the highly diverse, urban, and suburban American schools systems such as San Diego, Philadelphia, Washington, DC, and San Antonio, voluntary and mandated restrictive school dress policies—initially designed to change a school's environment and social climate by reducing clothing competition and increasing perceptions of order—have been adopted as interventions functioning to positively influence student attitudes, behavior, and academic outcomes (LaPoint, Holloman, and Alleyne, 1992; Stanley, 1996). There is an ongoing debate and little empirical evidence to support or disprove whether dress codes or uniform policies are actually linked to positive outcomes such as safer and more cooperative school environments (Brunsma and Rockquemore, 1998; Murray, 1997; Stanley, 1996).

Numerous anecdotal accounts and descriptive studies report finding that implementation of restrictive school dress policies (especially those mandating standard dress) impacted students and school communities.

For example, Newmann and his associates (1989) report that perceptions of increased orderly student behaviors (less student misbehavior, less substance abuse, and improved attendance) often occurred when students wore mandated school dress. In the Long Beach school district in California, a survey was conducted assessing the impact of mandated school dress on perceptions of school safety (Stanley, 1996). Descriptive results showed that adults, especially school administrators, perceived the strategy of mandating school dress codes as having a positive impact on student behavior, and held beliefs that there was an actual relation between dress codes and reported decreases in crimes, vandalism, weapon possession, and substance abuse. In spite of numerous reports from districts extolling the direct positive influence of restrictive school dress policies, empirical studies to test these reports are literally nonexistent (Holloman, LaPoint, Alleyne, Palmer, and Sanders, 1996; Murray, 1997). Because the term "uniform" is never defined in all of these studies, it is unclear which types(s) of student dress were actually studied. It seems quite likely that most of these studies investigated aspects of dress codes such as standard (common) dress, *not* true uniforms (which are group identifying).

Because there is so much at stake when dress codes or uniform policies are implemented, it is important to know whether the specified type of restrictive school dress makes a difference for students. Speculation and anecdotal or descriptive reports suggest that school dress effects exist, and may not only positively influence student feelings of safety and identification with the school community, but also (mediated through uniform effects on school academic and social climate) have indirect effects on motivation, achievement, and other school-related student outcomes (Battistich and Hom, 1997; Roeser, Midgley, and Urdan, 1996). However, previous reports from the few empirical studies specifically investigating actual school uniforms or standard dress (dress codes, nonuniforms) indicate that study results have been mixed or unsuccessful in finding evidence to confirm the existence of real effects related to school apparel (Brunsma and Rockquemore, 1998; Murray, 1997; Tanioka and Glaser, 1991).

SCHOOL DRESS POLICIES AND STUDENT OUTCOMES: A PROPOSED MODEL

In response to the obvious need for more strenuous research on school uniforms, a preliminary investigation was designed to test whether *true* school uniforms impact a school's academic and social climate to produce direct or indirect effects on school-related student outcomes. The research goal was to determine *empirically* whether school-identified uniforms were related to important motivational aspects of school climate thought to foster a sense of community in schools, specifically, *the relation established through the development of a distinctive group identity and a sense of school-related belonging.* This research study tested hypotheses that middle school students' school-related perceptions and beliefs differ by type of school dress, gender, ethnicity, or grade level.

Though measures of perception are commonly used to assess factors contributing to school climate (Welsh, 2000), research data representing perceptions are open to criticism because perceptions are "are not objective reflections of 'reality,' [being] prone to influence by subjective factors" (Owens, 1987, p. 298). In this school uniform study, however, *the concern was not school dress or uniform policy itself, but student perceptions of belonging and safety in their school community.* The thrust was not to look for or check objective reality, but rather to assess students' underlying perceptions of the degree they felt connected to and safe in their school community. The intent was *not* to evaluate whether a school community *really* was welcoming or safe.

This belief in the validity of using perceptual data is supported by research suggesting that the school climate impacting members of an organization (such as a school community) is not the physical sum *reality* of physical and psychological factors in that organization, but rather the *perception* of the nature of the organizational climate (Anderson, 1982; Halpern and Croft, 1963; Welsh, Stokes, and Greene, 2000). "The point is that whatever people perceive as their experience is the realty to be described" (Owens, 1987, p. 298). The perceived "sense" of security and community *is* reality to students: In such instances subjective perceptions tend to translate into objective reality.

To better explain the relation between school dress policies (school-identified uniforms) and student outcomes hypothesized in this study, a theoretical model based on the McMillan-Chavis (1986) community model and the model of prosocial development developed by Brown and Solomon (1983) was proposed, as shown in Figure 4.1. This composite model illustrates how school uniforms might play a role in student motivation, emotions, social interactions, and academic behaviors. It is hypothesized that school dress policies (uniforms) influence student out-

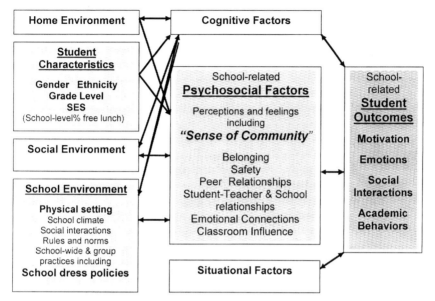

Figure 4.1   Suggested Determinants of School-Related Motivation, Affect, and Behaviors

comes, functioning indirectly through mediating psychosocial factors including student perceptions of their school as a community: These "sense of community" factors include perceptions of belonging, emotional and social relationships, and feelings of security and safety in school.

The rest of the chapter is divided into nine sections in which (a) the categories of school dress are defined, (b) theoretical foundations and (c) previous relevant research are summarized, and (d) the research hypotheses are introduced. The fifth section (e) details study sample demographics, school dress policies, design, methods, and analyses. The final three sections include (f) a summary of study results, (g) discussion of the research results, (h) suggestions for ongoing school uniform research, and (i) concluding remarks.

DEFINITIONS FOR SCHOOL UNIFORM RESEARCH

Uniforms have been defined as dress characterized by distinctive design (style, color) and/or features (pictorial representations, wordings, logos) and worn by the members of particular group (such as soldiers, police, Girl and Boy Scouts) as a means of public and self-identification (Neilson, Knott, and Carhart, 1958). Joseph (1986) defines uniforms as visible and concrete symbolic reminders prompting engagement and execution of role- and context-appropriate behavioral schemas. Joseph also suggests that clothing becomes a uniform when it (a) serves as a representation (emblem) of a group, (b) authenticates group/institutional legitimacy by disclosing members' relative status (subordinates or superiors), and (c) suppresses individuality. For this study, detailed definitions meant to differentiate several types of school apparel were developed. To more precisely define variations in restrictive school dress, this study included one unrestricted dress category and four relatively exclusive categories.

No Restrictions on School Dress

The *no restrictions* category applies to school dress that is not subject to any school guidelines, rules, or restrictions: This category allows students free choice to wear any manner of clothing desired. Though not documented by research findings, anecdotal reports suggest this category is not common in contemporary American schools. Even when schools do not endorse a specific dress code (such as identifying appropriate language for T-shirts, requiring belts, or banning baggy clothing), schools tend to have at least gender-specific appearance guidelines (such as a specific skirt length for girls and maximum hair length for boys).

General Dress Code

The *dress code* category may be applied to any school dress that meets certain standards meant to ban objectionable school clothing. This form of appearance control attempts to decrease the incidence of undesirable student behaviors through control of general appearance and dress. Controls include banning individual items including such elements as torn clothes, gang scarves or colors, objectionable slogans, gold jewelry, or baggy clothes that could conceal weapons (Holloman et al., 1996). Dress codes do not mandate school-specific clothing items (clothing readily identifiable with a specific school): Dress codes most often tell students what *not* to wear.

Specific Dress Code: Standard Dress

The *standard dress* category meets stricter standards that specify clothing style and color options, usually restricting the approved styles and colors of school clothing. This differs from a general dress code because clothing styles or features are mandated to some extent, with students usually told *exactly* what to wear. For example, a standard dress school outfit might include khaki-colored traditional-style pants or knee-length skirt worn with a solid color white or dark green polo-type shirt and plain belt. However, similar to less restrictive dress code school clothing, standardized dress items do not have distinctive features that identify them with a specific school.

Logo Uniforms

To be classed a "school (i.e., *logo*) uniform" for this study, a school's dress standard was required to mandate specific clothing item(s) that had distinctive applied iconography (words or symbols such as a visible logo, crest, name, initials, design, or mascot design) unique to, or readily identified with, a *specific school*. Specifically, a logo is a character or symbol that represents a word or concept, shortened or condensed for the sake of brevity and parsimony (Neilson et al., 1958, p. 1453). A school name, school name initials, or a school-identified graphic (mascot, etc.) printed or otherwise attached to an article of clothing could be considered a logo: It identifies a specific school and can communicate information about the school to wearers and observers alike. Dress or "body supplements" (Roach-Higgins, Eicher, and Johnson, 1995), including insignia that could be attached, adhered, or clipped to student clothing, are capable of visually communicating statements about an individual such as gender (Cahill, 1989), age, social class, religion, and school affiliation (Johnson, 1977; Johnson and Lennon, 1999).

THEORETICAL FOUNDATIONS

Sense of Community and Belonging in Schools

Why is it considered important to develop and maintain positive perceptions of a sense of community in schools? Battistich and Hom (1997) suggest that increased positive perceptions of sense of community aspects (including motivational elements of belonging and positive interpersonal relationships) play *indirect* or *mediating* roles in positive academic motivation and social-intellectual development through enhanced identification with school. Other research has provided additional evidence that feelings of belonging and relatedness are important mediating factors in teacher-student relationships (Roeser, Midgley, and Urdan, 1996) and students' sense of, and identification with, their school community (Battistich and Hom, 1997; Solomon, Watson, Battistich, and Schaps, 1996; Voelkl, 1996). Many educators strongly believe that the creation of a "true community of learning" not only is the "glue that holds the school together," but also is the "most essential element" of effective schools (Baker, Bridger, Terry, and Winsor, 1997, p. 589). They suggest that high levels of sense of community in neighborhoods and schools might serve as a protective factor against individual and social problems.

Defined on an individual level, the general term *belonging* describes the processes of building or maintaining attachments, friendships, intimacy, commitment, and involvement and avoiding feelings of social isolation or separateness (Wehlage, Rutter, Smith, Lesko, and Fernandez, 1989). School-related belonging (school membership) consists of personally held beliefs that one is a significant member of the school community, is accepted and respected in school, has a sense of inclusion and social support in school, and includes school as part of one's self-definition (Goodenow and Grady, 1993; Voelkl, 1996).

When students feel significantly connected to each other and to their school through majority membership or other social processes, it is thought that such feelings promote or reinforce school spirit and "esprit de corps," enhancing a greater sense of community in schools. Research reviewed by Osterman (2000) concludes that a sense of belonging contributes to students' positive self-perceptions of competency, self-determination, identity, and a greater liking for school and helps enhance intrinsic academic motivation, engagement, participation, achievement, and retention in school (Calabrese and Poe, 1990; Goodenow, 1993b; Goodenow and Grady, 1993; Voelkl, 1996). Researchers found that school reforms undertaken to enhance a sense of community in schools play a crucial role in student/teacher satisfaction, student motivation and resiliency, and subsequent educational outcomes (Manning and Saddlemire, 1996; Zimmerman and Arunkumar, 1994).

Uniforms and Identity

Shared Social Identity

Creation of a shared social identity (a perception that one is similar to others) is a factor contributing to feelings of affiliation (belonging) and community in schools. When the highly visible individual differences created by clothing styles are minimized, it becomes simpler to create artificial bonds supporting personal identification with the larger group of the entire school community. Social theory suggests that it is possible to impose a "super group" onto separate groups; that is, artificially creating one new all-encompassing group by merging formally separate groups (Gaertner, Dovidio, Mann, Murrell, and Pomare, 1990).

Research suggests that the more intensely a group is viewed as a whole (rather than an aggregate), the more favorably former out-group members (now within the group) are regarded: This promotes a greater sense of unity and social identity (Baird and Rosenbaum, 1992; Gaertner et al., 1990). Individuals sharing a social identity would literally "rub elbows" with a wide array of individuals (Baird and Rosenbaum, 1992, p. 13). Others optimistically suggest that individuals who became part of a diverse group partnership and adopt a group's shared social identity will be in a better position to work cooperatively within the group and to be challenged by specific experiences that contradict established stereotypes (Aronson, 1999; Gaertner et al., 1990).

Because of the ability to convey information about the group uniforms represent, Joseph (1986) theorized that uniforms exert a normative group influence, providing social feedback to group members. Thus the type of dress, such as fashionable clothes or uniforms, provides social feedback that can contribute to a sense of belonging (Chubb and Fertman, 1992; Goodenow, 1993b; Goodenow and Grady, 1993; Joseph, 1986; Voelkl, 1996). Goffman (1951/1959) suggests that "collective symbols" on clothing (insignia, logos, etc.) function to suppress differences between categories (such as within-school subgroups) allowing members of varied subgroups to come together as "a single moral community" (p. 294).

Especially for adolescents, as noted by Erikson (1968), identification with peer groups is a natural part of identity development; middle schools provide an especially fertile ground for the construction, deconstruction, and reconstruction of arrays of social affiliation groups (Milgram, 1985).

Creating Identity With Uniforms

For over a century, theorists have speculated on the function of clothing and uniforms in the general context of identity. Uniforms are a common form of a "status symbol" having both categorical significance (identifying social status) and expressive significance that conveys the values, rights, and duties of the wearer (Goffman, 1951/1959): Uniforms serve as representative or emblematic forms of dress that function to translate abstract values into concrete meanings (Firth, 1973). Stone (1962) describes an individual wearing a uniform as one assuming a specific identity: This identity would subsequently elicit certain responses from viewers and prescribes a behavior pattern for the uniformed individual. The individual's identity and that of the uniform merge; the uniform does not mold the person, but rather the uniform *is* the person (Carlyle, 1883; Johnson, 1977). Historically—for a wide variety of organizations such as military units, sports teams, business groups, private schools, and professional medical groups—uniforms were worn to create specific identities. Uniforms were visual and psychological identification, encouraging bonding with a specific group.

In a school setting, one might think that school uniforms would facilitate student activation of a range of school-related role schemas and identities such as classmate, learner, or school community member. Though school uniforms might not maintain student individuality, they do provide a means for students to identify directly with their individual school. For example, medical students attend a ceremony during which new students are presented with short white jackets emblazoned with their medical school emblem. Donning the school emblem immediately transforms an unidentifiable gathering of diverse students into a highly visible, identified group with instant bonds to their school and profession. The cohesion created by this uniform-stimulated bonding process facilitates the creation of a group perceived as the in-group *us* with the in-group members, denoting all others not wearing the group's specific uniform as the out-group *them*.

Uniform Logos: Communicating Identity and Status

Even in literature, the notion of communication through clothing symbols has been noted. Nathaniel Hawthorne (1850) symbolically represents the social stigma of adultery in colonial America through the letter "A" embroidered on the clothing of character Hester Prynne in *The Scarlet Letter*. In Virginia Woolf's 1938 political satire, *Three Guineas*, the clothing of men in powerful positions in English society is described: "Every button, rosette, and stripe has its symbolic meaning and its specific rules regulating its use" (Woolf, as quoted in Roach-Higgins et al., 1995, p. 199).

Various shades of meaning (depending on the social context) can be prompted by cues provided by clothing characteristics, such as additions (names/words, insignia, logos), properties (color, shape), novelty (Kaiser, Nagasawa, and Hutton, 1995), or unusual and complexly patterned or brightly colored objects (McArthur and Post, 1977; Miller, 1982; O'Neal, 1998). These findings lent credibility to the possibility that even minimal body attachments (small badges or nametags) can communicate wearer identity status as effectively as an all-encompassing astronaut's space suit. A single property of an item of dress (a logo supplement) could be a more critical indicator of an individual's identity than the whole outfit (shirt and pants or blouse and skirt). A group name or simple initials, an organization-specific graphic (a logo supplement) attached to school dress—if it attracts attention or is visually memorable—could be more important to communicating group identification and status than other distinctive apparel properties that are not unique to a specific group (such as color, pattern, or style).

Individuals have many domain-specific identities making up their total "self," each relevant to a specific situation or context. This suggests that not only is the logo worn on apparel to create a uniform important in communicating status to observers, but also relevant is the *context* in which a logo is worn. Although individual political affiliation is not normally expressed through dress—during a political campaign, at a convention, or at a protest—political affiliation may be made temporarily visible by wearing logo pins, badges, or armbands (Hambleton, 1972).

Military and Gang Logos

Military, fraternal, or scouting organizations utilize a wide array of insignia: emblems, badges, crests, cords, or pins to indicate the status of the uniform wearer to both the wearer's self and to those observing the uniformed individual. It is not required that the entire uniform be symbolic. The literal size or extent of the symbol is not the most important element, but rather the visibility, character, and novelty of the symbol. For example, military groups may indicate rank or membership in elite groups (status differentiation) by a single, relatively small, symbol. Status differentiation might include different colored berets with unit number, Navy Seal insignia, paratrooper parachute symbol, or pilot wings.

In World War II, membership in the notorious German Schutzstaffel elite guard (universally shortened to "SS") was communicated simply by a discreet lightning SS insignia attached to soldier's regular uniforms; the same small insignia was tattooed on the underside of a soldier's upper arm. The SS logo uniquely identified the soldier not only to the SS group internally, but also, when viewed by outsiders, instantly communicated the dreaded reputation of the SS to the rest of the world (Snyder, 1976).

Gangs or other groups may use less formal symbolic insignia, such as a tattoo, special scarf, or jewelry. Gang membership is publicly communicated by the intentional wearing of prescribed clothing. San Antonio police described gang identification typical of local gangs as including pictorial tattoos, rags (bandanas), hats with embroidered names, religious symbols and rosary beads, and special colored shoelaces with beads attached (Forney and Forney, 1995).

Logo Supplements on School Dress

School belonging (affiliation and membership) in a school community is internal and normally not visible, but belonging could be made visible if a school-identifier logo is included as required elements of school dress. In this context, a school logo element functions in the management of appearance as an external and very visible indicator of school membership status. Logos function to superimpose a very specific identity on students—an identity that creates instantaneous recognition as a group member via nonverbal communication. This addition renders a simple and anonymous standard dress into a school-specific *uniform* imparting both physical and emotional information to the wearer and viewer. This means that students wearing uniforms outside of the school community can be instantly recognized, and in turn identify other members of their in-group as distinct from out-group nonmembers. Families walking on the street, or attending a graduation party for their child in a local restaurant, can immediately classify other children present as schoolmates, or *not* schoolmates, if these other children are wearing school-identified uniforms.

RESEARCH ON SCHOOL DRESS:
DRESS CODES AND UNIFORMS

A variety of psychological effects of clothing—ranging from a study assessing the effects of clothing style and color on perceptions of intelligence and achievement (Behling and Williams, 1991) to an investigation of personality characteristics in relation to aggressiveness and clothing color—is well documented in the research literature. In contrast, there are few reports in peer-reviewed journals of empirical studies investigating *school dress* effects: Most studies reporting investigations of school apparel or dress codes have been theses or dissertations (Hughes, 1996; chapter 3, this volume; McCarty, 1999), purely descriptive studies (Stanley, 1996), anecdotal reports, or nonstringent empirical studies published in education-related print media (Adami and Norton, 1996; Murray, 1997).

Of interest from the education media is a brief empirical study of school climate by Murray (1997). This study was the first to report a significant association between the type of school dress policies and reported levels of the sense of school as a community, finding that urban students from a school with a "school uniform policy" (p. 106) reported more positive perceptions of school safety and school community than students in a similar middle school without a similar school dress policy. However, this study has come under widespread criticism for methodological problems, ranging from a restricted and biased sample to unaccounted-for intervening and confounding variables (Brunsma, 2004; Fosseen, 2002). Despite the interpretative and generalization limitations imposed by the methodological problems found in the Murray (1997) study, one might cautiously suggest Murray's results provide some hint of a direction for more rigorous empirical studies testing for "real" school uniform effects.

For example, a rigorous definition of the term *school uniform* raises the provocative question: Was Murray's (1997) study actually an investigation of *school uniforms* as reported? Murray and other researchers appear to universally use the term "school uniform(s)" to describe a range of different clothing types mandated by school dress codes or school district policies. Not a single research report found presents a description of the specific student dress or dress code policy under investigation. This suggests a possible and startlingly simple reason why few real effects of school dress have been found and reported: *Authentic school uniforms have not been studied.*

Rather, the results from studies investigating dress codes (which include standard dress, often misnamed "uniforms") actually misstate their findings as school "uniform" effects (or noneffects). For example, a study by Hughes (1996; see chapter 3 this volume) finds no relation between "school uniforms" and student attendance, discipline referrals, and classroom environment. Brunsma and Rockquemore (1998) find no relation between mandatory so-called school uniforms and student attendance, behavior problems, or substance abuse. Neither study report describes which elements of dress defined the type of school dress being investigated in the respective study. It is highly probable that dress codes, not uniforms (as specifically defined by this study), were the actual variables in these earlier studies.

In contrast, Tanioka and Glaser (1991) studied a group of Japanese high school students wearing school-identified uniforms (i.e., authentic school uniforms). The dress type serving as a variable in this study *was* described and met the definition of a real uniform: Worn on Japanese students' school apparel, the school-identified uniform logo was a visible indicator of belonging in a specific school. Because students who wore their uniforms after school perceived their uniforms to function to identify them as members of a specific school group, these uniformed students were less likely to report involvement in delinquent behaviors than students not wearing uniforms after school. The finding of a significant causal relation between the variability of student perceptions related to school uniforms (cause) and subsequent behaviors (effect) reported by Tanioka and Glaser is especially noteworthy, illustrating three important points: (a) This study report provides a description of the type of school apparel variable (a school-identified uniform), accurately classifying it as an (authentic) school uniform; (b) when authentic school uniforms (those utilizing school-identified logos) are studied, effects *have* been found, providing a rationale for further school uniform research; and (c) these results provide preliminary evidence that school uniforms *do* make a positive difference for students.

Empirical research investigating the existence of effects related to school-identified (logo) uniforms is nonexistent. Even anecdotal reports relating to school dress logos are scarce. Of the few, a report from the Long Beach, California, school district described the pattern of disciplinary actions at an urban public middle school where school logos were included on (voluntary) standardized school dress. The rationale for introducing a school-identifying logo on school dress was explained by the school principal: School-identifying iconography was a visible indicator that promoted membership, identity, and school pride. Because these symbolic representations conveyed school pride, school administration felt there was a need to incorporate school identification (such as a logo) on standardized apparel (Loesch, 1995). The principal's report further indicated that students not wearing these true uniforms (created by the logo addition) were referred for discipline infractions at a rate 22 to 1 over students who voluntarily wore logo uniforms.

RESEARCH QUESTIONS AND HYPOTHESES

An important question underlying this study is whether students really perceived school dress (specifically group-identifying uniforms) as conveying identification with peers and enhancing a sense of belonging in their school community. Based on aspects of psychosocial identity theory, this study hypothesizes that collective symbols such as school emblems (logos) would function to assign instant identity. A presumption presented in our study is that plain standard dress clothing merely homogenizes the outward appearance of students and effects little or no changes in student psychosocial attitudes, including identity. Rather, it is the crucial *addition of a school-identifying logo* that differentiates a uniform from standardized dress: The logo functions to transform anonymous standard dress clothing to a uniform symbolic of a specific school community.

This research study tests hypotheses that students' school-related perceptions and beliefs differ by type of school dress, gender, ethnicity, and grade level. Research suggests that clothing in general, and uniforms specifically, might positively influence social interactions and identity; perceptions and motivation; and school climate. This study hypothesizes that perceptions of belonging, safety, emotional connections, peer relationships, teacher and school relationships, and classroom-influence aspects of "sense of school as a community" differ significantly by two categories of mandated school dress (logo uniforms and standard dress).

Previous research found that gender, ethnic status, and grade level in school were significantly related to individual differences in student perceptions and beliefs. Therefore, the second hypothesis consists of three parts: Do perceptions of belonging, safety, emotional connections, peer relationships, teacher and school relationships, and classroom-influence aspects of *sense of school as a community* differ significantly by (a) gender, (b) ethnicity, or (c) school grade level?

SCHOOL UNIFORMS IN MIDDLE SCHOOLS: STUDY DETAILS

Demographic Information

Study participants included 1,032 sixth, seventh, and eighth grade students from 10 economically disadvantaged middle schools in Houston and San Antonio, Texas. Eight Houston schools supplied 89% of the total study sample; two San Antonio schools, 11%, with participation averaging 9% of the students enrolled at each school. Of the 677 girls and 355 boys in this study, 34% identified themselves as Hispanic, 25% as White/Anglo, 15% as African American, and 9% as Asian American. The 567 participants from "standard dress" schools in San Antonio and Houston represented 55% of the students involved in this study; the remaining 465 participants were from "logo uniform" schools in Houston ISD.

School Dress Policies

San Antonio ISD

At the time of data collection, district-wide dress code policy required standard dress for all San Antonio ISD students (elementary through high school). SAISD dress code did not mandate or allow school-specific identifiers as part of standard dress outfits. Therefore, students from San Antonio were not represented in our study's logo uniform subsample. To date, the SAISD dress code policy in effect during this study has not been changed.

Houston ISD

From data collection, continuing unchanged to the present, Houston ISD policy did not stipulate a district-wide dress code. Rather, district policies assigned formulation of school dress rules to the individual school level, allowing principals to mandate school-specific guidelines. Four of the eight participating Houston middle schools required students to wear logo uniforms (standard dress with the addition of a school-specific identifier logo on shirts). Though logo schools did not differ in average enrollment from standard dress schools, these logo schools were more affluent and had a higher academic status (based on standardized test scores) than standard dress schools. Four of the participating HISD schools mandated a dress code based on nonidentified standardized dress. After this study was conducted, and continuing to the present, two of the four standard dress schools instituted grade-level identification by assigning a logo-free shirt of a specific color to each grade level.

Policies Common to Both Districts

When the study was originally designed, several participating schools allowed students free choice of school clothing options. By the time of data collection, and continuing to the present, widespread compliance with standardized dress codes or uniform policies—on either a voluntary basis (HISD) or a district-wide mandate (SAISD)—meant no middle school in either district allowed students the option of free choice for school clothing.

STUDY DESIGN, METHODS, AND ANALYSES

Design

A causal-comparative, factorial between-subjects design was selected for this preliminary empirical study. The goal was to assess whether there were links, that is, relations, between the required type of school clothing (dress type) and students' psychosocial perceptions of their middle school communities.

Independent Variables

School dress type. Based on the first hypothesis, the independent variable of primary interest to us was category of school dress. Participants were assigned to groups by the type of school dress mandated at their middle school; students were designated as members of one of two groups: (a) those attending *logo uniform* schools or (b) those attending *standard dress* schools. The uniform for the first group, *logo uniform*, was defined as a mandated school uniform that required students to wear a specified type of school-identified outfit. For logo uniform schools, a school uniform was defined as standard school dress differentiated by the addition of an individual school's full school name, school initials, or school name and school mascot graphic printed or embroidered permanently on all standard dress shirts and blouses.

The uniform for the second group, *standard dress*, was defined by a school dress code that required students to wear a type of standardized school outfit. In general, this category specified a plain shirt or blouse and pants or skirt of specific colors. Depending on the individual school, the specific style of the clothing might also have been specified. However, the dress code rules of all participating standard dress schools specified that shirts would not be ornamented with any graphics or school identification.

Gender, ethnicity, grade level, and school-level SES: Demographic information about gender, ethnicity, and grade level was gathered from responses to five self-reported items included in the student survey and from school-level socioeconomic status (SES) information from school district reports. These variables were included because prior research provided convincing evidence that these factors were significantly related to the psychological processes of interest in our study, such as identity, school bonding, and perceptions of community in schools (Arhar and Kromrey, 1995; Battistich, Solomon, Kim, Watson, and Schaps, 1995; Bryk and Thum, 1989).

Because the students in this study attending logo uniform schools tended (on average) to be *less* economically disadvantaged than students from standard dress schools, a confounding of *logo uniform* school dress with *low income* (as opposed to *very low income*) school-level SES was anticipated. To statistically account for any modifying effects or interactions of SES with school dress type, school-level SES was included as an independent variable in analyses. SES, measured at the school level, was represented by the percent of students eligible for free/reduced school meals at each school. Participating schools fell into two distinct clusters of students eligible for free school lunches, labeled *low income* (25–50%) and *very low income* (75–100%).

Dependent Variables: Sense of Community Items

Dependent variables were student scores on six scales made up of Likert-scale response type items designed to assess students' perceptions of the degree to which they felt their school was a caring community. These included individual perceptions of school belonging (generalized emotions, acceptance, fitting in, being appreciated, and feelings of alienation and negativity toward school membership); peer and teacher interpersonal relations in schools; and feelings of physical and emotional security (safety, victimization, caring, liking). Student perceptions of safety were represented directly by their responses to items rating the degree to which they felt safe in school, and indirectly in terms of their reports of the frequency of aggressive behaviors (fights) and criminal behaviors (theft, vandalism) at their schools.

Survey items were selected from a variety of existing measures, with some items modified to reflect a focus on middle schools. Most items were from the "Psychological Sense of School Membership" instrument (PSSM, Goodenow, 1993b) and the "Student Sense of [Classroom and School as a] Community" measure (Battistich et al., 1995; Roberts, Hom, and Battistich, 1995). Five safety items were selected from two studies (Anderman and Kimweli, 1997; Griffith, 1997), while the remaining items were adapted from two others (Battistich et al., 1995; Voelkl, 1996).

METHODS AND ANALYSES

Based partly in theory and partly on empirical results from factor analyses, survey items were divided into six variables and then divided into two groups for analyses. Survey scoring procedures entailed computing average scores for the individual items grouped together in the six individual subscales. Study hypotheses were evaluated using two multivariate Custom General Linear Models (Type III sum of squares). For data analyses, the multivariate Wilks's statistic (essentially a MANOVA analysis) was utilized, including main effects, and all first-order interactions with Alpha probability levels were set at $p < .05$. A Bonferroni adjustment of $\alpha/3$ or $\alpha/6$ was used in conjunction with univariate F-tests and multiple comparisons. Three dependent variables, represented by scores on measures of belonging (8 items, $\alpha = .76$), safety (5 items, $\alpha = .71$), and emotional connections (6 items, $\alpha = .67$) made up the first model used in analyses; the second model consisted of scores on peer relationships (14 items, $\alpha = .86$), teachers/school relationships (11 items, $\alpha = .82$), and classroom influence (4 items, $\alpha = .73$). For both models, the independent variables included 2 categories of school dress $\times$ 2 categories of gender $\times$ 4 categories of ethnicity $\times$ 3 grade levels.

RESULTS

A significant overall relation (main effect) was found between school dress and students' perceptions of belonging in school. This significant result ($p < .05$), though tempered by its relatively small statistical effect, provided evidence that the type of school dress worn by students (logo uniform versus standard dress) was related to the degree students felt a personal connection and belonging in their school. On average, students in this study wearing a school-identified type of dress (logo uniform group) reported significantly more positive perceptions of belonging in their school community than reported by students in the standard dress group. *This finding is of great interest because research has shown school-related belonging is a major motivational dimension of the school environment and plays an important role in the development of a sense of community in both schools and other community environments* (Goodenow, 1992; McMillan and Chavis, 1986; Osterman, 2000; Sergiovanni, 1994; Solomon et al., 1996).

When this study looked at student perceptions in relation to both school dress type *and* gender, it found a link of school-specific identification (logo) to more positive perceptions of school community aspects that *became much more apparent when gender differences were factored in, especially for boys*: There were significant interactions of gender with school dress type on four of six sense of community components (belonging, safety, peer relationships, teachers/school relationships). But once again, these interactions, though significant, had very small strengths of effect, accounting for less than 2% of the total effects found in these analysis models.

Surprisingly, few significant effects for ethnicity, grade level, or SES were found. No significant relations were found between school dress type, perceptions of school community, and students' ethnicity or grade level. This study did find, however, that the *low SES* student group reported significantly different perceptions of school-related safety, emotional connections, and classroom influence from students in the *very low SES* group. But in analyses of survey responses grouped by students' school dress type *and* SES group, significant relations were found only for perceptions of feeling safe in school. The following sections discuss study findings in greater detail: These sections concentrate on the relations found between school dress type, gender, and student perceptions of the belonging and safety aspects of a school-related sense of community.

DISCUSSION

School Dress Type and Belonging

Results from study analyses indicate that the group of students wearing logo uniforms (school-identified dress type) tended to score significantly higher (more positive) on school-related belonging items than the group wearing standard dress (nonidentified school dress type). Finding this significant association between school-identified dress and positive perceptions of belonging was not surprising considering the well-known motivation and engagement functions of group identification and membership (Battistich et al., 1995; Maslow, 1968; Vygotsky, 1978). As a group, students expressing more positive school-related belonging perceptions appeared to feel more accepted, appreciated, and respected; felt more comfortable and not very different from others; and felt that other school community members frequently extended friendship to them.

Interestingly, as also found by Goodenow (1993b) and Goodenow and Grady (1993), this study found that absolute levels of reported student attachments to school were not very positive. Students tended to be neither strongly negative nor strongly positive about aspects of school as a community, and their perceptions ranged (on average by group) from some disagreement (2.0 on a scale of 5.0) to some agreement (3.6, on the same scale).

Although not specifically tested in this study, one might postulate that the mechanism responsible for the association of wearing a logo uniform with more positive perceptions of school belonging might be attributed to a combination of factors. The common (standardized) dress aspect of the school-identified uniforms worn by study participants made individuals' general appearance more homogeneous, presenting a visible similarity across all students, helping students to feel less different, and increasing feelings of "fitting in" as a school community member. At the same time, the school-specific iconography on the students' uniforms provided students with a psychological and visually distinctive link with their specific school community and distinction from all other schools.

School-specific logos serve as visible *reminders* of school affiliation to students and other school community members and as *identifiers* to outsiders. Though informal school surveys, such as those often found in the popular press, often report that most students deny liking any school dress codes, there are other reports suggesting many students actually perceive logo school uniforms as engendering respect and status from school staff and other individuals outside the immediate school community. In addition, there is some speculation that logo uniforms, by heightening the feelings of comradeship between students through a uniformity of appearance within the group, possibly reduce barriers to friendship development (Joseph, 1986; Loesch, 1995).

Belonging: The Gender Factor

In order to rule out the possibility that gender alone might account for differences in student perceptions, one-way ANOVAs were conducted on the sense of community outcome variables: There were no significant existing differences by gender. However, results from subsequent multivariate analyses showed a significant main effect of gender on belonging perceptions, with girls reporting more positive feelings of belonging than boys. Because a two-way group interaction between school dress and gender on belonging was also significant, interpreting the general relation (main effect) between gender and belonging without reference to dress type could be misleading. The post-hoc analysis conducted to determine which groups were significantly different found a significant and positive relation between school-specific dress type (logo uniform) and student perceptions of school-related belonging.

Specifically, *for girls only*, those girls wearing logo uniforms scored significantly more positive scores on belonging items than girls wearing standard dress. *For boys only*, those boys wearing logo uniforms scored significantly more positive scores on belonging items than standard dress boys. Interestingly, though both girls' and boys' perceptions were positively associated with wearing logo uniforms, this relation was found to be much more dramatic, shown by a greater positive magnitude of difference between boys in the logo uniform group over boys in the standard dress group, as illustrated in Figure 4.2.

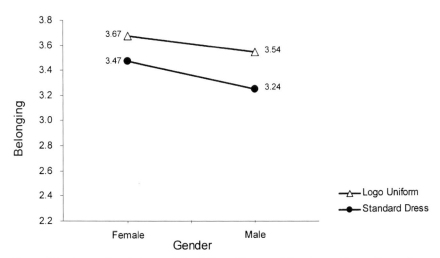

Figure 4.2 Interaction Between School Dress Type and Gender on Perceptions of School Belonging

As a group, girls reported more positive perceptions than boys across the sense of community dimensions of belonging, peer, teacher, and school relationships. This is consistent with earlier reports that girls were more bonded to school than boys (Arhar, 1992; Arhar and Kromrey, 1995; Goodenow, 1993a, 1993b; Goodenow and Grady, 1993; Osterman, 2000; Welsh, Greene, and Jenkins, 1999). It is of considerable interest that the degree of association of school dress identification to perceptions of school-related belonging seems strongest for boys, especially with boys identified by research as most in need of enhanced connections to school (Baker et al., 1997; Calabrese and Poe, 1990; Everett and Price, 1995; Finn, 1989; Welsh et al., 1999). Girls may seek to fulfill their relationship needs by stressing positive social interactions with classmates or teachers and by frequent involvement in school community activities. Boys, in contrast, may be less comfortable engaging in these types of school-related social interactions, be less likely to experience belonging, and feel less connected to school (Arhar and Kromrey, 1995; Solomon et al., 1996).

Though not specifically tested by this study and mindful of small effect sizes, one might speculate that the positive effect of logo uniforms for boys might be related in part to several factors. First, logo uniforms may positively influence perceptions of boys' behaviors by teachers or other adults through a Pygmalion effect. More positive perceptions of behavior would be likely to benefit student and teacher relationships, communication, and sense of community perceptions.

Second, again for boys, wearing a logo uniform (visually identifying a specific school community by name or symbol) might foster belonging effects through mechanisms that reduce the degree of competition among boys and that foster perceptions of the school community being equivalent to a team or a positive form of a gang. Though one might expect both girls and boys to benefit equally from increased bonding to school facilitated by reducing competition and conferring identity or status, such social bonding forms seem to be *especially* important to a broad population of adolescent boys (Arhar, 1992; Forney and Forney, 1995; Jenkins, 1997; Welsh, 2000). Thus, based the findings from earlier research and this study, there seems to be evidence to support forecasting that logo uniform interventions—functioning to help students feel more connected to school—would show greater benefit (for belonging-related effects) for boys than for girls.

Third, logo uniforms might confer *both* affiliation *and* status (membership, prestige, cachet) to the wearer. Moore and Boldero (1991) speculated that although belonging has been equated with affiliation for girls, boys may also equate belonging equally with affiliation *and* status— suggesting boys might value status even more than girls do. That boys could receive the benefit of both affiliation *and* status from school-identified dress might partially explain gender differences found related to school dress types. This could account for (a) why perceptions of school belonging of boys grouped by logo uniform were not only more positive than those of boys grouped by standard dress, but also that (b) the degree of difference between dress types for boys appeared to be proportionately greater than the corresponding positive difference between girls grouped by logo uniform over girls grouped by standard dress.

School Uniforms, Belonging, and Community: Theory and Policy

Historically, theorists have advocated the importance of relatedness as a foundation for caring connections with others and an essential element promoting positive psychosocial functioning as a prerequisite to learning (Erikson, 1968; Maslow, 1968; Sergiovanni, 1994). More specifically, belonging fosters intrinsic motivation and a stronger sense of identity and personal autonomy, and promotes self-regulation and a sense of social competence, school participation, and liking school; in contrast, psychological alienation and disconnection lead to classroom problems of low interest and achievement, aggression, violence, and high suicide rates (Battistich et al., 1995; Osterman, 2000; Solomon et al., 1996)

Important implications for policy and practice in schools stem from the links between school dress type, school-related belonging, and motivation. Current interest in investigating the motivational dimensions of school environments to guide both policy and applications stems partially from proposals by researchers in the early 1990s suggesting that the focus on changing the child (behavior) should shift to a focus on altering motivational aspects of school environments. Osterman (2000), in a review of belonging research, suggested that a psychological sense of school belonging could affect students' behaviors and achievement *indirectly* through its influence on motivation; Roeser and colleagues' (1996) study found belonging *directly* linked to levels of greater academic efficacy.

The community model formulated by McMillan and Chavis (1986) defines boundaries between groups as an essential element in the creation of stable, viable communities. Individuals use dress or other context variables (language, landmarks, passage rites) as boundaries to satisfy needs, delineate who can be trusted, and provide social protection against threats from outside the specific community. As defined in the current study, logos (emblems, names) are used as a collective symbol to represent all members of a school group: Logos function as a visual boundary for that group. Such "symbol systems" (McMillan and Chavis, p. 10), are especially important to create distinct visual boundaries that do not exist naturally in the highly diverse, heterogeneous populations making up contemporary communities. Although adolescent peer culture may establish standards for dress and behavior through fashion or gang-identifying clothing, this "teen fashion" might not contribute sufficiently to satisfy student needs for belonging—except in the area of peer relations (Solomon et al., 1996). Thus, one might extend this study's findings to suggest that perhaps school uniforms may serve the *overall* belonging needs of adolescents better than their preferred "teen fashion."

School Uniforms and Perceptions of School-Related Safety

School Dress Type and Gender Interactions

In this study, the logo uniform school dress type was linked to an enhanced sense of belonging for students. It was speculated that the significantly more positive sense of school as a safe environment also reported by the logo uniform group over safety perceptions reported by the standard dress group could be logically linked to the positive relation between school uniforms and enhanced perceptions of belonging: A school uniform (visible, school-specific identification on school dress), through the relation to student belonging, could function to help provide uniformed students with personal sense of protection, security, and order by fostering positive feelings of emotional and physical safety afforded by group membership.

In contrast to prior studies finding no relation between gender and student perceptions of school safety (Anderman and Kimweli, 1997) this study found that students' perceptions of safety in school differed significantly by both by gender and school dress type in a school dress by gender interaction, as shown in Figure 4.3. Though logo uniforms were linked to increased feelings of safety in an interaction with gender, this relation was less dramatic than that seen for that of logo uniforms with belonging. This finding actually might reflect the supposition already presented that the primary link of school-specific dress identification to school-related outcomes was through belonging.

These results indicated that for the group of *girls only*, the group of girls wearing logo uniforms scored significantly higher (felt safer) on school safety items than girls wearing standard dress. For *boys only*, the group wearing logo uniforms also scored significantly higher on school safety items than the group of boys wearing standard dress. Surprisingly, logo uniform boys also scored significantly higher on safety than logo uniform girls. However, no significant differences were found on scores of perceptions of school safety between standard dress girls and standard dress boys. It was especially interesting to note that the largest gender difference found was for the group of boys wearing logo uniforms.

Logo uniform boys (on average) reported feeling significantly safer in school, even over the group of logo uniform girls: Although the group of

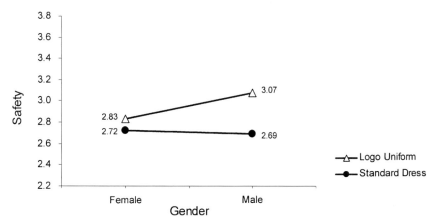

Figure 4.3 Interaction Between School Dress Type and Gender on Perceptions of School Safety

logo uniform girls felt significantly safer than both girls and boys wearing standard dress, the positive difference of the logo uniform group over the standard dress group was substantially greater for boys than for girls. This result is of interest as boys more than girls are seen as physically aggressive, implicated frequently in school misbehaviors, more often victims or perpetrators of school violence (Anderman and Kimweli, 1997; Everett and Price, 1995; Welsh, 2000; Welsh et al., 1999), receive lower grades than girls (Anderman and Kimweli, 1997), and are at increased risk for school dropout (Calabrese and Poe, 1990). The results of this study provide preliminary evidence that a decrease in such negative behaviors and outcomes could be facilitated by interventions proven to be effective for boys: If the relation between identified school dress and safety is found to be of practical significance in subsequent investigations, logo school uniforms might be an environmental intervention of choice to aid in violence reduction in schools where incidents perpetrated by alienated boys and male gang members are an identified problem.

School Dress Type and SES Interactions

In addition to finding that the SES category of student schools was related to how safe students felt in school—participants attending *low*-income schools feeling safer than those attending *very low* income schools—these relations differed significantly by school dress type (a school dress by SES interaction). Though significant, the effect was very small. This study also found that in the more affluent (*low* SES) schools represented in the current study, logo uniform students felt safer than standard dress students: This was a hypothesized and expected outcome. But for the poorest schools (*very low* SES), the results were unexpected: Logo uniform students felt *less* safe. One explanation of this deviation from the expected relation might stem from the fact that the only participating *very low* SES logo uniform school was located in an area where crime and gang activity was known to be very common.

School Uniforms and Social Relationships in School Contexts

A second analysis on the dependent variables of peer relationships, teacher/school relationships, and classroom influence did not indicate a significant general (main) effect for uniform type, but a significant main effect was found for gender. In addition, several interaction effects attributed to a combination of student school dress type and gender were found. For both boys and girls, wearing logo uniforms appeared to be related to more positive perceptions of the quality of relationships with peers in the school community (peers as more interested, appreciative, helpful, and caring as school community members). As found for school safety, the magnitude of difference in relation to peer relationships was found to be greater between logo uniform boys and standard dress boys than the corresponding difference between logo uniform girls and standard dress girls.

Goodenow (1993b) reported that girls in general felt more positive about teacher relationships in school than boys, but these findings were only partially duplicated in this study. On average, standard dress girls, logo uniform girls, *and* logo uniform boys reported significantly more positive perceptions than standard dress boys, but the effect was very small, suggesting that school dress had little effect on the perception of these relationships. In absolute terms, both dress groups felt ambivalent about relationships with teachers, their principal, how much they liked school, and how proud they felt to be a school member.

Where Do We Go From Here?

This investigation of school uniforms yielded a number of significant results: Though preliminary, these findings are important. School dress type contributed significantly to students' perceptions of belonging and to perceptions of safety for boys. However small, these results can be considered meaningful.

There is a need for additional investigations to replicate the findings of the current study and to further delineate the relation of school uniforms to students' perceptions and school motivation through replication and extension studies. Such research could help address confounding factors (such as the confounding of logo uniform with school location in safer neighborhoods) and determine if these findings would hold and generalize to new settings. In addition, future research could address the issue raised by Paliokas and Rist (1996) that changes in the school community implemented at the same time as dress codes (such as policing policies, other new safety practices, Hawthorne or halo effects, or a natural decline in violence independent of new programs) might be factors related to the degree of feeling safe in school reported by students.

Other aspects of school uniforms not addressed in this preliminary study provide research questions for future investigations. Because logos define school uniforms, the question of whether differences in logo design impact student perceptions needs to be raised. For example, in this preliminary study logo designs on student shirts ranged from small embroidered school initials to large motifs on T-shirts. Would the addition of other *very* distinctive dress features—such as a unique, distinctive patterned fabric— incorporated into the school uniform contribute to additional school uniform effects?

Enforcing the distinction between different types of school dress became a driving force when results from this study were communicated. Of even greater importance for future research will be to understand and take into account these distinctions between common school dress and logo uniforms.

CONCLUSION

This preliminary study defined critical terms to reduce existing confusion, developed a theoretical base, and tested hypotheses that school-identified uniforms were related to student perceptions of their school as a supportive and safe community.

In light of the preliminary nature of this study, plus the fact that effect sizes of the significant relations found between group-identified uniforms and student perceptions of school-related belonging and safety were small, perhaps the major contribution of this study was to bring issues of the definition of school dress to the forefront. Adequately defining variables is crucial to ensuring the validity of empirical research. Once this flaw—*the omission of definition*—in the existing research was identified during the course of this research study, it became apparent in other school dress studies that it was highly probable that reported effects were merely artifacts rather than true school uniform effects.

Based on the definitions developed in this study (which make clear distinctions between true uniforms and dress codes) the viewpoint taken in this chapter suggests that dress codes (including standard dress) cannot create within-school identity or interschool differences. *There is a difference between standard school dress and school uniforms.* This hypothesis was supported by the study's differential results: School-identified (logo) uniforms do make a difference, specifically in relation to student perceptions of school-related belonging and safety. Dress codes are not designed to create feelings of belonging or security, but rather, as detailed previously, function simply to minimize difference—to homogenize student appearance. Also, with true uniforms, goals are set a priori; iconography creates distinctions and differences between systems (in this case, between schools).

This research-based empirical evidence also clarifies reports from anecdotal accounts suggesting that restrictive school dress reduces clothing competition and fosters social bonding among students (Evans, 1996; Holloman et al., 1996; LaPoint et al., 1992): Standard dress does not merely facilitate group bonding; distinctive logo type uniforms facilitate bonding and security feelings among students by emphasizing a distinct school identity apart from other schools.

In 1996, Roeser and his associates reported finding that school-related belonging was significantly related to positive school affect and motivation. These findings provide preliminary evidence to link school uniforms and this belonging factor. By maximizing interschool differences while eliminating intraschool differences, authentic uniforms help set the scene for developing identity and fostering relational school communities. The significant results from this preliminary study contribute needed *empirical* validity and basis in theory for ongoing school uniform research by providing evidence to strongly support the hypothesis that school-specific dress identification (school uniforms) may be important in facilitating feelings of belonging and cohesion among middle school students.

The significant link between school uniforms and safety found in this investigation is noteworthy. This preliminary finding provides support for previous reports suggesting dress codes and school uniforms are designed to positively change a school's environment and social climate by increasing perceptions of orderly student behaviors (Brunsma and Rockquemore, 1998; Murray, 1997), thus contributing to safer and more cooperative school environments (Holloman et al., 1996; Murray, 1997; Newmann, Rutter, and Smith, 1989; Paliokas and Rist, 1996). The link of school uniforms to more positive perceptions of school safety compliments earlier research finding that students who report feeling safe in school tended to also report lower incidence of school disorder and misconduct (Welsh et al., 1999): A higher degree of school bonding measured in 11-year-old boys was related to noninvolvement in violence in middle school, even for aggressive male students identified as at the greatest risk to become participants in school violence (O'Donnell, Hawkins, and Abbott, 1995).

Finding school uniforms related to more positive perceptions of personal security and school as a safe environment, especially for boys, provides evidence that school uniforms, by promoting belonging and social bonding, might prove an effective intervention to help reduce violence and enhance safety in schools. This would be especially important in gang-active central city neighborhoods where research has found boys in public schools feel less safe than others students (Welsh, Stokes, and Greene, 2000). If these findings are replicated in broader contexts, the indirect link (through belonging and safety perceptions) of school uniforms to positive school outcomes will add a modest piece to the process of understanding how uniforms function in school-related contexts and offering some suggestion that learning more about school uniforms could contribute useful information to the search for interventions facilitating more relational, supportive, motivating, and safer school environments.

Finally, it is crucial to re-emphasize that, as defined by this study, *group-identified uniforms in school contexts serve different functions and purpose than nonidentified dress codes typically confused with genuine uniforms.* As explained earlier, the purpose of a school dress code is to eliminate discrimination, functioning only to *eliminate* differences, homogenize appearance, and eliminate within-group (i.e., within-school) differences. In contrast, authentic uniforms (group-identified dress) function on multiple levels: In school contexts, uniforms incorporating standard dress features not only function to homogenize appearance within a school, but most importantly, differentiate between schools. Uniforms function to create identity and identification with a specific group, maximize between-group (i.e., between-school) differences, and help facilitate important cohesion and bonding processes.

Standardized school dress and formal school uniforms have been widely criticized as being unrealistically appealing to parents, teachers, and policy makers by being readily visible and understandable, simplistic and immediate, cheap, and relatively cost free to taxpayers (Brunsma and

Rockquemore, 1998). If continuing research provides more positive evidence that school-specific uniform identification may help students with the process of connecting to their school community, these criticisms may instead become strengths. Finally, it is extremely important to stress that a valid uniform *does not need to incorporate common dress*: The critical element in creating a uniform is the addition of group-identifying iconography. In practical terms, a logo uniform need not be an expensive custom-made outfit, as typified by many private school uniforms. Rather, the link of logo uniforms to positive student outcomes could be achieved using a highly visible and distinctive—yet simple and inexpensive—school-specific pin or badge attached to standard dress outfits or student clothing meeting less restrictive dress code rules.

Student Uniforms and School Climate: The Urban Middle School Teacher's Perception

Winston H. Tucker III

As of the fall of 2004 the Saint Paul Public Schools is the largest school district in Minnesota, serving 41,085 students (Saint Paul Public Schools, 2004). It was also the first public school district in Minnesota to implement a mandatory student uniform policy at one of the 73 traditional public schools in Saint Paul. This school, Hazel Park Middle School, began the process of seeking approval from the board of education in 1995 to require student uniforms and implemented a mandatory uniform program for all students in 1997. Currently, there are 14 elementary and 3 middle schools that require their students to wear uniforms in the Saint Paul Public School District.

PROCESS OF UNIFORM IMPLEMENTATION

Several important issues arose as the proposal to require student uniforms at Hazel Park Middle School gained momentum. Some issues included student rights to freedom of speech (Nelson, 1997), school climate (Murray, 1996, 1997), student safety (Nelson, 1997), peer pressure (Kaiser, 1990), reducing distractions (Nelson, 1997), increasing school unity (La-Point, Holloman, and Alleyne, 1992), decreasing gang activity, and increasing staff safety (U.S. Dept. of Education, 1996). Local issues such as open enrollment, uniform costs, and parental concerns also arose. The forum for staff, student, and parental input as well as questions and concerns of the board of education and superintendent were items to be resolved before uniform implementation could proceed and be formally approved. The initial step was to seek staff input regarding this proposal. It was essential that the vast majority of the teaching staff support this proposal before it could advance.

Discussing the pros and cons of requiring student uniforms resulted in many spirited educational and philosophical discussions among the staff. These discussions centered on the role of public education versus the role of private education, students' rights to freedom of expression, school climate, public perception, and parental support and opposition. After much discussion and debate the majority (at least half) of the staff voted in favor of proceeding with the approval process. All building staff were allowed to vote on this proposal.

The second step involved seeking student and parental input before seeking official approval from the board of education. Students were asked to share their feelings via the student council, and informational meetings were held to present the rationale for the uniform implementation to parents. At a meeting with an audience of approximately 100 interested and concerned parents, the principal, some teachers, and a parent presented some educational articles that supported uniform implementation as well as news articles regarding school districts around the country that were beginning to implement uniform programs. The limited research that was presented focused only on the positive aspects of uniform implementation. The presenters only presented the benefits of a uniform policy and then fielded questions from the audience.

Students were also present during the presentation and were modeling the uniforms. Parental reaction to the presence of students modeling the uniforms ranged from praise and support to vehement frustration and the perception that students were being used as a manipulative tool to force uniform implementation on the entire student body. Parents were given the opportunity to ask a variety of questions. These questions centered on the rationale for uniforms in a public school setting, approximate costs for parents, expected impact on the students' morale, and level of teacher support. Parents were also given time to express their support or resistance to this policy proposal. Parental statements of support centered on the perception that uniforms would result in improved student behavior and improved academic achievement. Statements of parental resistance revolved around the feeling that this idea was a step backward to a more oppressive time in education and society as well as a concern that students would lose the right to freedom of expression if a uniform policy was adopted. Parents were also concerned about the added expense of having to purchase clothes that are worn only for school.

The proposal was presented to the board of education in 1996, and a decision was made to allow parents at Hazel Park Middle School to vote on the issue. Ballots were distributed via a mailing to parents, and of those who voted, at least 75% supported the implementation of a uniform program, which was required before the proposal could proceed. Several key arguments were used to either support or refute the uniform policy proposal. The rationale in favor of uniforms revolved around improving school climate and school spirit (Kaiser, 1990); increasing academic achievement (Stanley, 1996); improving student behavior (Nelson, 1997); minimizing the expression of gang affiliation via student dress, making it easier to identify any middle school–aged outsider who did not belong on campus (U.S. Dept. of Education, 1996); and reducing clothing cost for parents. The bases for opposing uniforms were concerns such as the oppression of student speech and expression (Nelson, 1997), loss of student individuality (LaPoint et al., 1992), increased costs for parents who would have to purchase clothing for school use only, and the inability of students to attend their attendance area school for those students whose parents were opposed to uniforms.

One of the main issues that arose was the dilemma of what to do with the students whose parents refused to follow the proposed uniform policy if adopted: the classic compliance issue (Bernet, 2003; Tillman, 1999). Although the Saint Paul district has an open enrollment policy, it did not seem fair to have students leave Hazel Park after the completion of their seventh grade to attend another Saint Paul middle school for their eighth grade school year if they and/or their parents refused to abide by the uniform policy. For this reason a 3-year phase-in policy was adopted and required by the board of education. The 1st year of uniform implementation was voluntary for all students. A small cohort of approximately a dozen students and about six staff wore uniforms on a semiregular basis. The 2nd year there was a requirement for all entering seventh grade students to abide by the uniform policy, while the eighth grade students were exempt. In the 3rd year of implementation, in the fall of 1997, all students at Hazel Park Middle School were required to abide by the student uniform policy (see appendix at the end of this chapter). Another issue that arose was whether or not staff could be required by the building administration to abide by a staff uniform policy. It was a strong belief of the principal and assistant principal that the administrators and teachers were to be role models for professional dress for the students and should therefore wear uniforms as well. The proposal was for staff uniforms that closely resembled the student uniforms in style and color. This proposal was very divisive among the staff and was vehemently supported and opposed by a number of staff members. Many staff members felt that as professionals they should not be required to dress like the students in any type of uniform. This raised a myriad of issues and discussion related to the teacher contract, increased clothing expense for staff, freedom of expression, union rights, and the debate of the purpose of a public school versus the purpose of a private school.

In some of the informal discussions at the building and district level the issue of creating an elite middle school among the eight middle schools in a public school district was also an issue that was of concern for some, but was never formally discussed at the building level or at the board of education. There was concern that Hazel Park, with the new uniform requirement, would draw the majority of the academically oriented students, resulting in an elite middle school as compared to the other middle schools in Saint Paul. Issues of fairness and equity between schools were of concern to some. All of the above were salient issues as the proposed student uniform policy proceeded toward implementation.

ADOPTING THE UNIFORM POLICY

Prior to adopting a uniform policy the school had a generic student dress code, which was enforced and fairly consistently followed by the student body. This dress code was fairly typical of most public schools and prohibited clothing that was vulgar or offensive, promoted alcohol, drugs or cigarettes, or revealed an inappropriate amount of a student's body. The rationale for adopting the first uniform policy in a public school went far beyond the issue of student dress, however. The underlying reasons for implementing the uniform policy included improving the learning environment and school climate (Murray, 1997), improving student behavior, and reducing distractions in the classroom (U.S. Dept. of Education, 1996), creating a sense of equality among disparate socioeconomic groups, reducing peer pressure related to clothing, and increasing the level of school spirit and unity among the diverse student body (Kaiser, 1985).

There were two strong underlying reasons for implementing a uniform policy, which were shared by the building administration and several staff members alike, but not always verbalized in a public forum. The first reason was to attract students of a higher academic caliber. It was believed that being the only middle school in a large urban district with open enrollment, having a uniform policy would attract those parents and students who were more serious about academic rigor and achievement than the average family. The second underlying reason was the assumption that Hazel Park could attract students who were more focused and better behaved than the average junior high school student. It was assumed that the type of students who would submit to their parents' insistence to attend a uniform school or who were themselves motivated to wear uniforms were more likely to obey their parents and as a result obey their teachers and behave in a more appropriate manner. This assumption has not always come to fruition, since some parents looked for a uniform school if their child was experiencing increasing behavior problems at home and in the community. It was also hoped that the school would draw some students who had previously attended parochial schools due to the new uniform policy.

Uniform policies around the country were being implemented in several public school districts with apparently positive results. Long Beach, California, implemented a district-wide uniform policy, and the media reported statistical improvements in the learning environment, which helped provide further impetus to Hazel Park Middle School's efforts to implement a uniform program (but see chapter 7 for a critique of this study, as well as Brunsma, 2004).

The momentum for implementing a uniform policy was also bolstered by the fact that President Clinton stated his support for uniforms in the public school in a State of the Union address in 1996. President Clinton instructed the United States Department of Education on February 24, 1996, to distribute the *Manual on School Uniforms* to over 16,000 school districts. This manual provided legal advice on how to implement and enforce a student uniform policy in public schools. The timing of these national educational issues played an important role in setting the stage for uniform implementation for the first time in the Saint Paul Public School District and in the state of Minnesota.

ANALYSIS OF SCHOOL CLIMATE
AND STUDENT UNIFORMS

As a teacher at Hazel Park, I was privileged to watch and participate in the interesting social and educational experiment of mandating student uniforms in a public school for the first time in Minnesota. After the uniform policy was successfully implemented, parents continued to send their students to Hazel Park, and enrollment remained steady. Many staff members informally commented that the uniforms helped improve the school climate. Despite this perception there was no data analysis being conducted related to the mandatory uniform policy and possible effects on the school climate. A few years later, when I changed from serving as the role of teacher to assistant principal at Hazel Park, I felt a desire to analyze the current state of the uniform policy on a more formal basis. My enrollment in a doctoral program at the University of Minnesota provided further impetus to study this issue in a broader context as I began my dissertation. By the fall of 1998 another middle school in the Saint Paul Public School District, Cleveland Middle School, implemented an identical uniform policy, which broadened the research base, allowing for deeper comparative analysis. In addition, the new principal of Hazel Park Middle School was very supportive and encouraged my analysis of the impact that student uniforms had on the school environment.

Four middle schools in the Saint Paul Public Schools were selected for data collection during the 1998–1999 school year. These schools were Battle Creek Middle School, Cleveland Middle School, Hazel Park Middle School, and Washington Middle School. These four schools are somewhat similar in their demographic data, but important differences exist between the schools.

Battle Creek Middle School is located in a predominantly lower middle to middle class socioeconomic section of Saint Paul and serves primarily students from a lower to middle class socioeconomic background. Seventy-seven percent of the students were on free or reduced lunch. There were 921 students and 58 full-time licensed classroom teachers employed at Battle Creek Middle School during the 1998–1999 school year (Saint Paul Public Schools, 2004). The student racial/ethnic breakdown in grades six through eight for the 1998–1999 school year was 45% Asian American, 3.5% American Indian, 13% African American, 3.5% Hispanic, and 35% Anglo-American.

Cleveland Middle School is located in a predominantly lower middle to middle class socioeconomic section of Saint Paul and serves a similar population as compared to the other middle schools in the district. Eighty-five percent of the students were on free or reduced lunch. There were 364 students and 27 full-time licensed classroom teachers employed at Cleveland Middle School during the 1998–1999 school year (Saint Paul Public Schools, 2004). The student racial/ethnic breakdown in grades six through eight for the 1998–1999 school year was 50% Asian American, 0.5% American Indian, 18.5% African American, 8% Hispanic, and 23% Anglo-American.

Hazel Park Middle School is located in a predominantly lower middle to middle class socioeconomic section of Saint Paul. Although having the highest percentage of Anglo-American students of the four middle schools studied at the time, it serves a fairly diverse constituency. Sixty-five percent of the students were on free or reduced lunch. There were 953 students and 42.5 full-time licensed classroom teachers employed at Hazel Park Middle School during the 1998–1999 school year (Saint Paul Public Schools, 2004). The student racial/ethnic breakdown in grades six through eight for the 1998–1999 school year was 29.2% Asian American, 0.8% American Indian, 16% African American, 8% Hispanic, and 46% Anglo-American.

Washington Middle School is located in a predominantly lower middle to middle class socioeconomic section of Saint Paul. Eighty-one percent of the students were on free or reduced lunch. There were 786 students and 43 full-time licensed classroom teachers employed at Washington Middle School during the 1998–1999 school year (Saint Paul Public Schools, 2004). The student racial/ethnic breakdown in grades six through eight for the 1998–1999 school year was 37% Asian American, 2% American Indian, 26% African American, 7% Hispanic, and 28% Anglo-American.

These four middle schools share several factors in common. These schools are all part of the Saint Paul Public Schools and are located in urban neighborhoods of similar socioeconomic status. Well over half the students in each school were receiving free or reduced lunch. They served a diverse student population of students in grades six through eight. Currently only one of the original four schools still has sixth grade; the other three now serve only grades seven and eight.

These four middle schools also have several factors that make each one unique. Cleveland Middle School was in the first full year of requiring uniforms, and Hazel Park Middle School was in the second year of uniform implementation at the time of this study. While these schools are located in similar socioeconomic neighborhoods, they serve students from throughout Saint Paul. In addition, the student population at Cleveland Middle School was smaller than the other schools. The pupil:teacher ratio also varied from a low of 14 to 1 at Cleveland Middle School to a high of 23 to 1 at Hazel Park Middle School. These factors may have been variables in the teachers' perception of school climate.

STUDY METHODOLOGY AND FOCUS

The purpose of my study was to determine the effect of a student uniform policy on the climate of urban middle schools. The issue of school climate has been an escalating concern nationwide (e.g., Murray, 1997). Student uniforms were becoming a growing trend for climate transformation, and there was little substantive research to verify the impact of uniform policies on school climate. The areas of school climate explored include school safety, student achievement, peer interactions, feeling of community among students, teacher-student interactions, and student behavior.

The research methodology was exploratory and sought to gather a variety of data to examine the possible impact that student uniforms might have on perceptions of school climate. This study utilized both quantitative and qualitative research methods. The quantitative research included the administration of the NASSP CASE climate survey and a supplemental survey to 113 teachers in four Saint Paul public middle schools, two with and two without a uniform policy. Battle Creek had 29 respondents, Cleveland had 21 respondents, Hazel Park had 30 respondents, and Washington had 33 respondents. Cleveland and Hazel Park both had uniforms at the time of this study. This allowed for a comparative analysis of the climate of middle schools with uniforms and those without uniforms. An analysis of variance was utilized to check for statistical differences. The qualitative research included focus group interviews of 27 teachers in the two uniform schools to gain a deeper understanding and examine similarities and differences in perception of teachers' perspective of the impact of student uniforms on the climate of their school. A computer program designed for qualitative data analysis based on the transcripts of the focus group interviews was used to sort the data for prevalent and reoccurring themes.

The focus of this study was on teacher perception and understanding of how student uniforms affect the climate of urban middle schools. One potential limitation of this study was that the unit of analysis was confined to the individual teacher's perception of student uniform policies and their relationship to school climate. This is a limitation because the view of only a sample of teachers who volunteered to participate in the focus groups was gained, as opposed to a sample of the entire faculty. A broader sample of teachers may have produced more contradictory perspectives and opinions. It is possible that those staff who self-selected to participate in the focus group interviews were staff who supported the uniform policy and participated to express their support of student uniforms. A second potential limitation was the use of focus groups as a research method. Because the teachers participating in these focus groups were familiar with each other, individuals may have been hesitant to share information that is controversial or political, or that would make them appear uninformed or adversarial. A third limitation in this study was the use of the CASE school climate survey. While this survey measured factors of school climate, there may not be a direct correlation between the climate factors and the uniform policies. A fourth limitation in this study was external validity or generalizability. This study took place in a Midwestern urban school district at a middle school level. Due to the size of the sample and where it was administered, it would be difficult to generalize across all samples in different settings.

Only teacher perceptions were utilized in this study. No effort was made to explore the perceptions of students, parents, community members, administrators, or other school staff. This narrow focus was intentional, and only teachers' perceptions were utilized as the basis for research since they have the most direct contact with students in the educational setting in which face-to-face instruction occurs. Other diverse input would have been beneficial to gain an additional perspective and would serve as the purpose for a future research study. This study intentionally examined only what teachers perceived as the impact on school climate due to the implementation of student uniform policies. By examining the teachers' perspectives during this time period in education, this study made a contribution to a limited body of literature that lacked in teacher perception, opinion, or lived experience. Many of the educational articles involving school uniforms focused mostly on the perspective of the school principal or district administrator at the time of this study. This study did not explore the impact of uniforms in private, charter, or parochial schools. It did not examine public educational systems in rural or suburban settings. The opinions of elementary and high school teachers were not sought in this study either. This study explored how middle school teachers in an urban setting perceived the effects of uniform policies on the school climate.

The central research question was what impact does a student uniform policy have on the climate of urban middle schools in the Saint Paul Public Schools? These six subquestions guided my research study:

1. Has there been any impact on school safety that might have resulted from the implementation of a student uniform policy?
2. What has been the effect on student achievement since the implementation of a student uniform policy?
3. Have there been any changes in peer interactions as a result of the implementation of a student uniform policy?
4. Have teachers perceived a change in the feeling of community among the students as a result of the implementation of a student uniform policy?
5. Has the teacher interaction with students changed in any way as a result of the implementation of a student uniform policy?
6. Has there been a change in student behavior as a result of the implementation of a uniform policy?

RESULTS

An increasingly important issue in education today is school safety. One of the reasons public schools are adopting uniforms is an attempt to make their schools safer. The CASE school climate survey results revealed that the teachers' perceptions of security were statistically similar between the four schools regardless of two schools having a uniform policy when an analysis of variance was conducted on the data (F = 1.19, df = 3, p = .317). However, the focus group interviews revealed that teachers perceived that their schools were safer with a uniform policy. Teachers stated that school staff were more readily able to identify outsiders because their students all wore uniforms. Staff felt that students would be less able to hide a weapon since the clothes were not as baggy and the students had to tuck their shirts in their pants. It was also observed that there was less conflict around clothing issues and that uniforms suppressed the visible presence of gang affiliation. Teachers indicated in the focus group interviews that an increase in school safety is an important change in the school climate.

A paramount issue in education, especially with the requirements of the No Child Left Behind Act, is student achievement. One of the underlying reasons for adopting a uniform policy is to raise the levels of student proficiency with the hope and intention that students will be more focused on their lesson if dressed somewhat professionally in a school uniform as opposed to their normal street clothes. The CASE survey results revealed quite similar perceptions in student academic orientation between the four schools regardless of any uniform policy (F = 2.12, df = 3, p = .102). When the mean results were combined for the two uniform schools (51 responses) and the two nonuniform schools (63 responses), however, the teachers at the uniform schools had a more positive perception of academic orientation (M = 14.55) as compared to the nonuniform schools (M = 13.28) (F = 5.23, df = 1, p = .024). The focus group interviews revealed that these middle school teachers did not perceive a direct relationship between the adoption of a uniform policy and levels of academic achievement. Teachers did indicate that they perceived that student uniforms had an indirect influence on academic achievement. One teacher stated,

I think achievement increases. I was fortunate to be here when we didn't have uniforms and still be here when we implemented them one hundred percent. Kids at this age have a tendency to daydream or think about what someone is doing across the room or sitting next to them and I don't see students looking at each other for what type of shirt they are wearing or what type of pants they are wearing, which takes them away from being on task. I just don't see that. I think they focus more on their work because of that.

The way in which middle school students treat each other in a school setting is an important indicator of school climate. A positive school climate is marked by respectful peer interactions in which students support one another and feel like they belong in the learning community. The CASE survey results demonstrated on the Student-Peer Relationships Subscale that the teachers in the two uniform schools had a more positive perception of peer interactions than the two nonuniform schools. Uniform schools reported more positive perceptions of the role that uniforms play in improving peer interactions than nonuniform schools ($F = 4.81$, df = 3, $p = .004$; Tukey Post-Hoc tests available upon request). The focus group interviews revealed that the middle school teachers believe that peer interactions improve with uniforms. They felt that student uniforms are social equalizers in a diverse student body, decrease status related to clothing, decrease teasing centered around clothing, decrease obvious cliques among students, decrease tensions among students, decrease physical conflicts among students, and provide greater flexibility for interaction among diverse student groups. One teacher stated,

I think that there is, at least for our kids, I think there is a socioeconomic class equalizer that is very much needed, if kids that go to school here or kids that live near here will get into fights over clothing it tells me that there is some desperation attached to being poor. When you get to where you've got to grab onto and hold onto these items that you cover your body with and they are pretty much functional, and they get excited about that and get aggressive and get mean, it tells me something: the uniforms are good because it gets rid of reasons to have conflict.

Educational leaders are working harder than ever to create a positive feeling of community amongst the student body. The Student-Peer Relationships Subscale on the CASE school climate survey revealed that the teachers in uniform schools had more positive perceptions of peer interactions than did the teachers in nonuniform schools in this study. The teachers in the uniform schools reported more positive perceptions of the role that uniforms play in improving the sense of community than did the teachers in the nonuniform schools. In the focus group interviews teachers reported that the sense of community among students has improved as a result of implementing a uniform policy. Teachers perceived a decrease in tension among students, less obvious factions among students, and an increase in the sense of belonging and unity among students. Teachers expressed that uniforms facilitate a sense of collective identity and common ground for a diverse student body. One teacher noted this about the students:

> We don't all speak the same language, and we don't all have the same customs, we don't all have the same expectations, except we are in uniform. This is an expectation we all share. That is common ground, and for some that might be the only common ground. It is a coming together, an equality, that does not exist outside of a uniform setting. It didn't exist before we had uniforms. There has been a positive change in the sense of belonging. They dress for it.

Research is very clear that the relationship between middle school students and their teacher is a critical factor in how students behave and to what level they engage in their academic studies (Mullis, Rathge, and Mullis, 2003). On the Teacher-Student Relationships Subscale the uniform schools had more positive perceptions of teacher-student relationships than did the two nonuniform schools. Uniform schools reported more positive perceptions of the role that uniforms play in improving teacher-student interactions than nonuniform schools (F = 7.20, df = 3, p = .0002; Tukey Post-Hoc Tests available upon request). The focus group interviews revealed that teacher perceptions of students were positively altered with uniforms. Teachers stated that they had to get to know students as individuals as opposed to making assumptions based on dress and that they were less likely to make negative judgments based on a message derived from clothing. One teacher stated, "We see past what kids are wearing and what they have on, and we don't pre-judge them based on what they are wearing." Teachers stated that in some cases students were perceived as less threatening since they were dressed in a school uniform. Teachers also stated that they felt they were put in a position of greater authority since the students wore uniforms in school. The improvement in teacher-student interactions was perceived as the most important change in school climate resulting from implementation of uniform policies according to several teachers. It is important to note that the statements above represent perceptions and are not substantiated by more objective and quantifiable forms of research data.

How students conduct themselves in middle school has been, and continues to be, an important issue in education. On the Student Behavioral Values Subscale on the CASE survey, the four schools had similar perceptions of student behavior ($F = 2.16$, df $= 3$, $p = .097$). When means were combined by uniform and nonuniform schools, however, uniform schools ($M = 9.65$) reported more positive perceptions of the role that uniforms play in improving student behavior than nonuniform schools ($M = 8.54$) ($F = 6.38$, df $= 1$, $p = .013$). The focus group interviews revealed a consistent perception that student behavior is positively altered with uniforms. Teachers reported that uniforms create positive behavioral expectations resulting in an improvement in behavior that is most noticeable when students are in large groups. Teachers noticed a reduction in inappropriate behavior directly related to implementing uniform policies. A teacher commented, "It immediately sets up an expectation that the kids have to fulfill and do so just by showing up in a uniform, and that sets a standard that we expect them to behave in a uniform and look proper and ready for school." Six of the 27 teachers (22%) interviewed in the focus groups reported that student behavior was perceived as the most important change in school climate resulting from the implementation of uniform policies.

Hazel Park Middle School, the uniform school that had the policy in place longer, frequently reported higher climate ratings. Both uniform schools noted a change in clientele as a result of the policy, which was feasible due to the district's open enrollment policy. This change in clientele raises an essential question regarding uniform policies. Does requiring student uniforms change students' behavior and conduct, or does requiring uniforms attract a more subservient clientele in a district with open enrollment, thereby resulting in a perceived improvement in student conduct and school climate?

Teachers noted a slight reduction of behaviorally challenging students, which they felt was due to the uniform policy. Teachers also cited a slight increase in academically oriented students and the potential for recruiting private school students. Both uniform schools share some frustration regarding the implementation of a uniform policy. The consistency in enforcement among teachers is an ongoing issue among teachers. A public school uniform policy requires an extensive uniform loan system, and with that come the time and energy to launder those clothes that have been borrowed and returned. Both uniform schools revealed very similar perceptions of the relationship to the uniform policy and school climate.

IMPLICATIONS AND CONCLUSIONS

Schools must carefully consider their objectives concerning school climate and whether or not a uniform policy will impact the learning environment as perceived by educators and parents alike. It is imperative that schools conduct a needs analysis before attempting to implement a uniform code. A formal needs analysis was not conducted at any of the middle schools in Saint Paul prior to implementing a uniform policy. Securing the support of the teachers, parents, administration, superintendent, the board of education, and, if desired, the student body is required for effective implementation. In Saint Paul the schools effectively gained the support of the above adult constituent groups before implementing a uniform policy. This may be one reason that the middle schools still continue to require student uniforms.

Schools should have measurable outcomes regarding school climate to analyze the effectiveness of any uniform policy. Uniform policy guidelines must be simple, clear, specific, and reasonable. There must be an understanding and sensitivity for students from households with few material and financial resources. There are children who through no fault of their own will come to school in a soiled uniform, which is especially noticeable if a white shirt is a required component of the uniform code. In a public school setting, human, physical, and monetary resources are imperative for the implementation of a uniform requirement. The Saint

Paul middle schools requiring uniforms have effectively allocated the necessary resources to enforce a uniform policy on a daily basis. Students may not be denied an education because they were not able to wear a uniform on any given school day. School personnel must work with parents in need to assist in procuring school uniforms when necessary. The uniform schools in Saint Paul provide uniforms for those students and families who could otherwise not afford them. Public schools must have a loaner clothes program to assist those students who for various reasons come to school with dirty or stained uniform clothing that would embarrass a student if he or she wore it during the day or for those students who come to school without one or all parts of their uniform. An effective loaner program is in place at the uniform middle schools in Saint Paul.

This research study allowed teachers' perspectives and lived experiences to be shared and published. It also confirmed that uniform policies can have positive impacts on various aspects of the perceptions of school climate. It provided useful data for the Saint Paul Public Schools as well as useful data for schools and districts considering the adoption of a uniform policy. This study helped expand the research base on student uniforms and the impact on school climate in public urban middle schools. Perhaps most importantly my research was a confirmation that uniforms are not a cure-all for school climate challenges and the hard work and dedication that are necessary on the behalf of public school educators to help all children succeed to their highest level.

In the fall of 2001, one of the two nonuniform schools that participated in the study, Battle Creek Middle School, adopted a uniform code for all of its students. As of the fall of 2004 there are 3 middle schools and 14 elementary schools in the Saint Paul Public School District that require student uniforms. Whether a Saint Paul school adopts a uniform policy or not is still a local school decision that requires board of education approval, and 80% of the families of the entire student body in the school must vote in favor of uniform adoption for implementation to proceed. The site council is often the decision-making body that takes the lead on this issue and conducts the vote and presents their request to the board of education. The process has become more formalized since the implementation of the district's first uniform policy at Hazel Park Middle School in 1997. It still remains a local decision and will most likely remain so under the leadership of the current superintendent since her philosophy supports the concept of schools, parents, and students having an array of choices relating to their child's education.

In Saint Paul, the uniform selected must not be characterized as gender-specific, and schools must make provisions for those students whose families cannot financially afford to purchase uniforms. Schools must implement positive reinforcement measures to encourage compliance with the uniform policy. The uniform expectations, rationale, and benefits of the uniform policy must be communicated to families and fully understood by students and parents alike. The district does suggest having a phase-in policy when possible, but it is not a requirement. The color style of the uniforms and any phase-in procedure is to have school-wide and district support. Of the 17 Saint Paul schools that require uniforms there are variations in the colors that are permitted, with some schools allowing students to choose between several colors.

Other implications of the uniform policy arose relating to the climate and operation of the school. These include a mixed public perception of the schools that require uniforms. One perception is that a uniform school is one that is structured, orderly, and well managed and has high expectations for students and academics, since uniforms are required and very visible to the public. A contradictory perception by the public is that the school has such difficult students and so many problems with discipline and gangs that they had to require uniforms to keep the students in control and keep the learning environment orderly.

Another implication for uniform schools is providing uniforms for those students whose families are in economic hardship. This has resulted in increased fundraising, grants, and partnerships with outside agencies and area businesses. Since all or part of a uniform is also loaned out to some students on any given day for various reasons, it essential to have personnel available in the morning to distribute loaner clothing and in the afternoon to collect loaner clothing from students. In addition a staff member must assume the responsibility of washing and sorting the loaner clothes for reuse by students in need.

Another issue that has impacted the climate and operation of the school among teachers is the ongoing issue of uniform policy enforcement. Students at the junior high level are amazingly creative at finding various ways to test the limits and requirements of the uniform policy. While this is a natural stage of development for adolescents, it does lead to frustration among the staff when there is inconsistency in enforcement. Some staff are oblivious to uniform violations or noncompliance, while others can be overly zealous and picky regarding a student's uniform. This leads to student and staff frustration and usually ends up being addressed and resolved by the building administration.

Reflecting on the implementation process that was utilized at Hazel Park Middle School, it is obvious that the district process is now more formalized and standardized resulting in a uniformity of implementation across the district. I feel it would have been wise to keep the issue of student and staff uniforms separate and focus on a professional dress code for staff. Tying the two issues together caused a great deal of controversy and resistance among many of the staff members. While the concept of leading by example is admirable and necessary for educators, there may be more prudent and less divisive ways in which this issue could have been addressed.

The requirement of a phase-in process of the student uniforms by the board of education was probably necessary at the time of implementation, but it created an obvious division between the seventh and eighth grade students that was not positive for school spirit, climate, or the sense of community. The district process currently suggests a phase-in policy, but not one that will result in one grade required to wear uniforms and one grade not required to wear uniforms. The current phase-in policy suggests that uniforms are voluntary the first year and mandatory the second year, allowing those families who are vehemently opposed to a uniform requirement to have adequate time to choose another school that does not require uniforms.

Overall it can be surmised that the implementation of student uniforms at 17 of the schools in the Saint Paul Public School District has been positive and is generally supported by the district, staff, parents, and even many students. Not one of the 17 schools that adopted uniforms has repealed their policy, and the overall feeling is that student uniforms are one variable in improving the school climate by creating a greater sense of unity among disparate student groups while helping to improve the learning environment. Student uniforms are by no means a cure-all for the challenges that educators and families face today. They are no substitute for effective school management, utilization of research-based best instructional practices, and the support of the students, parents, and community members for a quality educational learning environment. In a district such as Saint Paul, with an urban, multicultural setting and a substantial rate of poverty, student uniforms are not a significant equalizer that overcomes the barriers to learning and student achievement. The support of parents, community, students, and educators working collaboratively is necessary to allow all children to achieve to their highest potential whether or not they wear a school uniform.

There were many variables in this study that were factors in perceptions of school climate as they relate to requiring student uniforms. This research study was a snapshot in time in which the uniform policies had recently been implemented. The size of the survey respondent group participants (113) and the size of the focus group participants (27), as well as the narrow focus on teachers' perceptions of school climate, make this study limited in scope and difficult to generalize about across all educational settings. The important issue of selectivity, in which some at-risk students may not have chosen to attend one of the two schools that require uniforms, might have resulted in a change in student population that could have skewed teachers' perceptions in favor of a uniform policy since they perceived fewer behavioral problems once uniforms were implemented. Yet in reality it may not have been the uniforms but the change in student population that resulted in the perception of an improved school climate and learning environment. Other variables may have influenced teacher perception of school climate, such as the student population, class size, building leadership, racial and ethnic diversity, parental support, and poverty levels.

It would be interesting and prudent to conduct follow-up research at these uniform schools to ascertain whether or not teachers, students, and parents perceive that uniforms currently play a role in shaping the school climate. A long-term analysis of student achievement and discipline data across the junior high schools in Saint Paul would provide additional insights as well.

There are many variables that impact a school climate and student achievement levels. Uniforms are just one tool used to attempt to improve the climate of a junior high school and raise student achievement. At this point in education the effect of a uniform policy on school climate may just be in the eye of the beholder.

APPENDIX: HAZEL PARK MIDDLE SCHOOL UNIFORM GUIDELINES, SAINT PAUL PUBLIC SCHOOL DISTRICT, 2004

Tops

White collared shirt that has been purchased at Hazel Park OR a shirt that matches the photo provided.

White, navy, or black sweaters or sweatshirts without hoods or zippers are acceptable to be worn over the white collared shirt.

Bottoms

Navy or black dress pants. (Denim, sweat pants, and wind pants are not acceptable.) Belts will be brown, black, or navy and have plain buckles.

Accessories

Accessories will be school appropriate. (No headwear, medallion necklaces, or key lanyards.)

All clothing will be worn appropriately for school. Example: All clothing will be an appropriate size for the student, shirts must be tucked in, collars showing, and pants pulled up.

ALL students are required to follow Hazel Park's Uniform Policy.

Part 3

SCHOOL UNIFORMS: CRITICAL AND
COMPARATIVE PROCESSES

6

School Dress Codes and Uniforms: Perspectives on Wearing Uniforms in Korea and the United States

Yunhee Kim and Marilyn Delong[1]

In general, the motivation for stricter dress codes in schools is the perception that some clothing worn to school may be distracting in an academic environment and may increase errant behaviors in youth (Behling, 1994; Davison, 1990; Paliokas, Futrell, and Rist, 1996). School uniforms are sometimes proposed as a concrete means of reasserting school order and safety. However, some schools choose to adopt a dress code while others are focusing on a uniform policy. What is needed for learning to take place within schools? How important is expression of individualism and development of a sense of community? The U.S. value of freedom of expression is perceived as being violated by adopting uniforms, but perhaps not by a dress code. A different perspective may result when what is needed to develop a sense of school community is considered (Kohn, 1996). This study was implemented to reveal the various perspectives in the uniform debate and the complex factors related to community, school, and those individuals involved in making decisions about what is right for students.

According to Joseph (1986), the uniform is a category of perception with culturally determined values and with certain designated relationships within an organization as well as with the external public. He states, "Implicit in the use of uniforms is an underlying mental set or cluster of values and norms which supports these relationships. Successful changes in uniform require concomitant changes in the accompanying norms and values" (p. 2). The rules for wearing a uniform are usually quite explicit, but may be flexible within a given school setting. Groups adopting uniforms must conform to certain standards of appearance and behavior, and thus uniforms lend themselves to a variety of controls. Uniforms enable an organization to establish membership and enlist the public as external censors to enforce organizational codes. Thus the uniform and the perception of the uniform are dependent upon audience and setting, which we called context.

Joseph enumerates the basic characteristics of the uniform as follows: (a) Uniforms are a designator of an organization; (b) a visible indicator of status as a member within that organization, (c) which also indicates the relationship between wearer and organization and implies at least a two-tiered organization/wearer and a superior who supervises conformity to group regulations; and (d) a suppressor of individual idiosyncrasies of behavior, appearance, and physical attributes (Joseph, 1986, p. 68). Implicit in adoption of the uniform is not just the form it takes, but also the implied relationships of students within the school and with the parents and teachers in that school. The decision to adopt school uniforms is most often made by a school advisory board consisting of parents, teachers, and administrators. Though students are the ones most affected by a uniform policy, school administrators may not consider students' opinions about wearing school uniforms.

The objective of these studies was to compare the perception of students, teachers, and parents concerning wearing school uniforms in private schools with varying degrees of dress code and within two cultural settings: the United States and South Korea. It is most pertinent regarding the wearing of school uniforms to determine motivations, attitudes, and values that persist within each cultural context. Looking at a situation from a different point of view often discloses similarities and differences in cultures and may open possibilities and new perspectives about whether uniforms would ultimately be accepted in a different context. This study combines results of two similarly structured but separately published studies, each within a different culture. Comparable data were available only with male and female students attending private schools, and therefore results must be interpreted within this limitation of private rather than public schools.

HISTORIC BACKGROUND AFFECTING
UNIFORMS IN KOREA

Koreans have a long history of wearing uniforms for both middle school and high school throughout most of the 20th century. In the 1980s, they ceased the uniform policy (DeLong, Kim, and Koh, 2002). A primary reason was the perception that not wearing uniforms would allow for more student expression and individuality (Wickliffe, 1999). However, several years later increasingly frequent reports of juveniles involved in delinquent behaviors brought up this issue of wearing uniforms again in some schools. Today the majority of Korean students in both middle and high school wear uniforms once again (DeLong, Kim, and Koh, 2002). Motivations and the cultural value of maintaining a neat and modest appearance is part of the Confucian tradition handed down from generation to generation (Geum and DeLong, 1992). Even during the time when school uniforms were out of favor, Koreans preferred a somewhat more formal appearance than in the United States. Currently, the trend toward globalization has been placed into consideration for the Korean family, which is described as incorporating both Confucian and Western cultures. Respect for those in authority, such as parents and teachers, is important. However individualism is also perceived as influencing students today, with the result that parents and teachers are losing some of their former respect and dignity, previously taken for granted.

Korea was introduced to wearing uniforms by the Japanese during their occupation from 1910 to 1945. Originally Korean uniforms came from Japan when they were in military power. The same Japanese-style uniforms were adopted in Korea, as described by McVeigh (2000). For males, uniforms were quite severe, closed forms, dark navy or black piece suits of one color with a high collar. For the girls, uniforms were a sailor-style top and pleated skirt of similar dark colors and worn with a white blouse or skirt. Even though Korean uniforms have changed into other styles and forms, the Japanese have continued to wear those severe uniforms, the same in style, color, and materials, for 100 years in all schools.

With independence from Japan and before the Korean War in 1945, Koreans accepted the flexibility of fashionable dress and the importance of appearing up to date. During the Korean War, fashionable dress was often abandoned because there was a lot of uprooting of families as they moved back and forth across the 38th parallel as either North or South Korea gained ground. Koreans were concerned with family background. As survival became critical during this time, Koreans came to realize the importance of family and social order. Today Koreans still value social order and a hierarchical society. One way to break away from the social order is through education, so education is viewed as very important. Historically a Korean's status was determined from birth; the only exception of raised status was if a person passed an extremely difficult test and then could become a government official. This may have been the origin of the respect that Koreans continue to have toward education.

After the Korean War, Koreans identified less with birth background, and movement within the society was more accepted. Still, Koreans who rise to the top do not wear casual clothing such as jeans. They want to keep their status, once achieved, and prefer to wear a dark business suit. In Korea, education is highly valued. Educational systems are monitored and evaluated regularly by the government. Koreans believe teachers should be respected for their ability to help mold and challenge a student.

Uniforms were worn until the 1980s when the president of Korea proclaimed, "No more uniforms" because they stifle creativity of students. Then uniforms ceased to be worn but were reintroduced several years later. When reintroduced, uniforms were adopted that suited Korean society and meshed with their beliefs and values.

Korean Values and Education

Koreans chose to play down Buddhism and increase emphasis on Confucianism from 1392 onward. In Confucian philosophy a "we" consciousness is valued, in direct contrast to an "I" consciousness. Decisions that are usually considered to be individual in the United States become family decisions in Korea (Rohner and Pettengill, 1985). The individual in Korea is still viewed as a part of a more significant whole (Song, Smetana, and Kim, 1987). Overall, strong friendships develop among Korean high school students as a result of Confucianism (Lavin, 1999). The consciousness of "we" helps to influence a Korean's use of language. Word restrictions include the heavy use of "I" and "you." These are in accordance with status rules. "I," which indicates individualism, is not used when around the family. Before a person is an individual, the family and others around the person should be considered. Koreans therefore prefer to use the word "we." Finally, Koreans are racially homogeneous with a long and continuous tradition, and this may decrease an individual's separation and conflict within the population (Korean Overseas Information Services, 1993). This strong Confucian tradition and homogenous population may impact perceptions of school uniforms.

A Confucian value requires a disciplined personality emphasizing teaching and learning and a general disregard for material comfort. Education was originally developed to train men to be competent government officials. Eventually Korean parents became aware that the way to a successful career was through education (Lavin, 1999). School pride is defined solely through academic achievement, rather than through activities such as sports. During the 1950s and 1960s exams stipulated school placement, and the uniform as a badge of that school signified the rankings among schools and indicated academic levels. Many Korean high school students attend school through the evening, so attending school may occupy a major portion of a student's time. Because Korean parents know that the way to a successful career is through education, education of children is considered the highest priority of parents (Delong, Kim, and Koh, 2002).

Korean philosophy growing out of Confucianism contrasts with the U.S. value of individualism and emphasis on freedom. In one study focusing on perceptions of students regarding parental control, in Korea strict parental control is perceived by adolescents as maternal control and parental warmth with high involvement and low neglect. On the other hand, U.S. students tend to perceive strict parental control as hostile and tend to reject the idea (Rohner and Pettengill, 1985). From the perspective of Korean students, respect for parents and teachers is important. Korean teachers (74.7%) thought that they should be allowed to discipline students using physical measures ("Majority of Parents," 1999). In respect for authority, Koreans are less likely to negotiate with their instructors in school. Korean students seemed to have a more difficult time thinking about inappropriate behavior in more situations than their U.S. counterparts (Delong, Kim, and Koh, 2002). In the 1950s and 1960s Koreans respected their parents and teachers as role models. Individualism is perceived today as influencing students, with parents and teachers losing some of their respect and dignity. Though Koreans today are not as authoritarian or as formal as previously, they still show respect for their teachers.

ADOPTION OF SCHOOL UNIFORMS/DRESS CODES IN THE UNITED STATES

School uniforms can be adopted from early childhood onward, but adolescence is a time when uniforms may be adopted in the United States (Kim,

DeLong, and LaBat, 2001). At what age uniforms are introduced in schools would seem an important consideration. Adolescents may struggle over their self-identity, with appearance an important part of nonverbal communication used to establish credibility in roles (Fuhrmann, 1986; Honess, 1992; Stanley, 1996). Adolescents may wear certain clothing to show their individuality or membership in a specific group. Some attempts to be accepted in a group by looking and dressing in certain ways may seem strange or ridiculous to adults. Certain types of clothing and accessories have come to symbolize lifestyles relating to drugs, violence, and disrespect for authority (Hethorn, 1994).

Johnson (1982) notes that the uniforming of students has been a traditional means of differentiation of status and identity based on clothing difference. Elite schools traditionally employ the uniform as an obvious mechanism to reinforce high status and identity relative to other subgroups within local school systems. Dress regulations in the form of dress codes were not developed to promote conformity, but to diminish the importance of clothing (LaPoint, Holloman, and Alleyne, 1992; Stevenson and Chunn, 1991). However, they were meant to blur economic difference between wealthy and nonwealthy students. Today a school may adopt a dress code without adopting the practice of wearing a school uniform. Thus dress codes can vary from a mild expression of the type of appearance desired within a school context to a full-fledged uniform policy. While in some countries, such as Korea, uniforms are a matter of course, in the United States such policies are slow to be adopted except in some private and religious schools (Kim, DeLong, and LaBat, 2001). However, as public school environments become increasingly unruly, administrators are searching for solutions that include the adoption of a school uniform policy.

Interest in a uniform policy or dress code is based on a desire by school staff and parents to focus student attention on learning rather than diverting attention to appearance (Kim, DeLong, and LaBat, 2001). The appearances of students may include wearing a range of inexpensive to expensive designer clothing (Stevenson and Chunn, 1991). A pervasive trend in the United States is to dress more casually, so uniforms counter this trend by forcing students to dress more formally (DeLong, Kim, and Koh, 2002). For U.S. students, wearing uniforms may be viewed as too formal in a casual school atmosphere and too limiting of individuality. Parents may perceive that uniforms are less expensive than what would ordinarily be worn everyday. Parents may be interested in uniform policies as a means of alleviating competition for expensive clothing that drains family budgets and lowers the self-esteem of students who cannot afford the expensive clothing. Parents believe that wearing expensive clothing removes attention from the real purpose of school and may even encourage illicit activities (Stevenson and Chunn, 1991). Elementary school staff and parents often favor establishment of a uniform policy to encourage better discipline (Ellicott, 1988). Parental support of a uniform policy is critical for the success of school uniforms. Often uniform policies require the permission of parents (Archibold, 1998). Many schools that have successfully created a uniform policy survey parents first to gauge support for school uniform requirements and then seek parental input in designing the uniform. Parental support is also essential in encouraging students to wear the uniform (Kim, DeLong, and LaBat, 2001). However, students responding to mandatory school uniforms do not perceive uniforms as positively as adults (Stanley, 1996). A variety of factors may contribute to discrepancies found between adult and student perceptions. Though students indicated they were bored with uniforms, wearing uniforms had a positive impact on student's self-image, and this was confirmed by positive comments from the community (Hoffler-Riddick and Lassiter, 1996). On the other hand, Wilkins (1999) points out that students are keenly aware of economic status, regardless of uniformity of clothing, and so parents and teachers may overestimate the effect uniforms have on student behaviors.

METHOD

Development of Questionnaires

For both studies, three questionnaires for teachers, parents, and students, similar in scope, were developed to address the specifics of the differing roles each has in regard to the school uniform. It was expected that students' perceptions toward wearing school uniforms would be affected by their past or current experiences of wearing uniforms in school. Each subject group was also asked open-ended questions related to wearing a uniform. Questionnaires for the Korean study were the same as the ones used for the U.S. study of Kim, DeLong, and LaBat (2001). The questions were translated into Korean, and some words were modified slightly to make them more equivalent for each school (DeLong, Kim, and Koh, 2002).

The questionnaire for students consisted of 28 questions, for the parents, 22 questions, and for the teachers, 22 questions. Most of the questions were designed to be answered using a numeric rating scale. The first 14 questions were the same for all subject categories, with slight wording modifications necessary for some questions to make them more equivalent for the nine schools.

Schools Selected Based on Dress Codes and Uniform Policy

In the United States, three private Catholic coeducational high schools in Minneapolis and Saint Paul, Minnesota, were selected and gave approval to distribute questionnaires. The three schools were almost identical in their religious affiliation, urban location, racial composition, and socioeconomic class. Each had a dress code but a different uniform policy varying from more restrictive to flexible to no uniform: (1) The restrictive school uniform policy requires students to wear specific items of apparel, such as school jackets and skirts; (2) flexible school uniform policy is based on the requirement that a student's ensemble conform in certain ways such as the school's color choice of black skirts or trousers and white shirts with the school monogram; and (3) no school uniform policy, but with a dress code that does not require a school uniform (Kim, DeLong, and LaBat, 2001).

In Korea, coeducational schools are less common, so additional schools were added to make up a similar grouping of students. Six private high schools, three boys' schools and three girls' schools, were selected for the study in order to compare with respondent data from the U.S. study. Subjects included teachers, parents, and students from schools in the northwest area in Seoul, South Korea. All six schools were similar in urban location and socioeconomic class. One boys' school was paired with a girls' school with similar dress codes. Each pair of schools was selected because they had a different uniform policy ranging from (1) a restrictive school uniform policy that required students to wear specific items of apparel; (2) a flexible school uniform policy that allowed a choice for one garment in the uniform; and (3) no school uniform policy (DeLong, Kim, and Koh, 2002).

RESULTS

Perceptions Toward Wearing Uniforms in the United States

According to the study of Kim, DeLong, and LaBat (2001), students didn't believe that they experienced much ridicule from friends about what they wore. Parents and teachers were more concerned about peer pressure regarding the type of clothing students wore. Students reported that they experienced some peer pressure about wearing fashionable clothing and did not think that wearing school uniforms would help to remove peer pressure concerning the clothing they wore.

Students responded that school uniforms didn't help to improve environment or behavior. Parents and teachers reported that wearing uniforms could protect students from gang presence in school; but students disagreed. It is possible that students believe that gang presence is visible through clues other than clothing such as hand signs, postures, jewelry, and tattoos. Parents and teachers may believe that gangs would not be allowed to get into school buildings without wearing uniforms. Because most of the gang members may not be students, they could more easily linger around the school if uniforms were not worn. When questioned whether wearing uniforms makes economic class differences less visible, students were doubtful about the positive impact of a school uniform because clothing is not the only way to show economic differences or gang identity.

Students did not perceive that wearing uniforms would create an improved self-image or a stronger sense of belonging or greater pride. When wearing uniforms, students felt greater pressure to express themselves than when wearing regular clothing. Parents reported that wearing uniforms helps students learn that style of dress does not make the person.

Reduced cost of a student's wardrobe is a benefit explored in this study. Parents were more concerned than students about cost of school clothing. Parents and teachers agreed that wearing school uniforms might help decrease the family budget for school clothing.

Based on the viewpoints of parents, teachers, and students in the U.S.

schools studied, a flexible dress code could be a useful compromise for parents, teachers, and students. Such a flexible code could include a color stipulation, which means that with color the only restriction, various styles and types of clothing could be worn and combined into various ensembles. Flexibility could include various types of garments to be combined into layers based on preferences of the students, instead of only a single ensemble choice. This would address some of the students' concerns for maintaining individuality, as well as parents' perception that wearing uniforms improves student behavior.

Students' concern about clothing comfort and current trends can also be reflected in a dress code and explicit uniform policies. Students reported poor fit of uniforms as a source of dissatisfaction. In the long run a somewhat higher cost for a better fitting uniform might increase satisfaction. Because fit usually denotes a more formal type of clothing, acceptance of formal to casual types in the United States would need to be examined further.

A flexible dress code and a variety of garments to be layered according to the weather can provide another source of satisfaction and comfort. Parents emphasized the importance of comfort, and allowing for seasonal layering of garments would be a means to that end. Discomfort caused by only one choice of uniform that did not adapt well enough to temperature changes was also an issue for students. However, if many uniform items were added, costs of the uniforms would increase.

This U.S. study showed that the longer the history of students wearing uniforms, the more positive they are about wearing them. If a school dress code with a uniform policy were started at the grade school level, acceptance could be more positive in middle and high school. Then when grade school students become high school students, wearing uniforms would not be as difficult to accept. A uniform policy for grade school students could appeal to parents' concerns about school clothing costs as well.

Perceptions Toward Wearing Uniforms in Korea

In the study of DeLong, Kim, and Koh (2002), students did not agree that uniforms helped to eliminate peer pressure and to improve school climate or students' behaviors in school. Teachers and parents were more likely to disagree with students. However, all three groups, teachers, parents, and students, positively responded to an increased sense of belonging to a school due to wearing uniforms. The reasons for this connection could reflect the culture's still pervasive "we" attitude.

When asked whether students' pride improves when students wear uniforms, teachers and parents responded positively more than did students. This could be a result of the long history of wearing school uniforms in Korea, and therefore Korean adults associated a school reputation with wearing school uniforms. However, with equalization of schools in academic level and administrative system, students did not believe that school pride would be improved because of uniforms.

Korean students were more concerned with losing their individuality than parents and teachers. Students responded that individuality declined when they wore uniforms. Teachers and parents supported that wearing uniforms helps students in learning that style of dress does not make a person. But it wasn't supported as much by students.

Students didn't consider the cost for school clothing as much as parents and teachers. Teachers felt more obligated to protect students from gang violence. Students thought that clothing or appearance is not the only way to show their economic differences. So they disagreed that wearing uniforms makes economic differences less visible. Teachers agreed with the idea more than did the parents.

The study of DeLong, Kim, and Koh (2002) revealed that while students expressed a desire for individualism they also indicated a desire to adopt the school uniform. Both male and female students preferred formal uniforms more than uniforms of flexible dress codes or casual wear. A major reason given was that it was easy to select what to wear every morning. In addition both female and male students said they preferred the clean, neat appearance of the uniform.

Perceptions of school uniforms reflected the traditional perception of gender in Korean society. Boys preferred uniforms that looked masculine. The value of the traditional Korean female role might be reflected by appearance, such as how the girls want to look. Female students indicated preferences for clothing related to their gender, and a feminine look was considered a significant point of difference rather than comfort or individuality.

This study on the Korean perspective reflected the influence that cultural context had on perceptions of school uniforms. Students supported wearing uniforms and at times preferred uniforms for reasons that can be linked to gender role cultivated by Korean cultural values.

CONCLUSION

Both in Korea and the United States, teachers and parents had a more positive attitude toward students wearing uniforms than did students. Adults might think that students' behaviors will be changed by what they wear. In the United States, parents seemed to expect uniforms to serve several functions. They believed that wearing uniforms helps students identify with each other and with their school community because uniforms tell observers from the outside community that the wearer is a student. Therefore, parents may expect that when students wear uniforms, they feel pressure not to commit delinquencies because the uniform is a visible and identifiable sign of belonging to a particular school, especially when worn outside the school in the community.

As students move into the secondary school years, they might be confused by the school environment that changes both in scope and complexity. Therefore, parents may expect that wearing uniforms could help teenage students to reduce role conflicts. Parent's positive beliefs about uniforms may be influenced because elite schools traditionally adopt the uniform as a way to show an obvious school identity. In Korea, teachers were just as positive about uniforms and were often more positive than parents were about wearing school uniforms. Teachers could feel more responsible for students' welfare in school because students spend so much time there and education is valued highly in Korean culture.

Unlike Korean students and teachers, U.S. students and teachers indicated a preference for casual dress, so that uniforms were more likely to be acceptable when they were a part of a flexible dress code resulting in a casual appearance. (Kim, DeLong, and LaBat, 2001). However, most Korean students supported wearing uniforms, and more preferred formal uniforms than uniforms resulting from flexible dress codes (DeLong, Kim, and Koh, 2002). For U.S. students, alternative solutions may cater to individual values by allowing students to choose among a wider variety of school uniforms. Students could differentiate themselves by altering a portion of their uniform. Even though globalization is spreading throughout Korea, traditional Confucianism that reveres a disciplined mind is still reflected in Korean students' preference for wearing formal uniforms.

While U.S. students reported their uniforms did not fit well (Kim, DeLong, and LaBat, 2001), in Korea easy access to alterations has eliminated such fitting problems. Such a solution of altering to fit could help reduce U.S. students' dissatisfaction with wearing uniforms.

Contrary to the long history of school uniforms in Korea, the underlying values of the United States may be in opposition to the idea of the school uniform. For the United States to be successful may require thoughtful adaptation of the characteristics of uniforms and what is implied with adoption of a uniform in any culture. Though Korea had a time of cessation of uniform policy to encourage students' individuality, the outcome was not favorable, and the result was a return to students wearing uniforms.

Wearing school uniforms is not just a panacea for larger social and behavioral problems. These studies point to the value of exploring the notion of wearing school uniforms within the context of cultural values. Whether the uniform could be associated with promoting acceptable student behavior in the classroom remains a question for further research.

NOTE

1. Thank you to Dr. Karen LaBat for review of the manuscript and to Dr. Ae-Ran Koh for help with data collection.

The Implementation and Impact of Mandatory School Uniforms in Long Beach, California

Viktoria Stamison

On February 24, 1996, then President Bill Clinton appeared in Long Beach, California, to commend the Long Beach Unified School District for implementing a bold mandatory school uniform program. In an address to a standing crowd, the president solemnly declared that "our children cannot learn in schools where weapons, gang violence and drugs threaten their safety or where plain unruliness and disorder and lack of discipline make learning impossible" (Clinton, 1996b, p. 367). President Clinton underscored the fact that his administration had worked hard toward the end of achieving safe schools. In his closing remarks, Clinton promised the audience that he would steadfastly promote school uniforms. The former president was so convinced that school uniforms were effective violence-fighting agents that before returning to the nation's capital, he invited Long Beach Superintendent Carl Cohn to participate in a leadership conference on drugs and violence at the White House (de Vise and Yarborough, 1996).

President Clinton's decision to travel to Long Beach at that particular juncture was, in part, politically expedient. In fact, just hours before his Southern California visit, Clinton signed an executive order directing the Department of Education to prepare a manual on school uniforms to be sent to all 16,000 public school districts in the country. The manual's rationale is unequivocally stated:

> In response to the growing levels of violence in our schools, many parents, teachers and school officials have come to see school uniforms as one posi-

tive way to reduce discipline problems and increase school safety. (U.S. Dept. of Education, 1996, p. 1)

Upon his return from Long Beach, President Clinton asked Attorney General Janet Reno, in conjunction with the Department of Education, to draft voluntary guidelines for school districts across the nation interested in adopting a school uniform policy.[1] Consequently, the Long Beach Unified School District's plan is not only one of several uniform policies included among the "model" policies in the federal Department of Education's *Manual on School Uniforms*, but it is the first one to be showcased.[2]

WHY SCHOOL UNIFORMS?

School violence is routinely mentioned as one of the most serious problems facing America's public schools (Clinton, 1996b; Crews and Counts, 1997; Trump, 1996; Polakow, 2000). Therefore, it should come as no surprise that school safety and student misconduct issues are often of greater concern to Americans than mediocre or poor academic achievement (Graham, 1997, p. R1). The urgency of this problem has prompted countless school administrators, frustrated by the failure of other measures, to adopt school uniform policies (Wilkins, 1999, p. 19).

Mandatory school uniform policies have been accepted by some as the panacea to the scourge of gang violence that occurs on or near many of the nation's public school campuses. Hundreds, perhaps thousands, of school uniform policies have been implemented across the country to combat the problem (Isaacson, 1998).[3] Support for school uniforms in this capacity is so widespread that at a 1998 national summit on school violence, the U.S. Conference of Mayors' National Action Plan on School Violence and Kids endorsed school uniforms (Wilkins, 1999).

Still other rationales have been offered in defense of school uniforms. Some school districts have adopted voluntary school uniforms in an effort to improve school spirit and student camaraderie, while others believe school uniforms can enhance academic achievement (Brown, S. S., 2002). While multiple justifications exist, gang violence in school remains the most compelling and, ostensibly, the most legally defensible.[4] In fact, the vast majority of early mandatory school uniform experiments, including the subject of this study, cite gang-related violence as the impetus behind the policy (see Bishop, 1992; Davis, 1994; Figneroa, 1994; Sardella, 1995; Tawa, 1993). Therefore, one must pay close attention to the gang violence rationale.[5]

The Long Beach Unified School District (LBUSD), located in Southern California, was the first public school district in the country to implement mandatory school uniforms on a district-wide basis. Commencing in the fall of 1994, the Long Beach School Board, with the notable exclusion of high schools, required students at its 70 elementary and middle schools to wear uniforms. Within months, the school district attributed extraordinary developments to the introduction of school uniforms, from a sharp reduction in gang-related violence, to impressive attendance records, to enhanced academic achievement. Concurrent with the actions taken by the LBUSD, the California legislature amended the state education code to permit any public school district the right to mandate uniforms as part of its school safety plan. As was the case with the LBUSD's unprecedented action, thwarting gang violence was also the impetus behind the California School Uniform Law.

This chapter presents the California School Uniform Law and Long Beach Unified School District case study. The chapter's primary objective is to provide a comprehensive consideration of the implementation of school uniforms by the LBUSD and the subsequent statute passed by the California legislature that sanctions this course of action. Special attention is given to key policy actors at both the school district and state level. The chapter opens with a review of the LBUSD's school uniform pilot program and the myriad forces that shaped its design. Next the chapter examines the impetus behind the California School Uniform Law and the various factors that influenced its passage. The final section of the chapter is devoted to assessing the effect of school uniforms as measured by the LBUSD. Here I review specific district-generated reports concerning the benefits of school uniforms. The chapter concludes with a critique of the validity of the empirical substantiation offered by the school district to corroborate its claims of success.

THE PILOT PROGRAM

In the early 1990s Long Beach parents requested assistance from the LBUSD for help with what they perceived to be a growing and dangerous

problem. According to reports from several parents whose children attended Whittier Elementary School, their students' safety was jeopardized
as they walked to and from their neighborhood public school (D. Van Der
Laan, March 10, 1997;[6] see also Barbarosh, 1995). The parents feared that
their children were becoming victims of gang violence because they un-
wittingly dressed in "gang colors" (Van Der Laan). The idea of a school
uniform was suggested as a solution because, it was surmised, a uniform
would neutralize the appearance of the students, in effect, decreasing the
likelihood of their being mistaken for gang members.[7] Carl Cohn, the superintendent of the LBUSD, remarked,

> Our uniforms thus provide a safe passage for children who must negotiate
> their way through gang territories going to and from school. Our students
> clad in uniforms need not worry about gang colors and styles. They don't
> have to focus undue attention upon making sure they or their parents select
> clothing colors or items that avoid inadvertently advertising one's self as a
> gang member. Uniforms go a long way toward providing a neutral coat of
> arms for children whose clothing might otherwise make them targets.
> (Cohn, 1996, p. 23)

The impetus behind the adoption of school uniforms was, according to
Cohn: ". . . safety, pure and simple" (Sterngold, 2000, p. A23).

The Long Beach Board of Education, persuaded by parental and community appeals, agreed to initiate a pilot program.[8] In 1991, Whittier Elementary School, located in an economically depressed Long Beach neighborhood, launched the first school uniform pilot program ("A Uniform
Solution," 1996; see also de Vise, 1994a). By 1993 four more schools,
two elementary and two middle schools, augmented the scope of the pilot
program (de Vise, 1993). The pilot program eventually included eight elementary and three middle schools.[9] In the end, the experiment was labeled
a huge success as administrators in the participating schools reported considerable improvements to "school climate" (Cohn, 1996, p. 23).

DISTRICT-WIDE IMPLEMENTATION

Ed Eveland, Long Beach Board of Education member, spearheaded the
effort to extend the experimental program district-wide for all elementary

and middle schools. The school uniform idea, however, was not Eveland's brainchild (de Vise, 1994a). Instead, Long Beach families served as the inspiration behind this undertaking.[10] Many parents had not only heard of the experiment that was underway in several of the local schools, but for those who had passed one of the participating schools, it was impossible to miss the sea of blue and white uniformed children (de Vise, 1994b). Armed with district reports that the pilot program was successfully countering a range of problems, it is not surprising that the number of supporters began to swell.

Support for the LBUSD's far-reaching initiative to "counter the influence of gangs" was pervasive (see "Guidelines and Regulations," 1994, sec. I, p. 1). A district provision stipulating that two thirds of Long Beach parents consent to the school uniform policy was easily met ("A Uniform Solution," 1996, p. 224). Parents continued to show overwhelming support for the uniform measure.[11] Although not an official factor, a *Long Beach Press-Telegram* survey reported that more than 80% of its readers who responded to the questionnaire favored the school uniform measure.[12] The Long Beach Police Department also provided backing, albeit splintered, for school uniforms.[13] Those opposed to the school uniform policy, often identified as a vocal minority, were composed largely of civil libertarian organizations and the target population, the students.[14]

Bolstered by a broad spectrum of proponents, the school uniform proposal was passed unanimously by the school board in January of 1994 (de Vise, 1996d). With this single act, the Long Beach Unified School District, the third largest in the state, led the nation by instituting the first mandatory school uniform policy at the kindergarten through eighth grade level with a scheduled start date of September 1994. In the end, the expanded program affected approximately 60,000 students at 56 elementary and 14 middle schools (de Vise, 1994a, p. A1).

THE HIGH SCHOOL DILEMMA

Conspicuously absent from the district mandate, however, were the Long Beach high schools. In a move that surprised many observers, the board of education deliberately excluded the older students. Interestingly, the board's curious decision to exempt the student cohort most vulnerable to the dangers of gang activity was motivated entirely by the fear that they would refuse to wear uniforms.[15] Yet just 2 days after President Clinton lauded the LBUSD for its model innovation, Long Beach Unified administrators, perhaps buoyed by Clinton's historic visit, began discussing the idea of extending the policy to the high school level (Yarborough, 1996a).

The path to implementing school uniforms at the high school level, however, was not without obstacles. While the national media attention may have provided incentive for the action, the district soon discovered that the sweeping and often uncritical praise showered upon the earlier programs would not characterize the effort to bring uniforms into the high schools. One key difference involved a change in the demographics of support.

High school students were outraged, which prompted almost immediate mobilization. From the outset, high school pupils were in attendance at site meetings to protest what they considered an oppressive, ineffective policy.[16] The ranks of student opposition continued to increase as district and school administrators accelerated their plans. A survey conducted within 3 months of the proposal's announcement showed high school students rejecting school uniforms eight to one (de Vise, 1996c). Not only was the opposition among students remarkably widespread, it was fiercely expressed.[17] At Wilson High School, several students banded together to form the group Imitation is Suicide, an effort orchestrated specifically to defy the school uniform proposal (Hinch, 1996). According to one member of the student organization, "Kids are going to take this to the streets. This is not the Army and the school board is trying to treat the symptoms and not the problem" (Hinch, 1996, p. A1). Other students contended that the action the schools were seeking was "fascist and bigoted" in nature (Hinch, 1996). Students were not the only ones registering complaints about the slated change.

While mothers and fathers still generally favored school uniforms for high school students, a chorus of outspoken parents emerged and aligned with the teenagers' opposition cause (de Vise, 1996b). Among the concerns expressed was the belief that it was not within the schools' jurisdiction to dictate dress standards, and any effort to do so should be construed as an encroachment upon parental rights (de Vise, 1996b). Many parents also believed that the school uniform would unnecessarily stifle a student's freedom of expression (see "High School Uniforms," 1996; Yarborough, 1996g). High schoolers, some parents argued, deserve special consideration because they are virtually adults, and, for those students who have reached the age of consent, they are already adults (Yarborough, 1996e).

> The teen years are hard enough to go through—not just for the teens but for the parents. We have all these other things, like drugs and gangs and driving, to worry about that are at the top of the list. As long as they're dressed appropriately, dress is going to be pretty far at the bottom. (Yarborough, 1996e, p. A2)

Numerous Long Beach teachers also openly opposed the school uniform policy. Many instructors were especially troubled by the constitutional ambiguity of the plan (Yarborough, 1996f).

While the united front of students, teachers, and parents who sought to derail the drive for high school uniforms was ultimately unsuccessful, their efforts did directly affect the district's strategy concerning the measure. The board of education, of which all members favored extending school uniforms to high schools, had originally planned to vote on the issue in early November of 1996. The board was so certain that the high school uniform measure would receive the requisite community support, thereby ensuring its passage, that weeks prior to the official vote one trustee declared it was a "done deal."[18] Yet the vocal minority proved to be formidable enough to force, at least in part, a delay of the official vote. Shortly after the vote did not occur as scheduled, the school board president conceded that the governing body had decided to postpone the vote because it needed to devise a better method concerning the implementation of the policy.

> We were so euphoric that uniforms in kindergarten through eighth grade went so well and we got so much national publicity that we just did not fully look at what it would take to bring uniforms into high schools. (Yarborough, 1996e)

The board concluded that more input from the community was necessary if the measure was to survive.[19] Difficulty securing sufficient community support was not the only reason the board was growing increasingly frustrated with the high school uniform objective.[20] Another strategy employed by the board to expedite the high school transition, one that it had been pursuing concurrent to the consensus-building mission, was also encountering unanticipated resistance. This time the obstruction was not a by-product of student protestations. Instead, it resulted from the actions of unyielding state lawmakers.

Defending the Opt-Out Clause

During the fall of 1996, Long Beach officials dispatched lobbyists to Sacramento in an effort to persuade legislators to remove the opt-out clause from the California School Uniform Law.[21] The directive was a response to reports predicting that anywhere from 60% to 99% of high school students would seek an exemption if a school uniform requirement were imposed.[22] In the eyes of the school district, petitioning lawmakers was a necessary, preemptive measure if the school uniform program was to be successfully integrated at the high school level. After all, if there was no opt-out clause, the LBUSD would face little to no resistance from the students. According to one board member, "If the legislature could remove the opt-out provision, it would be a lot easier for us, because we know there will be a lot of opt-outs at the high school level" (Yarborough, 1996d).[23]

Board members also believed that lobbying legislators during an election year would result in a favorable outcome for the school district. The presumption was that legislators, under pressure to appease core constituencies, may be more inclined to support the actions of one of the largest school districts in the state (Yarborough, 1996e). The board, however, soon discovered that it would be almost impossible to strike the opt-out clause from the statute (Yarborough, 1996e, p. A2). By early December, after being informed that the reason the school uniform legislation passed was precisely because it stipulated the right to opt out, the board began pursuing other options.[24]

The school district eventually circumvented the opt-out loophole by taking several decisive steps.[25] The first major action involved the board's decision to implement school uniforms at only one of seven Long Beach high schools.[26] To make the transition even more acceptable to the targeted population, school uniforms were to be phased in gradually, starting with a program design that applied solely to the incoming freshman class.[27] The reasoning behind the school board's determination was transparent. The soon-to-be freshmen were already accustomed to wearing uniforms.[28] In fact, many of them had been donning them for eight years, since the inception of the first pilot program. Nonetheless, the news was dispiriting for the majority of high school freshmen because they had held out hope that high school would provide a "refuge from the uniform police" ("High School Uniforms," 1996).

It was the third step, however, that proved to be the coup de grace, a contrivance that afforded the district virtual insulation from potential legal challenges. In an effort to "get around the opt-out clause," Woodrow Wilson High was to be converted to a classical magnet school (K. Hansen, interview, October 14, 2002).[29] Under federal law, a magnet school offers an educational arrangement that is considered alternative in nature whereby no student is compelled to attend (L. Hartzler, personal communication, October 25, 2002).[30] The governing body of a school district is afforded tremendous latitude when establishing magnet schools in that it can "create a magnet for almost any reason" (Hartzler). It is therefore permissible for a school board to use school uniforms, as long as other options exist for students who do not wish to attend, as the orienting principle of a magnet school. But the LBUSD knew that a high school featuring school uniforms as its primary draw would likely suffer many defections. Losing students would be counterproductive because, by definition, a magnet school is created for the express purpose of attracting high-performing students from all over the district (Hartzler).

The suggested plan to adopt a classical curriculum proved to be precisely what the district needed to overshadow the deterrent of school uniforms. Under the rubric of a California classical curriculum, Wilson High would have to dramatically modify its core curriculum and increase its graduation requirements.[31] Moreover, students would also be required to hold a specified grade point average. Those students who failed to maintain the stipulated grade point average could face sanctions as severe as removal from the school.[32] To convey the seriousness of the new school standards, the students would be asked to sign a contract signaling their acceptance of all provisions, including school uniforms. In the words of one board trustee, Ed Eveland, Wilson High is "going to be like a prep school" (Yarborough, 1997a, pp. A1, A4). To better facilitate a smooth transition to a classical magnet school, LBUSD attorneys rigorously studied state law prior to the board vote and were quite "confident" that the Wilson proposal "meets the letter of the law" (Yarborough, 1997b, p. A1).[33]

While district administrators were ready to proceed, several teachers, parents, and students were not convinced. One cause for skepticism stemmed from the timing of the announcement. The board did not reveal its intentions until the 1st day of a 4-day holiday, with the vote scheduled to occur on the day classes resumed (Yarborough, 1997b). Thus, many parents, teachers, and staff members were extremely dissatisfied with the board because it allowed almost no advance time to debate the merits of the proposal.

As was previously true with the other school uniform trials, the opposition constituted a minority of community members.[34] Interestingly, most of the parents who disagreed with the school uniform mandate did not oppose the other suggested changes. In fact, parents welcomed the prospect of a more challenging academic environment because they envisioned the potential benefits associated with the classical magnet school curriculum. They did not, however, see the advantages of uniformed dress (Yarborough, 1997d). Not surprisingly, students were overwhelmingly opposed to what they believed to be an unjust policy. According to one student, whose comments are representative of hundreds of Long Beach students queried, the uniforms were viewed as little more than punishment: "I'm vice president of the student optimism club, so I'm trying to stay positive on this. But I think uniforms are unfair. . . . I'm being punished for what other kids act like" (Yarborough, 1997d, p. A10). With the obvious exception of students, the majority of Long Beach residents, including parents and teachers, were supportive of high school uniforms ("High School Uniforms," 1996).

As anticipated, on February 15, 1997, the Long Beach Board of Education voted unanimously to transform Wilson High into a classical magnet school. The 1997–1998 academic year, yet again, signified a marker in the LBUSD's nationally watched experiment with school uniforms.[35]

It would seem that the success achieved at Wilson should have precipitated similar policies at other Long Beach secondary schools; however, 6 years passed before another Long Beach high school implemented uniforms. In the fall of 2003, Millikan, located in what has been described as a suburban section of Long Beach, mandated that members of its freshman class dress in color-coded uniforms (Efychiou, personal communication, December 17, 2004).[36] Like Wilson, Millikan administrators decided that school uniforms would be introduced gradually to minimize student protests and ensure compliance. As is also the case at Wilson, Millikan's uniform requirement is nonnegotiable. Those students who oppose the concept of uniforms will be forced to enroll at another school in the district (Hanigan, 2003a). Yet unlike Wilson, Millikan's new directive received virtually no media attention and occurred without any fanfare (Efychiou). Currently, there are no plans to require uniforms at other Long Beach high schools (Efychiou).

THE CALIFORNIA SCHOOL UNIFORM LAW

Several years following the commencement of the Long Beach school uniform pilot program and 7 months after the Long Beach Board of Education agreed to extend the policy to all kindergarten through eighth grade schools, the California Legislature made a dramatic change to its education code that served to ratify the school district's action. In August of 1994, California became the first state in the country to allow any school district the option of instituting a district-wide school uniform policy. Specifically, the enactment of Senate Bill 1269 amended the California Education Code to stipulate the following:

> The children of this state have the right to an effective public school education. Both students and staff of the primary, elementary, junior and senior high school campuses have the constitutional right to be safe and secure in their persons at schools. However, children in many of our public schools are forced to focus on the threat of violence and the messages of violence contained in many aspects of our society, particularly reflected in gang violence. "Gang-related apparel" is hazardous to the health and safety of the school environment. . . . The adoption of a schoolwide uniform policy is a reasonable way to provide some protection for students. A required uniform may protect students from being associated with any particular gang. . . . Individual schools may include the reasonable dress code policy as part of its school safety plan pursuant to section 35294.1. (California Education Code, 1994)

As was the case with the LBUSD's unprecedented action, discomfiting hazardous gang influences were also the stimulus behind the California School Uniform Law. Consequently, as is unequivocally stipulated in the text of the legislation, the school uniform statute was designed to be part of a school's safety plan (California Education Code, 1994).

Statute Background

Both the problem of gang violence and the school uniform solution were broached by constituents in State Senator Phil Wyman's district (Weintraub, 1994). More precisely, the uniform cause was initially championed by high school student Jesse Atondo, who was concerned that his younger sisters, Lamont Unified pupils, were becoming too preoccupied with gang regalia.[37] Atondo approved of school uniforms because his parents were products of parochial schools in their native Mexico, and they believed that uniforms would help their children focus less on gang attire and more on school (J. Atondo, personal communication, October 7, 2002).

Wyman became involved after learning that Atondo's effort to implement uniforms at his sisters' public school was rebuffed by a Lamont Unified School District attorney who said that such a policy would be illegal (P. Wyman, personal communication, October 29, 2002). Senator Wyman, already a supporter of uniforms for their perceived "scholastic boost," was convinced that uniforms were a good idea and that the state legislature could help Lamont expedite its school uniform objective (Wyman). Wyman introduced the bill because he wanted to give "school administrators power to enact a uniform requirement without fear of being sued for exceeding their authority" (Ingram, 1994, p. A23). Invoking language almost identical to that spoken by LBUSD Superintendent Carl Cohn, Wyman declared, "School uniforms can provide a neutral coat of arms against gang colors and against gang intimidation of students" ("Wilson Expected to Sign," 1994).

The momentum behind the proposal was impressive. An overwhelming number of Lamont constituents registered concern about the perils of gang life and expressed unqualified support for the proposed solution of school uniforms.[38] The notion of school uniforms spread rapidly throughout Wyman's Central California Senate district, primarily because so many of his constituents had attended parochial schools and viewed school uniforms favorably.[39]

Contrary to what is commonly believed, the Long Beach experiment was not the impetus behind the California School Uniform legislation. That the state Senate introduced a school uniform bill the same month the Long Beach Unified voted to enact mandatory school uniforms was, quite amazingly, simply coincidental.[40] But the timing of the bill's introduction proved to be rather serendipitous for the LBUSD. Concerns regarding the legal foundation upon which its mandatory school uniform policy rested had begun to intensify.[41] The LBUSD knew that a state-sanctioned school uniform law would legitimize, and help insulate from possible attacks, their district-wide mandate. As a result, when the Long Beach Unified became aware of Wyman's pending legislation, a school district lobbyist was sent to Sacramento to help "push the bill forward" (P. Wyman, personal communication, October 29, 2002).[42]

Once in Sacramento the school district's lobbyists fought to preserve the bill's original form that would have allowed school districts to require uniforms with no opt-out stipulation (de Vise, 1994b). However, Democratic Assemblywoman Delaine Eastin, a candidate for state superintendent at the time, understood the importance of an opt-out clause and worked hard to ensure its inclusion in the final bill (de Vise, 1994c).

The American Civil Liberties Union (ACLU), the only formal interest group opposition, also lobbied on behalf of a student's right to opt out of the uniform requirement (P. Wyman, personal communication, October 29, 2002).[43] Early in the legislative process, the ACLU challenged the proposed statute on the grounds that it would stifle students' rights to freedom of expression. Recognizing the inevitability that the bill would become law, the ACLU fought tirelessly for the inclusion of an opt-out clause (E. Schroeder, personal communication, April 22, 2003).[44] The organization was also troubled by the absence of evidence to substantiate LBUSD claims that school uniforms reduced crime and improved the learning environment (Weintraub, 1994).

Other revisions were made to accommodate dissenting voices. Of particular importance were two changes advanced by Long Beach attorney and parent Gene Kinsey. Kinsey convinced an Assembly committee to include language that would prohibit school districts from discriminating against families who decided to opt out of the state law (Weintraub, 1994).

In addition, he urged senators to insert a stipulation preventing school districts from academically penalizing students who were not in uniform (de Vise, 1994b).

Numerous organized interests backed the school uniform bill. While the largest contingent of support came from a mix of California school districts, other interests were represented. Both the California Peace Officers' Association and the California Chiefs' Association favored the measure. Generally well liked by parents, the bill was also endorsed by the California PTA (Senate Bill 1269, 1994d).

The Legislative Response

The California School Uniform bill encountered little resistance in the state legislature. In an unlikely convergence of political minds, Democrats and Republicans scrambled to be associated with the measure. Conservative Republican Wyman had no difficulty recruiting Democratic Senator Teresa Hughes, who often clashed in ideological imbroglios with the lawmaker, as the Senate bill's primary coauthor (Ingram, 1994). Hughes was a proponent of school uniforms because she believed they would help instill school pride in young people ". . . at a time when they are being influenced by gangs, while reducing fierce peer pressure to wear expensive fashions" (Ingram, 1994, p. A3). In addition to Hughes, there were five other Senate coauthors, the majority of whom came from the Democratic Party.[45]

Notwithstanding the vast bipartisan popularity of the bill, a handful of outspoken Senate lawmakers voted to defeat the measure. Those who opposed it did so forcefully. Senator Tom Hayden, a liberal Democrat who championed civil liberties for decades, criticized what he called a "misplaced attempt to regain control over our kids" (Ingram, 1994, p. A3), an act that would do little more than frustrate the "inevitable friction" between parents and their children (Ingram, 1994, p. A3). Another lawmaker who disagreed with the legislation declared that the school uniform statute was intended primarily to appease the conservative Christian activists who sought to "impose their puritanical view on public schools." While the voices of the dissenting senators were heard, they were certainly not heeded. The bill sailed through the Senate with a huge margin of victory.[46]

The measure's backing was even more impressive in the State Assembly. The principal coauthor, Democratic Assemblywoman Betty Karnette, represented Long Beach (P. Wyman, personal communication, October 29, 2002). Five other Assembly members signed on as coauthors.[47] The Assembly support was broadly bipartisan, as is clearly illustrated by the ratio of ayes to noes; the bill passed on a 63–7 vote (SB 1269, 1994a).

While pending in the California legislature, Governor Wilson's official position on the bill remained uncertain. Once on the governor's desk, however, there was no doubt as to his support for the uniform law. In addition to the high school student who inspired the legislation, at least one dozen Central Valley students attended the bill-signing ceremony. The governor's office used this occasion to showcase the uniformed pupils as Governor Wilson spoke of how the scourge of gang violence threatens the lives of young people: "It used to be that students only had to worry about putting together clothes that matched. Today, the wrong combination can get you killed" (Weintraub, 1994, p. A3). With the stroke of the governor's pen, the state's public schools were afforded even greater discretion to control the lives of young Californians.

THE EFFECT OF SCHOOL UNIFORMS

Within a year of launching the pilot program, the LBUSD declared victory on the school uniform front. In addition to claiming great progress in the area of safety, administrators also asserted that uniforms effectively combated a "host of present day problems" (de Vise, 1994a, p. A5):

> In evaluating these pilot programs, the District found that use of school uniforms enhanced school safety, improved the learning environment, reduced ethnic and racial tensions, bridged socioeconomic differences between children, promoted good behavior, improved children's self-respect and self-esteem and produced cost savings for participating families. ("Guidelines and Regulations," 1994, p. 1)

While the achievement of nonviolence-related benefits appears impressive, it is clear from the text of the legislation that these were not the factors the California legislature relied upon when deciding whether to insti-

Chapter 7

tute a mandatory uniform policy (see Barbarosh, 1995; Sarke, 1998). Undoubtedly, such objectives could have been accomplished through less intrusive means. Therefore, precisely because the California School Uniform statute was conceived to be part of a school's safety plan, the most crucial measure of its legitimacy must come from its ability to demonstrate a link between school uniforms and a decrease in gang violence (Barabarosh, 1995, p. 1445).

Several pilot program participants were eager to share their accounts of success. Administrators at Whittier Elementary School reported a marked decrease in student absenteeism from previous years (Kennedy and Riccardi, 1994). In fact, improvement in the area of attendance was so significant that Whittier boasted the second lowest absenteeism rate in the entire district (de Vise, 1994a). At Franklin Middle School, the principal observed that the virtue of school uniforms lay in their ability to help students satisfy one of the school's nine keys to success: Look good.

One year after uniforms were mandated for all elementary and middle school pupils, the LBUSD claimed that Long Beach schools were remarkably safer. District-generated data suggested that elementary school suspensions dropped 28% during the 1994–1995 school year compared to the previous year (Stanley, 1996). Suspensions in the middle schools were down 36% when comparing data from the 1993–1994 academic year to 1994–1995. One district official, LBUSD public information officer Dick Van Der Laan, stated that the 1st-year statistics signaled a "dramatic reduction in crime" (Douglas, 1996).

Responding to surveys conducted by the school district, administrators reported that school uniforms improve student behavior, minimize classroom disruption, increase student cooperation, boost student attitude, increase work ethic, and contribute to more courteous students.[48] Other adults had similarly positive perceptions as to the effect of school uniforms. School counselors noted that students were more cooperative as result of school uniforms. Likewise, parents reported that after the introduction of school uniforms, they perceived an improvement in the school environment. Parents also believed that school uniforms positively affected citizenship grades, improved student interaction, and instilled in children the belief that "they were going to school to learn" (Stanley, 1996).

Following the release of the early data, LBUSD Superintendent Cohn announced that uniforms were a central feature of a "bigger picture, which includes setting higher standards of excellence for all students, not only in attire, but also in achievement" (Cohn, 1996). Cohn praised the district for numerous and "'dramatic' improvements including better attendance, fewer fights, far less school crime and violence and in some schools, significantly higher grades and student achievement" (Cohn, 1996).

After 2 years of implementation, the school district continued to report striking results. A sampling of data compiled by the LBUSD indicated that assault and battery decreased 34%; fighting decreased 51%; sex offenses decreased 74%; and vandalism decreased 18% (Stanley, 1996). According to LBUSD officials, during the same period, school uniforms also accounted for an extraordinary boost in school attendance levels. A district spokesperson stated that in the 15 years the LBUSD has been maintaining such data, attendance rates for kindergarten through eighth grade students had never been higher (Yarborough, 1996b). In fact, the school uniform policy has been touted in district literature as the primary factor behind the improved attendance rates (Long Beach Unified School District, 1999).

Five years subsequent to the kindergarten through eighth grade district-wide mandate, Long Beach data continue to reflect notable reductions in several categories of crime (*K–8 School Crime Report Summary*, 1999).[49] In short, the district maintains that since 1994, elementary and middle school crime has fallen 86% (*K–8 School Crime Report Summary*, 1999). While it is tempting to credit the school uniform with such an impressive drop in school crime, closer scrutiny of the data must occur before conclusive attribution is given.

DATA EVALUATION

The extraordinary results the LBUSD ascribes to school uniforms, ranging from safer schools to enhanced academic achievement, are not empirically substantiated. The data the Long Beach Unified relies upon are merely descriptive and represent incidents of specified types of behavior that have been compiled from one year to the next. While the LBUSD frequently invokes a heavily publicized survey it commissioned 1 year after district-wide adoption of school uniforms to demonstrate the merits of school uniforms, the research design measures participants' perceptions of school uniforms, as opposed to their actual effects (Stanley, 1996). Nonetheless, changes in the totals for a given behavior have ultimately been assigned to the school uniform. For example, after the 1994–1995 school year, the district reported a drop in several categories of school crime. In assessing the significance of the change, the LBUSD attributed virtually all credit to school uniforms.[50] In the end, however, district claims that school uniforms have caused certain outcomes are little more than conjecture based on anecdote and perception, not empirical analysis (D. Van Der Laan, personal communication, October 17, 2002).

In the absence of a systematic study of the school uniform and its effects, the LBUSD's data are inconclusive. Although district officials appear to understand the utility of multivariate analysis, such a project has yet to be undertaken.[51] For one thing, the difficulties associated with a "lean budget year" hint that a project of this nature is not likely to occur in the foreseeable future (D. Van Der Laan, personal communication, October 17, 2002). Furthermore, some Long Beach officials question the utility of multiple regression analysis in light of the quality of the LBUSD data.[52] One district administrator stated that methodological difficulties exist in several key areas, including the measurement of levels of implementation and the inability to "model" or formulate meaningful operational dependent variables (L. Winters, personal communication, October 21, 2002). Consequently, the school district's decision to base its claims of success on data of this type "makes their findings even more suspect."[53]

Other deficiencies threaten the integrity of the LBUSD data. While school uniforms have been promoted as the panacea for numerous ailments that afflict the Long Beach public schools, the school district stops just short of assigning them full credit. Concurrent with the implementation of school uniforms, the LBUSD instituted several programs designed to improve student behavior. For instance, at approximately the same time school uniforms were introduced, the district increased the number of teachers patrolling the hallways during class changes and imposed stiffer sanctions for violators (Siegel, 1996). Other efforts undertaken by the district at the same time include measures to facilitate greater parental involvement and school decentralization strategies (Gerstenzang, 1996).

A 1995 "Zero Tolerance" truancy ordinance that carries stiff monetary and educational sanctions may also have contributed to the increase in attendance.[54]

Beyond the actions initiated by the Long Beach district and community, pivotal California education statutes may also have affected student behavior, especially in the realm of academic improvement. The implementation of the highly publicized class size reduction legislation coincided with the adoption of school uniforms.[55] Dubbed the single most expensive education reform in California history, the legislation was crafted as an immediate response to an abysmal last place finish by the state's fourth graders on a national reading test (Helfand, 2000). Since its inception roughly 8 years ago, several studies indicate that students continue to make great strides in reading and math, as illustrated by enhanced Stanford 9 test scores (Helfand, 2000). While many observers are encouraged by the steady gains since the measure's passage, researchers are reluctant to attribute the improvements solely to smaller classes because the implementation of several other reforms, also designed to boost academic achievement, occurred at roughly the same time.

It has also been suggested that the Long Beach findings linking school uniforms to improved crime rates correlate to a larger national trend that schools have become much safer places, despite the use of school uniforms (Jones, R. A., 1999). This may help to explain why the Long Beach high schools, a group largely exempt from the uniform requirement, experienced a notable drop in crime (Douglas, 1996). Clearly, numerous variables exist that likely influenced the outcome the LBUSD credits almost entirely to the school uniform, but their explanatory significance has been either downplayed or never considered by the district. Until further study of these intervening variables is pursued, it will be exceedingly difficult to ascertain the efficacy of mandatory uniforms.

It is conceivable that the LBUSD has not pursued a multivariate analysis because of the likelihood that the findings would undermine its anecdotal assertions of success. More pointedly, it is possible that the district has deliberately avoided such a study for fear that it would expose their arguments as groundless (D. Brunsma, personal communication, November 6, 2002). The absence of empirical proof may explain, to some degree, why several district officials are extremely cautious when assessing the utility of school uniforms. A former coprincipal of Woodrow Wilson

Classical High offers tempered praise when considering the influence of school uniforms on student behavior: "It's not the answer, but it contributes. I don't think that the uniform does a whole lot, actually" (Sterngold, 2000, p. A23). Other Long Beach administrators are similarly restrained. Given the high number of new policies that were instituted at Wilson Classical High at approximately the same time school uniforms were introduced, a current coprincipal of Wilson Classical High is reluctant to credit school uniforms directly for the positive changes that have occurred since 1997 (K. Hansen, interview, October 14, 2002). Some are even more candid in their appraisal. According to a Long Beach middle school principal, uniforms offer only a superficial treatment of symptoms of a serious problem, one that can never be solved by mandating school uniforms (Garvey, 1998).

Prevailing scholarship concerning the relationship between student attire and academic achievement corroborates these suspicions. Social scientists have long questioned the actual effect of school dress codes (see Mahling, 1996). Many believe not only that there is no certainty that dress codes reduce school violence, but also that there is no collective consensus that dress codes even enhance academic achievement.[56] A growing literature indicates that there is no relationship between wearing school uniforms and the positive outcomes so often assigned to uniforms.

Two sociologists in particular have investigated the link between school uniforms and four key dependent variables: behavioral problems, reduced absenteeism, academic achievement, and substance abuse (Brunsma and Rockquemore, 1998). Using a nationally representative sample of students, their findings demonstrate that there is no statistically significant relationship between school uniforms and the four dependent variables. In fact, when considering the hypothesis that school uniforms improve academic achievement, the researchers discovered that, contrary to popular opinion, school uniform use actually decreased the standardized test scores of the cohort under examination.

The failure to ascertain a direct effect of school uniforms on absenteeism, academic achievement, behavioral problems, and drug abuse further underscores the need to more closely examine the rhetoric that fuels the uniform debate. This sociological study helps to expose the flawed logic that undergirds arguments advanced by school uniform proponents such as the LBUSD. While Long Beach school crime rates may have dropped for 2 consecutive years during a period that coincided with the adoption of school uniforms, there is no empirical evidence to suggest that this simple correlation is of a causal nature.

Brunsma and Rockquemore's (1998) study reveals that while school uniforms may have no direct effect on the dependent variables under investigation, they may still indirectly affect the school environment. The mere addition of such a highly publicized policy can influence the milieu of the school. Adopting a mandatory uniform policy is "a change which is immediate, highly visible, and alters the environmental landscape" of a school (Brunsma and Rockquemore, 1998, p. 13). While this modification is patently superficial, it nonetheless attracts considerable attention because of its conspicuous nature.

Furthermore, the act of mandating uniforms forces a change that affects not only students, but also parents, faculty, and other community stakeholders. Parents make an emotional and financial commitment to school uniforms; teachers and school administrators enforce their use on a daily basis and monitor their progress; and politicians provide credibility through their public endorsement of the proposal. When individuals become heavily invested in the outcome of a public policy, the creation of self-fulfilling prophecies is highly likely (Miller, K. A., 1999). More important than the uniform is the shared vision and collective commitment evidenced on behalf of the community.[57] According to one educational psychologist, "Students could be in bikinis and, if the parents are supportive, the school will do better" (Garvey, 1998, p. B2).

To argue, as the school district does, that the school uniform reduces absenteeism, enhances school safety, improves student comportment, and facilitates more cooperative behavior between students is akin to deceptive advertising. For while the LBUSD does not deny that its data are anecdotal, it is not forthcoming about the scarcity of empirical data.[58] Plainly stated, the LBUSD has failed to adequately substantiate its claims. Nevertheless, for many individuals, the wide appeal of mandatory school uniforms derives from their own intuition, shaped in large part by conventional wisdom, that school uniforms result in dramatic improvements to the school environment (King, 1998).

Mere perception is hardly a sufficient justification for sustaining a public policy, especially where student safety is concerned. As cited in the text of the California School Uniform Law and official declarations by the

LBUSD, school uniforms were conceived of as a countermeasure to the specific problem of gang violence. Therefore, ascertaining a nexus between gang violence and school uniforms is of crucial importance when evaluating the worth of the policy.

LBUSD Gang-Specific Data

When a public policy is enacted based on the principal rationale of gang violence, it is logical to expect the existence of gang-specific data to legitimize the mandate. However, at the time of the policy's adoption, neither the Long Beach Police Department (LBPD) nor the LBUSD maintained specific data on the number of gang members who attend the district's schools (R. Osborne, interview, March 10, 1997).[59] The Gang Division of the LBPD maintains only data on gang membership citywide; thus any attempt to determine the number of gang members who double as LBUSD students would be, at best, a rough estimate (Osborne). This means that no one knows exactly how many gang members are actually students within the LBUSD. Moreover, the number of gang members who commit crimes within the Long Beach schools is also unknown because the procedures utilized to document incidents of violence on the LBUSD campuses do not require administrators, teachers, or other school officials to record gang affiliation when cataloguing violent acts.

To illustrate, if Student A, who also happens to be a gang member, assaults Student B, a non–gang member, because he is provoked by B's clothing colors, the administrator documenting the incident will not indicate that gang membership may have been a factor contributing to the assault.[60] This appears to be a serious omission given the fact that gang violence was the primary impetus behind both the LBUSD and the California mandatory uniform policy. In short, any attempt to draw a connection between school uniforms and gang violence will be confounded by the absence of gang-specific data.[61]

Despite the fact that the district data do not account for gang membership, the LBUSD still claimed victory in the area of gang-related violence. In reality, district arguments that speak to a reduction in violence correspond to general categories of violence, rather than gang violence specifically.[62] Further confusing the reliability of early results is a statewide requirement that forced the consolidation of several categories of violence 1 year after the policy was implemented.[63] Consequently, the altered classification scheme utilized to gauge violence not just in Long Beach but across the state makes it especially difficult to accurately assess school violence data for this period.

Another difficulty presented by the school uniform data concerns the age of the affected population. According to LBUSD aggregate crime data, the group most severely affected by school uniforms, kindergarten through fifth grade students, is the cohort least likely to commit violent acts and also the population farthest removed from the tumult of gang violence (California Department of Education, 1997; California Safe Schools Assessment, 1997). In fact, the data suggest that middle school and, more frequently, high school students are the most inclined to commit violent acts, including assault, fighting, and property crimes. Furthermore, high school students are the most common users of drugs and alcohol, for which the levels of use remained constant despite the implementation of the school uniform policy. While elementary school students do engage in some incidents of misbehavior, it generally occurs on a much smaller scale and typically involves property crimes. It remains to be seen why the school uniform policy, with the exception of one high school, applies only to kindergarten through eighth grade.

The potential efficacy of the LBUSD's school uniform policy is further undermined when gang membership initiation norms are examined. According to one Long Beach Police Department Gang Division source, the average age of initiation characteristic of Long Beach gangs is 13–15 years of age (R. Osborne, interview, March 10, 1997). Furthermore, perpetrators who commit violent crime are likely to fall within the range of 15–23 years of age (Osborne). These data suggest that a representative eighth grader would fall somewhere between the ages of 13 or 14 years, while it is probable that a ninth grader is in the 14- to 15-year-old range. Based on this information, it is reasonable to conclude that students in grades 9–12 would be exposed to the greatest risk, both in terms of gang membership and propensity toward violent acts. Yet the mandatory uniform policy as currently administered includes the cohort least likely to join gangs (K–5) and largely excludes the group most likely to associate with gangs (9–12 students).

CONCLUSION

Analysis of the data presented by the Long Beach Unified, the state of California, social scientists, and other experts leaves many questions unanswered. For instance, one cannot help but wonder why the most vulnerable group of students, with the exception of Wilson High, would be excluded from the school safety, anti-gang mandatory uniform measure. Moreover, it is difficult to contemplate how the Long Beach Unified could have implemented such a prohibitive policy in the absence of hard data. To date, no systematic, multivariate study has been undertaken by the school district to conclusively corroborate its numerous anecdotal claims. How peculiar that a policy targeting gang violence could proceed without the existence of gang-specific data. A similar observation can be made in light of the California legislature's sweeping change to the state education code that occurred in the absence of meaningful data.

The lack of convincing data is even more perplexing when state guidelines that dictate a certain rigor in data collection are considered, particularly where the formation of public policies is concerned. California school districts are routinely advised by state offices to be cautious when developing strategies aimed at preventing school violence (National School Safety Center, 1996). The value of accuracy in reporting is seen by some agencies as the most important goal, especially if school crime statistics will be used to develop an understanding of the pressing issues confronting a school, district, or community (National School Safety Center, 1996). Anything less than this "is tantamount to gazing into a crystal ball to determine the safety needs of schools and districts" (National School Safety Center, 1996).

Yet the disappointment of school uniforms is not simply a function of inherently weak data; it has a great deal to do with the dubious rationale responsible for the California School Uniform Law. Because both the California School Uniform Law and official LBUSD policy declarations maintain that school uniforms were initially conceived of as a policy response to the specific problem of gang violence, identifying a link between these two variables is of great importance when evaluating the efficacy of the policy. As has been demonstrated, the LBUSD's highly lauded experiment failed miserably on this point. This chapter demonstrates that the claims made by Long Beach officials were based on little more than anecdote and perception, a shaky foundation for a problem as serious as gang-related violence.

One of the most important lessons learned from this project is that effective public policies must have a clear connection between means and ends. In other words, there must be obvious linkages between a public policy's objectives and its output. It is therefore incumbent upon policy makers at all levels to scrutinize whether or not a school uniform program, or any policy for that matter, has legitimate purposes. If it is determined that a policy does not advance its principal goal, then it should cease to be enforced. Having recognized the inadequacy of the California School Uniform Law as a safety measure, school officials and state policy makers alike should pursue substantive alternatives. The realization that a policy is feckless should encourage those in decision-making positions to take significant steps to find other solutions to address the problem, particularly when dealing with an issue as serious as gang violence and a target population as defenseless as school children.

NOTES

1. Clinton also dispatched Reno to Long Beach in December of 1995 to "underscore" his support for the school uniform measure and to investigate some of the legal issues raised by school uniforms. While in Long Beach, the attorney general met with parents, students, and community leaders to learn more about the policy. See Gerstenzang (1996); Clinton (1996b); and "Reno to Visit in Support of School Uniforms" (1995).

2. A few of the other examples featured in the federal guidelines include the 900-student large South Shore Middle School in Seattle, Washington, and its adoption of a mandatory school uniform policy in 1995; Kansas City, Missouri, and its mandatory uniform policy at a single elementary school affecting 320 students in 1990; and Phoenix, Arizona's, 1995 mandatory uniform policy at Phoenix Preparatory Academy, which affects 1,174 middle school students. Of the eight programs highlighted, none of them requires uniforms for their high students. Taken from the U.S. Department of Education web page, July 24, 2000 (U.S. Dept. of Education, 1996). The Long Beach Unified now requires uniforms at two of its high schools: Wilson Classical and Millikan. However, since the U.S. Department of Education first featured these schools: the Long Beach Unified

introduced school uniforms at one of its high schools: Wilson Classical High School.

3. School uniform policies have been adopted at the state level, the district level, and the individual school level. According to the ACLU website, 196 of the 328 public schools in Miami, Florida, alone require uniforms, and in Cleveland, Ohio, roughly two thirds of the public schools have implemented uniform policies (Tamar, 1997). According to the *California School News* (Isaacson, 1998), as many as 25% of the nation's public elementary, middle, and junior high schools were expected to implement dress-related policies during the 1997–1998 school year alone.

4. When considering the legality of school uniforms in public schools, some scholars have speculated that the preservation of safe schools is the only justification that would withstand governmental scrutiny: "It is unlikely that some of the purported benefits of school uniforms such as easing the economic burden of parents or improving school spirit constitute substantial government interests. The link between these objectives and enhanced learning in the classroom is tenuous. However, the state has a substantial interest in maintaining the integrity of its public schools and in providing a sound education to its students. School uniform policies can further these interests by ensuring a safe and productive environment" (Sarke, 1998, pp. 153, 171). See also Mahling (1996). American school districts have historically wielded great power in maintaining an environment conducive to education. However, the use of dress codes toward this end has invariably generated considerable controversy. When instituting prohibitions that appear to violate students' First Amendment rights, many school districts have been especially careful to offer compelling justifications, such as gang violence, in defense of their actions.

5. From the outset, and sufficiently corroborated in official policy statements, gang violence has remained the major justification behind both the California School Uniform Law and the Long Beach Unified School District's pioneering program. Therefore, the gang violence rationale is the single most important marker from which the efficacy of the school uniform policy will be measured. While other explanations may have since been offered to support school uniforms in California, many of which will inevitably be examined here, treating all rationales with equal consideration would, in effect, misrepresent the true purpose of the policy.

6. Dick Van Der Laan, public information officer, LBUSD.

7. In the words of Long Beach parent Shawn Ashley, school uniforms are all about safety because "Our students walk through very tough neighborhoods. . . . Now gang members leave them alone" (Korber, 1996, p. A9).

8. Superintendent Cohn remarked, "When parents and families told us they wanted school uniforms, we listened" (de Vise, 1996a, p. A4).

9. In total, there are 70 public elementary and middle schools in Long Beach (Cohn, 1996).

10. While canvassing the district's neighborhoods in an effort to increase interest in public school matters, Eveland discovered that Long Beach parents were raising the issue of uniforms "again and again" as a response to gang violence (de Vise, 1994a).

11. According to Daniel de Vise (1996b, p. A4) surveys continue to suggest that "most parents support the idea" of school uniforms, "while most high school pupils oppose it." An unofficial *Press-Telegram* survey conducted in the spring of 1994 found that "four in five parents agree that school uniforms are a way to safer schools, better behaved children and lower clothing bills" (de Vise, 1994b, p. A1).

12. This information is available on the LBUSD website at www.lbusd.k12 .ca.us/uniform/uniform.htm.

13. A Gang Division officer noted that while the measure was generally supported by the Long Beach Police Department, especially by the chief of police, it also had its share of detractors because many officers believed it was only a superficial measure that failed to address the root causes of gang violence (R. Osborne, personal communication, March 10, 1997).

14. The ACLU and the Legal Aid Foundation of Long Beach both waged courtroom battles, and a handful of Long Beach civil liberties lawyers also pursued legal action against the district. While students of all ages have spoken out against the school uniform policy, opposition was especially vocal at the high school level (de Vise, 1996c).

15. "The proposal does not include high schools because officials are not sure whether older students would accept uniforms as readily as younger pupils" (de Vise, 1994a, p. A1). Moreover, according to Sophie Yarborough, "District officials hesitated to spread the policy to high schools, fearing older students would refuse to wear uniforms" (1996a, p. A6).

16. Two days after President Clinton's visit, Long Beach's Lakewood High became the first high school to begin discussing the prospect of school uniforms. At a site council meeting, with roughly 20 people in attendance, all the students who were queried spoke out against the possibility of uniforms. Lakewood High junior Jennifer Wills said, "Wearing a uniform isn't going to turn me into a magically perfect person who sits in the classroom and twirls my thumbs. And anyone who thinks it will is living in a different world" (Yarborough, 1996a, p. A6).

17. Jordan High student Somaly Heng believed that she was free of the uni-

form burden forever when she left middle school, but was "horrified" to learn that the school district had every intention of extending the mandate to her high school. Heng, deeply troubled by the prospect, remarked, "Everywhere you go, you see the same people dressed the same way—it's sickening! It's going to spoil my whole senior year. I'm about to graduate and go off to college and people are still telling me what to do and how to dress" (Yarborough, 1996b, p. A1).

18. This belief seemed to reflect the general community feeling as well. Journalist Robin Hinch noted, "Although no formal board action has been taken, somewhere between May and October that proposal [school uniform] has been transformed into a fait accompli" (Hinch, 1996, p. A2). Many parents also expressed concern that efforts to solicit their input was merely window dressing and that the board really did not care what the parents had to say. According to Long Beach parent Rafael Palomo, Sr., "This uniform thing is a done deal. We're wasting our time" (Hinch, 1996). Other parents expressed indignation at the school board's arrogance. According to mother Debby Smith, who has a high school son in the Long Beach District, "I felt that we weren't really there to give our thoughts or opinions on whether we should or shouldn't have a uniform, but to implement it and design it. I was very offended by that. How would you feel if someone said to you that you can come and talk about it, but it doesn't really matter because we've already made up our minds?" (Yarborough, 1996f, pp. A1, A10).

19. Superintendent Carl Cohn's disappointment that consensus had not yet been reached was evident in his subtle condemnation to adults: "I've always said the high school uniforms would tell us more about the adults in the community than the kids" (Yarborough, 1996f, pp. A1, A10). Cohn then asked all teachers and parents to come together to support the school uniforms.

20. When board member Ed Eveland was informed of the postponement of the vote, he issued a rebuke to his colleagues: "They love all the accolades when it works, but it sounds to me like they get pretty chicken pretty fast when they think it won't work. I think they're afraid of telling me they're backing off" (Yarborough, 1996e, p. A1).

21. By this time, the California School Uniform Law had been in effect for roughly 1 1/2 years. Although the details of the California School Uniform Law have not yet been considered, it is crucial to note here that in spite of the fact that the legislature's action occurred pursuant to the LBUSD's directive, the Long Beach school uniform program must conform to the state law. LBUSD Superintendent Carl Cohn, in acknowledging that the state law supersedes his district's earlier action, declared that "Another challenge that we've had to face comes from those parents who have decided to opt their child out of the uniform policy.

The uniform legislation bill, which Governor Pete Wilson signed in August 1994, included a provision that required school districts to provide a 'method whereby parents may choose not to have their children comply with an adopted school uniform policy.' While our school district would have preferred a bill without that provision, we've been able to maintain an extraordinarily high level of compliance at all schools for a year and a half"(Cohn, 1996, p. 25).

22. When queried, students overwhelmingly expressed that they would opt out of the uniform requirement. Parents and educators alike also "predicted that if the policy was extended to high schools, most high school students will opt-out." Even maverick board member Ed Eveland, who often appeared myopic in his pursuit of uniforms, conceded that most students would opt out of the mandate (see Yarborough, 1996g, p. A6).

23. This statement was made by Long Beach School Board president Bobbie Smith. It is important to note that Long Beach administrators were also keen on removing the opt-out clause because they knew that although the plan had strong parental backing, the board discovered "that 18 year old students, who can sign their own absence slips, could probably sign their own opt-out forms as well" (Yarborough, 1996e, p. A2).

24. These remarks were made by Assemblywoman Betty Karnette, who served as an Assembly coauthor of the school uniform legislation (Yarborough, 1996f, p. A10).

25. This is not to say that these were the only steps taken by the board to get around the California law. Months prior to this action, the board anticipated that it would face considerable opposition and contemplated several scenarios. One in particular involved instituting a rigorous dress code for teachers. "Another way to sell uniforms to high school students, board members reasoned, is to enforce a dress code among adults. Officials of the teachers union, which fought earlier talk of enforcing the blue and white pupil dress code among adults, gave cautious support to this more liberal proposal" (de Vise, 1996c, p. A7).

26. Woodrow Wilson High School was selected to be the site the "pilot" program. According to Dick Van Der Laan, public information officer for the LBUSD, "We had pilots in the elementary and middle schools and it makes sense to pilot them in the high school" (Yarborough, 1997a, p. A4).

27. After the initial freshman cohort, each subsequent freshman class would be required to wear uniforms, until eventually all four grade levels would be outfitted similarly. This occurred during the 2000–2001 academic year (K. Hansen, coprincipal of Wilson Classical High School, interview, October 12, 2002).

28. A 15-year-old female Wilson High sophomore explained that because she had attended Long Beach public schools since first grade, she had grown accus-

tomed to wearing uniforms. While she was not necessarily happy to wear a uniform at Wilson, the policy was simply a fact of life. Several of her classmates who also participated in the discussion, including both males and females, agreed that they were used to the uniforms, but they stipulated that simply because they were in the habit of outfitting alike did not mean that they liked it (interview with author, October 14, 2002).

29. See also Yarborough's coverage, where she reports that "The Long Beach school district is expected to introduce high school uniforms this fall by turning Wilson High into the city's first all-magnet 'classical' high school" (1997a, pp. A1, A4).

30. Dr. Lynn Hartzler, Consultant on Magnet Schools, California Department of Education.

31. The feature that most readily distinguishes a classical from a nonclassical high school curriculum is the total number of units required for graduation. California law mandates that students must complete 220 units of coursework for a standard high school diploma; by contrast, 280 units are needed to obtain a classical diploma. At Wilson, all students are required to take seven courses each semester, one course more than what is expected at nonclassical high schools in California (Hansen, interview, October 14, 2002). As a result, Wilson's course requirements now exceed both the CSU and UC admission standards. See the Woodrow Wilson Classical High School "Code of Excellence" (Long Beach Unified School District, 2002).

32. According to the Wilson "Code of Excellence," "All students are expected to maintain a 2.0 GPA. A student who falls below a 2.0 at the end of the semester will be put on academic probation until the end of the following semester. Counseling and tutoring opportunities will be provided. If the student is still below a 2.0 at the end of the semester, s/he may be placed on a modified program or transferred to an alternative high school program."

33. According to Wilson coprincipal Keith Hansen, there has been only one lawsuit in 4 years. Because it is still pending, he declined to discuss the nature of the dispute. (Hansen, interview, October 14, 2002.)

34. In fact, "District officials say the opposition has not been overwhelming, and in some cases even less than expected" (Yarborough, 1997a, p. A4).

35. It is interesting to note, however, that almost 6 years after the high school pilot program, no other Long Beach high school has implemented school uniforms.

36. Christopher Efychiou, Acting Public Information Officer, Long Beach Unified School District.

37. Then state senator, and later assemblyman, Wyman remarked that the issue of school uniforms was brought to his attention by "Jesse Atondo, a young Hispanic male whose sisters were tempted by gang attire" (P. Wyman, personal communication, October 29, 2002). Lamont is a tiny, primarily Latino, immigrant community in Wyman's Central California Senate district, just outside of Bakersfield. See Ingram (1994). Atondo became especially troubled when his sisters expressed interest in obtaining a Raider's jacket, outerwear that had become synonymous with gang membership. Believing that his parents, Mexican immigrants who worked long hours as farm laborers, were not in the position to take on the issue, he decided to take action on their behalf (J. Atondo, personal communication, October 7, 2002).

38. When Jesse Atondo contacted Lamont Unified with his school uniform idea, the superintendent asked him to get feedback from the community. The very next day, Jesse showed up at the local supermarket and began circulating a petition of his own design. Within a matter of days, Jesse had collected over 1,000 signatures from parents and community members who supported public school uniforms. (J. Atondo, personal communication, October 7, 2002.)

39. In addition to its large Latino immigrant community, Wyman's Senate district included 90,000 Hmong immigrants in Fresno, the largest contingency in the United States, many of whom had worn school uniforms as children. (P. Wyman, personal communication, October 29, 2002)

40. When asked pointedly if the Long Beach model influenced his bill, Wyman stated, without hesitation, that the inspiration behind his school uniform legislation "came from tiny Lamont and Jesse Atondo." And he added that, at the time, he "had no idea what was going on in Long Beach" (P. Wyman, personal communication, October 29, 2002).

41. When Superintendent Carl Cohn was asked about the legal implications of the LBUSD's proposed mandatory school uniform policy, he replied, "I think there are probably some issues that could be contested. But one thing the board clearly wants to do is to get Sacramento to recognize that we need help in this area. We're in many ways putting out a call to the Legislature for help and support" (de Vise, 1994a, pp. A1, A5).

42. In January of 1994, the LBUSD recognized the necessity of "legislative support." According to board of education member Ed Eveland, "The superintendent has directed our lobbyists to seek legislative support for this initiative so that our efforts to make schools safer will have the full backing of State law" (Eveland, 1994, p. 2).

43. An official list of those who "support" and "oppose" the bill also recog-

nizes the ACLU as the only opposition to the pending legislation. California State Senate Committee on Education, *Staff Analysis of SB 1269 (Wyman)*, 1994, p. 2.

44. Elizabeth Schroeder, Associate Director, ACLU-Southern California.

45. Democratic State Senators Steve Peace (San Diego), Robert Presley (Riverside), and Art Torres (Los Angeles) signed on, along with one Republican, Tom Campbell (Palo Alto), and one Independent, Quentin Kopp (South San Francisco) (see SB 1269, 1994b).

46. The bill passed the state Senate with a 28–6 vote (see SB 1269, 1994d).

47. The remaining Assembly coauthors included Dean Andal (R-Stockton), Gil Ferguson (R-Newport Beach), Trice Harvey (R-Bakersfield), Willard Murray (D-Paramount), and Bernie Richter (R-Chico) (see SB 1269, 1994b).

48. According to the 2-year survey undertaken by the LBUSD, school administrators responded to a series of questions that asked if they "perceived" a change after the implementation of the school uniform policy. Thus all responses are anecdotal (see Stanley, 1996, pp. 424–435).

49. While certain categories of crime did drop during this period, other categories of crime increased. Yet the school district did not attribute the increase in incidents of sexual assault, for instance, to the introduction of school uniforms (D. Rockway, Senior Counsel, Legal Aid Foundation of Long Beach, personal communication, April 25, 2003).

50. According to Dick Van Der Laan, LBUSD public information officer, "I'd say the first year we had a pretty dramatic reduction in crime. School crime has decreased 36 percent (in elementary and middle schools). At high schools where we don't have school uniforms, there's been a five percent reduction in crime" (Douglas, 1996, p. A7). Karin Polachek, the former president of the school board, claimed that "Uniforms improve discipline, self-esteem, and self-respect. They focus attention upon learning and away from such distractions as fashion, competition and gang intimidation. Requiring uniforms enhances school security by permitting identification of non-students who try to enter the campus. Weapons have been concealed in jumpsuits, overcoat and baggy gang clothing" (Polachek, 1994, p. D5).

51. Van Der Laan said that the district had "not specifically" been approached by anyone with a plan to conduct such a study, but that he personally thought it was a "great idea" because "anecdotal" data cannot tell the real story behind school uniforms (D. Van Der Laan, personal communication, October 17, 2002).

52. Lynn Winters, Assistant Superintendent of Research, Planning and Evaluation for the Long Beach Unified School District, declared that there was "not a chance that multiple regression makes any sense in this situation" (Winters, personal communication, October 21, 2002).

53. David Brunsma, sociology professor at the University of Missouri, has conducted several multiple regression studies examining the effects of school uniforms on specific dependent variables. He is familiar with the LBUSD school uniform program and the favorable outcomes the district has imputed to the policy. He contends that data collected by schools individually, as opposed to the state or school district, are tenuous in the first place and thus "make their findings even more suspect" (D. Brunsma, personal communication, November 6, 2002).

54. A Long Beach city ordinance passed in 1995 made it illegal for anyone under the age of 18 to "loiter, idle, wander, stroll or play" outside of school between the hours of 8:30 and 1:30 p.m. on school days. Violators of the truancy law face fines as stiff as $250 and community service of up to 20 hours (Gerstenzang, 1996).

55. Class size reduction was significant legislation and one of then Governor Pete Wilson's crowning achievements in the area of education reform. Under the statute, class size from grades kindergarten through third grade is not to exceed 20 pupils. The decreased student-teacher ratio was believed to have many potential benefits, including higher academic achievement and a more manageable student population (see Anderson, N., 1998).

56. Education professor Pedro Noguera states that no data exist linking dress (whether it be a school uniform or a limited dress code) to academic achievement (see Davis, 1994).

57. Robert Walter, an education professor at Temple University, believes that "Uniforms in and of themselves will not have an impact on anybody. It's not the wearing of the uniform, but the shared vision and commitment to making the school a better place" (see Riechman, 1996).

58. The reference to anecdotal data is scarce to nonexistent in the published literature on the issue. As a result, there seems to be a presumption that the data are empirically tested.

59. Detective Roger Osborne, Long Beach Police Department, Gang Division.

60. This scenario was corroborated by various district sources, including Dr. Lawrence Burnight, Director of Student Assignment/International Student Registration, in an interview with the author, March 10, 1997, and Dick Van Der Laan, in a personal communication, March 10, 1997.

61. When queried as to whether or not gang conflict could be directly identified as the principal source of violence that afflicts young students as they walk to and from school, Osborne was reluctant to say yes. He stated that this is unknown and that much of the conflict and/or violence that impacts young people as they walk to and from school could also be racially motivated. He indicated that hostility is not uncommon where a perception of difference or otherness exists. Osborne, interview, March 10, 1997.

62. Such categories of violence include assault, vandalism (including property crime), and theft, among others. See the LBUSD website (www.lbusd.k12.ca.us/uniform/crime) for a complete picture of the crime classification scheme.

63. See the Long Beach Unified crime reports, such as the *K–8 School Crime Report Summary* (1999), available at the district website.

Postscript: Looking Back, Looking Ahead—On the Future of Educational Research and Training

Bart A. Reynolds

There is a perceived need for restructuring in public schools in the United States. To meet this need many school districts have implemented school uniforms to as a way to "improve the social climate" (Cornwell, 1995). School uniform enthusiasts state that such policies will accomplish several goals: reduce gang violence, increase attendance, raise academic achievement, and blur socioeconomic lines. On the other side, opponents contend that such policies will only act as a Band-Aid covering the larger problems and deeper scars facing public schools today.

As most of the contributors to this volume agree, the movement toward school uniforms received national attention in 1996 when then President Bill Clinton gave his support for uniforms based on the perceived success of the Long Beach Unified School District in his State of the Union address. This support came after Long Beach released statistics (see Stanley, 1996) supposedly showing the positive effects that school uniforms had on its student population (Clinton, 1996a).

The Long Beach Unified School District (LBUSD) was the first school district in the nation to require a uniform policy in 1994. This policy included all 70 elementary and middle schools in the district while excluding secondary high schools. The results were astounding on the surface and implied that the uniform policy was responsible for an increase in attendance and academic achievement as well as deceases in behavioral problems, gang activity, and substance abuse. Although most information regarding the LBUSD results failed to mention that other programs and policies were implemented at the same time as the uniforms, this research provided school districts across the country with the ammunition they needed to also implement uniform in their districts.

However, in 1998, the research and methodologies of the LBUSD "study" were scrutinized by David L. Brunsma and Kerry Ann Rockquemore. These researchers conducted an analysis of the assertions made by proponents in the Long Beach Unified School District. Using information from The National Educational Longitudinal Study of 1988, Brunsma and Rockquemore concluded that school uniforms alone do not have conclusive impact on substance abuse, behavioral problems, or attendance (Brunsma and Rockquemore, 1998). Since 1998, Brunsma has been the leading advocate for more research to be conducted on the effects of school uniforms on student behavior and academic achievement. His appeal for more researchers to study this issue using more rigorous longitudinal and experimental designs that will add significantly to our knowledge has been consistent.

Yet proponents of public school uniforms still cite the "success" of LBUSD and their "research" despite Brunsma's and others' evaluation of their impact in the above-mentioned analysis. For those who support uniforms in public schools, the claim, indeed assumption, that such policies will reduce crime and behavior problems and increase student achievement remains the central factor in deciding to implement school uniform policies in public schools.

From 1998 to the present day, Brunsma is one of the only researchers who have taken a critical look at the empirical research that has been conducted since the Long Beach study and concluded that our implementation decisions are being fueled by irrational fears in the face of scarce empirical evidence. Our understanding of these issues and the decisions we make to solve them must be grounded in research that is critical, thorough, and dedicated to uncovering those processes and policies that work for particular sets of social and structural conditions (Brunsma, 2002).

When reviewing the bulk of the research that has been conducted over the past 15 years, including the majority of the work included in this book, most of the research has been conducted as part of a partial set of requirements for an educational doctorate (EdD). The course work and training that students pursuing an EdD receive is light in most EdD programs. This is not a criticism, simply an observation after having gone through the process myself. Selecting a research design and following a methodology are critical if a cause and effect relationship is to exist.

The limitations that most EdD students encounter are the following: the ability to collect random samples; preserving internal and external validity; controlling for other variables and other variation in their models; receiving training in the chosen methodology; using an analysis suitable for the methodology; keeping information in the original design; and drawing conclusions that are supported by their data. Expecting students who are attempting research of this magnitude to accomplish all of this on their first attempt is a tall order—it is even a tall order for the experienced researcher.

Yet, when research is conducted, preserving the internal validity is one of the most important factors when one is trying to generalize the findings to other populations outside the study area. This is difficult to accomplish when one also has a stake in the outcomes of the research. With the exception of Brunsma, the authors of these studies also, in general, tend to work within or are associated with the schools and districts where the research was conducted. Having knowledge or being involved in the outcome of the data increases the chances of internal contamination and limits the validity of the study at hand.

One of the perpetual problems faced in conducting educational research, particularly in regard to school uniforms, is the collection of data. More often than not researchers conducting school uniform studies don't have the luxury of beginning prior to the implementation of the uniform policy. As a result, making a cause and effect interpretation is very difficult and presents a real problem when researchers, despite weak findings and questionable methodologies, still attempt to make such claims. Too often researchers step outside realistic boundaries in trying to interpret their findings as ones of cause and effect when the data simply won't support such an interpretation.

Researchers typically use descriptive methodologies, as in the present collection, because data such as attendance rates, truancy, test scores, and academic records are easily obtained from local, state, and national agencies. The trade-off, however, is that it is extremely hard to make causal statements or imply a cause and effect relationship. When researchers attempt to show a cause and effect relationship when data are limited or not collected properly, they step outside the reliable and realistic expectations of the given methodology.

It seems to be popular with researchers who utilize descriptive designs to want to predict outcomes or make certain claims. This is something to watch for when reviewing research and a significant problem if the data were collected after the implementation of the uniform policy or any other factors. Some of those other factors may include administrative or teacher changes, hiring of a truancy officer, implementation of closed campus policies, and/or the implementation of higher school standards—to name just a few factors that could account for the changes other than the uniform policy itself.

Experimental designs are rarely conducted largely due to the time element and cost factors involved. Again, the problem here is, more often than not, that the researcher begins the research after the implementation of the uniform. The opportunity to conduct pretests and posttests is not possible in such cases; therefore, as a result, researchers are forced to use descriptive methodologies out of convenience. Another issue is the inability to manipulate the independent variables within public schools. Districts have certain limitations they place on researchers due to moral, political, and ethical concerns. This results in many studies being conducted out of convenience, when data are easily available—the trade-off is that descriptive research does not prove anything.

This book breaks new ground in the field of school uniform research. Brunsma has collected some of the significant studies on school uniforms that have been conducted to date. The methodologies selected in these chapters meet their design, for the most part, and the framework for positive discussion exists. One of my overall concerns across these chapters is with the studies' external validity. In viewing this work, the ability to generalize outside the study location has certain limitations. The real value of educational research is in its transferability. For instance, is the research conducted in an urban district in Florida applicable to students in a rural district in Oregon? If the research was conducted where opt-out provisions were allowed, and the uniform consists of several colors and styles, does this limit the effectiveness, and can the results be expected, if one deviates from this format? In the end, the lack of standardization and the idiosyncrasies of each study make them almost impossible to duplicate outside the particular study area.

Where so many districts are making the decision to implement a uniform policy based on the claims of Long Beach and other districts, one must ask, how generalizable are the data being used? In viewing over 25 studies that have been conducted since 1992 (see Reynolds, 2004), my conclusion is similar to those of Brunsma and others who have stated something along the following lines: that there is insufficient empirical research to support a cause-effect relationship between the school uniform and increased student behavior and academic achievement.

Brunsma has led the charge in the United States in the area of school uniform research and presented compelling evidence for the need for additional research to be conducted. This research must reflect the rigors of critical research methodologies and be conducted before the implementation of the uniform policy so the independent variables can be properly controlled. This research must be conducted over a several-year period. If the Hawthorne effect is not taken into consideration, the school uniform movement will become a fad like many of the programs we have seen come and go over the years. Reform efforts of this nature need time to evaluate and must be tested using all methodologies and attention given to the research design used, making certain the methodology is strictly followed.

If educators are going to be the ones conducting this research using quantitative methodologies, then EdD curricula requirements need to include extensive training and mentoring by experienced researchers. Traditionally, the requirement for EdD students has not been as rigorous as the requirement for those completing PhD dissertations. Educational doctorates are typically completed by practitioners, while PhD students tend to gravitate toward research that is more painstaking. This may be an overgeneralization but nevertheless something that needs to be taken into consideration given the emphasis school districts are placing on relying on the research available.

One only has to look at the number of schools that were influenced by the Long Beach study to see the trust the president of the United States, as well as many other districts, placed in this particular study (the LBUSD study). Yet such faith has been undermined by the fact that the results claimed by LBUSD were related to factors other than the uniform. Today, 10 years later, LBUSD has distanced itself from the findings claimed shortly after the implementation of the policy.

Brunsma has successfully pointed out the need to examine the research on school uniforms carefully before making a rush to judgment. This book is a major contributing piece of work for school administrators and boards of education to consider before making a decision that will cost taxpayers hundreds of thousands of dollars. When one considers everything we now know, the results of research have not given a compelling enough reason to implement a school uniform policy. Political pressure, community values, or community consensus may force the implementation, but it should be noted that the research hasn't produced conclusive evidence.

References

Adami, R., & Norton, M. (1996). Not in my school you don't! Preventing school violence in the middle level school. *Bulletin of the National Association of Secondary School Principals*, 19–23.

Adleman, K. (1996, January 31). Dressing better for improved education. *The Washington Times*, p. A16.

American Civil Liberties Union (ACLU). (1988). *Personal appearance. The rights of students handbook*, 37–43.

American Federation of Teachers (1996). Is it time for uniforms? *American Teacher*, *80*(4), 8–9.

Anderman, E. M., & Kimweli, D. M. S. (1997). Victimization and safety in schools serving early adolescents. *Journal of Early Adolescence*, *17*(4), 408–438.

Anderson, C. S. (1982). The search for school climate: A review of the research. *Review of Educational Research*, *52*(3), 368–420.

Anderson, N. (1998, December 29). Smaller classes aid test scores, results show. *Los Angeles Times*, pp. A1, A23.

Archibold, R. (1998, March 18). Board to vote on a less rigid plan for school uniforms. *New York Times*, p. B4.

Arhar, J. M. (1992). Interdisciplinary teaming and the social bonding of middle level students. In J. L. Irvin (Ed.), *Transforming middle level education: Perspectives and possibilities* (pp. 139–161). Boston: Allyn and Bacon.

Arhar, J. M., & Kromrey, J. D. (1995). Interdisciplinary teaming and the demographics of membership: A comparison of student belonging in high SES and low SES middle-level schools. *Research in Middle-Level Education*, *18*(2), 71–88.

Aronson, F. (1999). *The social animal* (8th ed.). New York: Worth.

Ascher, C. (1982). Secondary school ethos and the academic success of urban minority students. New York: ERIC Clearinghouse on Urban Education. (ERIC Document Reproduction Service No. ED 235 247).

Ascher, R. (1986, September). You'd have to be crazy to want to wear a school uniform, right? *Seventeen*, 151.

Baird, R. M., & Rosenbaum, S. E. (Eds.). (1992). *Bigotry, prejudice, and hatred: Definitions, causes, and solutions*. Buffalo, NY: Prometheus Books.

Baker, J. (1987, November 30). Dressing to be successful. *Newsweek*, 62.

Baker, J. A., Bridger, R., Terry, T., & Winsor, A. (1997). Schools as caring communities: A relational approach to school reform. *School Psychology Review, 26*(4), 586–602.

Bandura, A. (1977). *Social Learning Theory*. Englewood Cliffs, NJ: Prentice Hall.

Barbarosh, A. (1995). Undressing the First Amendment in public schools: Do uniform dress codes violate students' First Amendment rights? *Loyola of Los Angeles Law Review, 28*(4), 1415–1450.

Barr, R., & Dreeben, R. (1983). *How schools work*. Chicago: University of Chicago Press.

Battistich, V., & Hom, A. (1997). The relationship between students' sense of their school as a community and their involvement in problem behaviors. *American Journal of Public Health, 87*(12), 1997–2001.

Battistich, V., Solomon, D., Kim, D., Watson, M., & Schaps, E. (1995). Schools as communities, poverty levels of student populations; and student attitudes, motives, and performance: A multilevel analysis. *American Educational Research Journal, 32*(3), 627–658.

Behling, D. (1994, October). School uniforms and person perception. *Perceptual and Motor Skills, 79*(2), 723–729.

Behling, D., & Williams, E. (1991). Influence of dress on perception of intelligence and expectations of scholastic achievement. *Clothing and Textiles Research Journal, 9*, 1–7.

Bernet, B. (2003, September 6). Trustees may change policy on uniforms. *Fort Worth Star-Telegram*.

Bishop, K. (1992, January 22). Schools order students to dress for safety's sake. *New York Times*, p. A18.

Bivens and Green v. Albuquerque Public Schools. (1995). 899 F. Supp. 556 (D.N.M. 1995).

Black, S. (1998). Forever plaid? *American School Board Journal, 185*(11), 42–45.

Blackham, G. J., & Silberman, A. (1980). *Modification of child and adolescent behavior*. Belmont, CA: Wadsworth.

Bollinger, L. S. (2002). *The effects of a mandatory school uniform policy on school climate and student discipline in an urban middle school*. Unpublished dissertation, University of Houston.

Boocock, S. (1980). *Sociology of education: An introduction* (2nd ed.). Boston: Houghton Mifflin.

Borg, W. R., & Gall, M. D. (1989). *Educational research.* New York: Longman.

Britt, J. (2001). *Teachers' Perceptions about the impact of school uniforms on the learning experience of students in an alternative public school.* Unpublished dissertation, Colorado State University.

Brown, B. (1981). Dealing with fear, stress, and anxiety in the learning environment. *Journal of Christian Education, 1,* 48–52.

Brown, D., & Solomon D. (1983). A model for prosocial learning: An in-progress field study. In D. L. Bridgeman (Ed.), *The nature of prosocial development: Interdiscipliniary theories and strategies* (pp. 273–307). New York: Academic Press.

Brown, S. S. (2002, August 29). Public schools try uniform approach: Growing numbers of educators embrace stricter dress codes. *Denver Post,* p. A1.

Brunsma, D. L. (2002). *School uniforms: A critical review of the literature.* Monograph for Phi Delta Kappan's From Inquiry to Practice series.

Brunsma, D. L. (2004). *The school uniform movement and what it tells us about American education: A symbolic crusade.* Lanham, MD: Scarecrow Press.

Brunsma, D. L., & Rockquemore, K. A. (1998). Effects of student uniforms on attendance, behavior problems, substance use, and academic achievement. *Journal of Educational Research, 92*(1), 53–62.

Bryk, A. S., & Thum, Y. M. (1989). The effects of high school organization on dropping out: An exploratory investigation. *American Educational Research Journal, 26*(3), 353–383.

Burke, N. D. (1993, April 8). Restricting gang clothing in the public schools. *Education Law Report, 513,* 391–404. Laramie: University of Wyoming College of Law.

Cahill, S. (1989). Fashioning males and females: Appearance management and the social reproduction of gender. *Symbolic Interaction, 12,* 281–298.

Calabrese, R. L., & Poe, J. (1990). Alienation: An explanation of high dropout rates among African-American and Latino Students. *Educational Research Quarterly, 14*(4), 22–26.

California Dept. of Education. (1997). California safe schools assessment, *School crime reporting form,* semi-annual district summary from 1993–1996. Sacramento, CA: Author.

California Education Code (1994, August 23). Chapter 325, sec. 35183, subsection (a), 1–3.

California Safe Schools Assessment. (1997). *School-by-school crime report summary,* July 1, 1995–June 30, 1996. Sacramento, CA: California Department of Education.

California State Senate Committee on Education. (1994). *Staff analysis of SB 1269 (Wyman)*, 2.

Camp, W. (1993). *The principal's legal handbook*. Topeka, KS: National Organization on Legal Problems of Education. (ERIC Document Reproduction Service No. ED 354 606).

Carlyle, T. (1883). *Sartor Resartus*. New York: Charles Scribners' Sons.

Caruso, P. (1996, September 6). Individuality vs. conformity: The issue behind school uniforms. *Educational Leadership*, 10–12.

Cho, E., & Grover, L. (1978). *Looking terrific*. New York: G. P. Putnam's Sons.

Chubb, N. H., & Fertman, C. I. (1992). Adolescents' perceptions of belonging in their families. *Families in Society: The Journal of Contemporary Human Services*, 387–394.

Clinton, W. J. (1996a, January 23). State of the Union Address. Reuter News Service Online.

Clinton, W. J. (1996b, February). The president's radio address. *Weekly Compilation of Presidential Documents*, *32*(9), 24.

Cocks, J. (1988, September 26). What the kids are wearing. *Time*, 76.

Cohn, C. (1996, February). Mandatory school uniforms: Long Beach's pioneering experience finds safety and economic benefits. *The School Administrator*, 22–25.

Cohn, C. (1996–1997). *School uniforms: Parents make the difference*. Long Beach Unified School District.

Coleman et al. (1974). *Youth: Transition to adulthood*. Chicago: University of Chicago Press.

Cornwell, T. (1995, October 13). True colours of uniformity (crime in Long Beach, California, schools). *The Times Educational Supplement* (Suppl. 4137), 18.

Crader, R. (1988). Should public school students wear uniforms? There are always dissenters. *American Teacher*, *73*(3), 4.

Crews, G. A., & Counts, M. R. (1997). *The evolution of school disturbance in America: Colonial times to modern days*. Westport, CT: Praeger.

Daily Report Card. [electronic newsgroup list.K12admin] (1996, January 22). Austin, TX: Tenet Education News.

Davidson-Williams, C. M. (1996). *Case study of the mandatory enforcement of a voluntary student uniform policy*. Unpublished dissertation, Arizona State University.

Davis, M. (1994, January 16). Fashion furor: Tougher school dress codes raise questions of safety and rights. *Los Angeles Times*, p. B1.

Davison, A. (1990). *Blazers, badgers and boaters: A Pictorial History of School Uniforms*. Horndean, UK: Scope Books.

DeLong, M., Kim, Y., & Koh, A. (2002, December). Perspectives on wearing school uniforms in Korea. *International Journal of Costume*, 2, 53–71.

de Vise, D. (1993, September 15). Summer's out, school's in for L.B., Downey. *Long Beach Press-Telegram*, pp. B1, B12.

de Vise, D. (1994a, January 1). Uniforms may be mandatory for K-8 pupils. *Long Beach Press-Telegram*, pp. A1, A5.

de Vise, D. (1994b, July 4). Clothes make the fighting man. *Long Beach Press-Telegram*, pp. A1, A7.

de Vise, D. (1994c, August 14). Long Beach students gear up for expanded uniform policy. *Long Beach Press-Telegram*, pp. J1, J10.

de Vise, D. (1996a, February 23). All dressed up for Clinton. *Long Beach Press-Telegram*, p. A9.

de Vise, D. (1996b, February 25). America is in your debt: President praises LBUSD for uniform effort to reduce violence in schools. *Long Beach Press-Telegram*, p. A4.

de Vise, D. (1996c, May 8). LBUSD to employees: Dress up. *Long Beach Press-Telegram*, pp. A1, A7.

de Vise, D. (1996d, May 14). A new round of reforms at Long Beach schools. *Long Beach Press-Telegram*, pp. A1, A2.

de Vise, D., & Yarborough, S. (1996, February 25). Clinton visits, but spotlight is on Cohn. *Long Beach Press-Telegram*, p. A1.

Douglas, T. (1996, August 27). Downey pupils put on uniforms. *Long Beach Press-Telegram*, pp. A1, A7.

Dowling-Sender, B. (2001, January). School law, disagreeing over dress: Can schools restrict student expression because it conflicts with the values they want to instill? American School Board Journal.com. Retrieved August 25, 2005, from http://www.asbj.com/2001/01/0101schoollaw.html.

Dress, right dress. (1987, September 14). *Time*, 76.

Dussel, I. (2001). *School uniforms and the disciplining of appearances: Toward a comparative theory of the regulation of bodies in early modern France, Argentina, and the United States.* Unpublished dissertation, University of Wisconsin, Madison.

Educational Testing Service. (2000). *Order in the classroom: The links among school discipline, student delinquency, and academic achievement.* Retrieved August 31, 2005, from ftp://ftp.ets.org/pub/res/order.pdf.

Ellicott, S. (1998, May 18). Public schools' new style. *San Francisco Chronicle*, p. B3.

Erikson, E. H. (1968). *Identity: Youth and crisis.* New York: W. W. Norton.

Evans, D. (1996). School uniforms: An 'unfashionable' dissent. *Phi Delta Kappan*, 78(2), 139.

Eveland, E. (1994, January 18). *Mandatory uniforms for all elementary and middle schools beginning with the 1994–1995 school year and action to obtain legislative authority for such requirement*, Long Beach Unified School District, Board of Education, 2.

Everett, S. A., & Price, J. H. (1995). Students' perceptions of violence in the public schools: The MetLife survey. *Journal of Adolescent Health, 17*, 345–352.

Figneroa, G. C. (1994, February 27). Youths could make a fatal mistake if they're dressed to kill. *Los Angeles Times*, p. B19.

Finn, J. (1989). Withdrawing from school. *Review of Educational Research, 59*(2), 117–143.

Firth, R. W. (1973). *Symbols: Public and private*. Ithaca, NY: Cornell University Press.

Florida Department of Juvenile Justice. (2004). *Juvenile justice statistics and research*. Retrieved August 25, 2005, from http://www.djj.state.fl.us/Research/statsnresearch/index.

Flugel, J. C. (1966). *The psychology of clothes*. London: Hogarth.

Forney, J. C., & Forney, W. S. (1995). Gangs of fashion: Influences on junior high student dress. *Journal of Family and Consumer Sciences, 87*(4), 26–32.

Fosseen, L. L. A. (2002). *School uniforms and sense of school as a community: perceptions of belonging, safety, and caring relationships in urban school settings*. Unpublished dissertation, University of Houston.

Fuhrmann, B. (1986). *Adolescence, adolescents*. Toronto: Little, Brown & Company.

Gaertner, S. L., Dovidio, J. F., Mann, J. A., Murrell, A. J., & Pomare, M. (1990). How does cooperation reduce intergroup bias? *Journal of Personality and Social Psychology, 59*(4), 692–704.

Garvey, M. (1998, March 22). Make a fashion statement. *Los Angeles Times*, pp. B1, B2.

Gathercoal, F. (1993). *Judicious Discipline*. San Francisco: Caddo Gap Press.

Gaustad, J. (1992). *School discipline*. Eugene, OR: ERIC Clearinghouse on Educational Management. (ERIC Document Reproduction Service No. ED 350 727).

Gerstenzang, J. (1996, February 25). Clinton praises school uniform pacesetter. *Los Angeles Times*, pp. A15, A16.

Geum, K., & DeLong, M. (1992). Dress as an expression of heritage: Exploring Korean culture. *Dress, 19*, 57–68.

Gilbert, P. (1993). Defense and safety: Their function in social behavior and psychopathology. *British Journal of Clinical Psychology, 32*, 131–153.

Gilligan, C. (1993). *In a different voice: Psychological theory and women's development.* Cambridge, MA: Harvard University Press.

Goffman, E. (1951/1959). *The presentation of self in everyday life.* Garden City, NY: Doubleday Anchor Books.

Gonzales, J. L. (2000). *Impact of school uniforms in elementary schools.* Unpublished dissertation, New Mexico State University.

Goodenow, C. (1992, April 20–24). *School motivation, engagement, and sense of belonging among urban adolescent students.* Paper presented at the Annual Meeting of the American Educational Research Association. San Francisco, CA.

Goodenow, C. (1993a). Classroom belonging among early adolescent students: Relationships to motivation and achievement. *Journal of Early Adolescence, 13*(1), 21–43.

Goodenow, C. (1993b). The psychological sense of school membership among adolescents: Scale development and educational correlates. *Psychology in the Schools, 30,* 79–90.

Goodenow, C., & Grady, K. E. (1993). The relationship of school belonging and friends' values to academic motivation among urban adolescent students. *Journal of Experimental Education, 62*(1), 60–71.

Graham, E. (1997, March 14). What's wrong—and right—with our schools? *Wall Street Journal,* pp. R1, R6.

Gregory, N. B. (1996). *Effects of school uniforms on self-esteem, academic achievement, and attendance.* Unpublished dissertation, South Carolina State University.

Griffith, J. (1995). An empirical examination of a model of social climate in elementary schools. *Basic and Applied Psychology, 17*(1–2), 97–117.

Griffith, J. (1997). Student and parent perceptions of school social environment: Are they group based? *The Elementary School Journal, 98*(2), 135–150.

Guidelines and regulations for implementing the mandatory uniform policy in grades kindergarten through eight. (1994, January 18). The Office of the Superintendent, Long Beach Unified School District. Sec. I, 1.

Gullatt, D. E. (1999). Rationales and strategies for amending the school dress code to accommodate student uniforms. *American Secondary Education, 27*(4), 39–46.

Halpern, A. W., & Croft, D. B. (1963). *The organizational climate of schools.* Chicago: University of Chicago.

Hambleton, K. B. (1972). Teenage appearance: Conformity, preferences, and self-concepts. *Journal of Home Economics, 64*(2), 29–33.

Hanigan, I. (2003a, January 15). Millikan parents, staff ask for student uniforms. *Long Beach Press-Telegram,* p. A1.

Hanigan, I. (2003b, February 1). Millikan dress code disputed policy: ACLU expects option for no uniforms, but LBUSD plans none. *Long Beach Press-Telegram*, p. A1.

Hanigan, I. (2003c, September 4). Freshmen dressed for occasion: Millikan High kicks off its uniform policy. *Long Beach Press-Telegram*, p. A1.

Hawthorne, N. (1850). *The scarlet letter* (1st ed.). Boston: Ticknor, Reed, and Fields.

Helfand, D. (2000, June 29). Cuts in class size show results, study suggests. *Los Angeles Times*, pp. A3, A23, A35.

Hethorn, J. (1994). Gang identity or self expression? *California Agriculture, 48*(7), 44.

High School Uniforms. (1996, October 3). *Long Beach Press-Telegram*, p. B6.

Hinch, R. (1996, October 2). Uniforms don't suit students. *Long Beach Press-Telegram*, pp. A1, A2.

Hoffler-Riddick, P., & Lassiter, C. (1996). No more "sag baggin." *NASSP Bulletin*, 27–28.

Holloman, L. O., LaPoint, V., Alleyne, S. I., Palmer, R. J., & Sanders, K. (1996). Dress-related behavioral problems and violence in public school settings: Prevention, intervention, and policy—a holistic approach. *Journal of Negro Education, 65*(3), 267–281.

Honess, T. (1992). The development of self. In J. C. Coleman (Ed.), *The school years: Current issues in the socialization of young people* (pp. 81–106). New York: Routledge.

Hughes, E. S. (1996). *Effects of mandated school uniforms on student attendance, discipline referrals, and classroom environment.* Unpublished dissertation, University of Houston.

Hutchins, R. M. (1943). *Education for freedom.* Baton Rouge: Louisiana State University Press.

In Schools with Uniforms: Attendance hits new high in LBUSD schools. Long Beach Unified School District. Retrieved August 31, 2005, from www.lbusd.k12.ca.us/uniforms/attend.asp.

Ingram, C. (1994, April 19). State Senate votes to let public schools require uniforms. *Los Angeles Times*, pp. A3, A23.

Isaacson, L. (1998, January). Student dress policies. *ERIC Digest, 117*, 2.

Jacobs, M. A. (1995, December 5). Court lets public school require uniform. *The Wall Street Journal*, p. B1.

Jahn, K. (1992, October). *School dress codes v. The First Amendment: Ganging up on student attire.* Paper presented at the Annual Meeting of the Speech Communication Association. Chicago. (ERIC Document Reproduction Service No. ED 355 595).

Jenkins, P. H. (1997). School delinquency and the school social bond. *Journal of Research in Crime and Delinquency, 34*(3), 337–367.

Johnson, K. K. P., & Lennon, S. J. (Eds.). (1999). *Appearance and Power.* Providence, RI: Berg Publishers, Inc.

Johnson, N. B. (1977, November 29–December 3). *Patterns of student dress and appearance: Aspects of resegregation in desegregated elementary school classrooms.* Paper presented at the Annual Meeting of the American Anthropological Association, Houston, TX.

Johnson, N. B. (1982). *Clothing and dress—Symbols of satisfaction in schools and in society: A descriptive study.* Chapel Hill, NC: Department of Anthropology, University of North Carolina. (ERIC Document Reproduction Service ED 218 166).

Jones, C. D. (1997). *Staff members' perceptions of middle school culture in middle schools that have implemented school uniform policies.* Unpublished dissertation, Pepperdine University.

Jones, R. A. (1999, August 13). Uniform, yes, but not all the same. *Los Angeles Times,* p. E3.

Joseph, W. (1986). *Uniforms and nonuniforms.* Westport, CT: Greenwood.

K–8 school crime report summary. (1999). Long Beach Unified School District. Retrieved August 22, 2000, from the LBUSD website, www.lbusd.k12.ca.us, p. 1.

Kaiser, S. B. (1985). *The social psychology of clothing and personal adornment.* New York: Macmillan.

Kaiser, S. B. (1990). *The social psychology of clothing.* New York: Macmillan.

Kaiser, S. B., Nagasawa, R. H., & Hutton, S. S. (1995). Construction of an SI theory of fashion, part 1: Ambivalence and change. *Clothing and Textiles Research Journal, 13,* 172–183.

Keat, J. Exploring the measurement of values. *Christian Education Journal, 5*(1), 37–42.

Kelly, D. (1996, March 17). Debating the dress code. *USA Today Online,* p. D1.

Kennedy, J. M., & Riccardi, N. (1994, August 25). Clothes make the student, schools decide. *Los Angeles Times,* pp. A1, A23.

Kim, Y. (1998). *Perception toward wearing school uniforms (dress codes).* Unpublished dissertation, University of Minnesota.

Kim, Y., DeLong, M. R., & LaBat, K. (2001, August). Perceptions toward wearing school uniforms. *Journal of the Korean Society of Clothing and Textiles, 25*(6), 1167–1178.

King, K. A. (1998). Should school uniforms be mandated in elementary schools? *Journal of School Health.* Retrieved August 31, 2005, from http://danenet.wicip.org/ncs/forumuniformseval.htm.

Kohn, A. (1996). *Beyond discipline*. Alexandria, VA: Association for Supervision and Curriculum Development.

Korber, D. (1996, February 25). Clinton learns firsthand about uniforms. *Long Beach Press-Telegram*, p. A5.

Korean Overseas Information Services. (1993). *Facts about Korea*. Seoul, Korea: Samhwa Printing.

Landen, W. (1992). Violence and our schools: What can we do? *Updating School Board Policies*, *23*(1), 1–5.

Lane, K., & Richardson, M. (1992). *School dress code law in the 90's: "Tinkering" with fashion and gangs*. Paper presented at the Annual Meeting of the National Organization on Legal Problems of Education. Scottsdale, AZ. (ERIC Document Reproduction Service No. ED 353 638).

Lane, K. E., Swartz, S. L., Richardson, M. D., & VanBerkum, D. W. (1994, March). You aren't what you wear. *The American School Board Journal*, 65–68.

LaPoint, V., Holloman, L. O., & Alleyne, S. I. (1992). The role of dress codes, uniforms in urban schools. *NASSP Bulletin*, *76*(546), 20–26.

Lavin, B. (1999, April 23). 'Work ethic' of Koreans legendary. *Korea Times*. Retrieved August 31, 2005, from http://www.hankooki.com/14-home/199904.

Lee, V. E. (1995). Effects of high school restructuring and size on early gains in achievement and engagement. *Sociology of Education*, *68*(4), 241–270.

Leslie, C. (1989, November 27). Hey, hairball! You're gone! *Newsweek*, 79.

Levine, M. D., & McAnarney, E. R. (1988). *Early adolescent transitions*. Lexington, MA: D. C. Heath.

Loesch, P. C. (1995, March). A school uniform program that works. *Principal*, *74*(4), 28.

Long Beach Unified School District. (1999). In schools with uniforms: Attendance hits new high in LBUSD schools. Retrieved August 26, 2005, from http://www.lbusd.k12.ca.us/uniforms/attend.asp.

Long Beach Unified School District. (2002, May). *Code of excellence*. Long Beach, CA: Author.

Mahling, W. (1996). Secondhand codes: An analysis of the constitutionality of dress codes in the public schools. *Minnesota Law Review*, *80*(3).

Majestic, A. (1991, January). *Student dress codes in the 1990's. Inquiry & analysis*, 1–7. (ERIC Document Reproduction Service No. ED 344 301).

Majority of parents supporting corporal punishment by teachers. (1999, May 5). *Korea Times*. Retrieved August 31, 2005, from http://www.hankooki.com/14-1/199905/t4151196.htm.

Manning, M. L., & Saddlemire, R. (1996). Developing a sense of community in secondary schools. *NASSP Bulletin*, *80*, 41–48.

Maslow, A. (1968). *Toward a psychology of being* (2nd ed.). New York: D. Van Nostrand.

Massare, J. A. (2004). *Staff and parent perceptions regarding the effects of mandatory school uniforms on elementary and middle school students in a New Jersey school district.* Unpublished dissertation, Wilmington College.

Mathis, N. (1996, February 25). Clinton urges student uniforms. *Houston Chronicle*, p. 6A.

McArthur, L. Z., & Post, D. L. (1977). Figural emphasis and person perception. *Journal of Experimental Social Psychology, 13*, 520–535.

McCain, D. (1988). Should public school students wear uniforms? The kids have a sense of pride. *American Teacher, 73*(3), 4.

McCarty, J. M. (1999). *The effects of school uniforms on student behavior and perceptions in an urban middle school.* Unpublished dissertation, Old Dominion University.

McGiverin, J., Gilman, D., & Tillitski, C. (1989). A meta-analysis of the relation between class size and achievement. *The Elementary School Journal, 90*(1), 52–55.

McMillan, D. W., & Chavis, D. M. (1986). Sense of community: A definition and theory. *Journal of Community Psychology, 14*, 6–23.

McVeigh, B. J. (2000). *Wearing ideology, state, schooling and self-presentation in Japan.* Oxford: Berg Publishers.

Milgram, J. I. (1985). The development of young adolescents. In J. H. Johnston & J. H. Lounsbury (Eds.), *How fares the ninth grade?* (pp. 5–9). Reston, VA: National Association of National School Principals.

Miller, F. G. (1982). Clothing and physical impairment: Joint effects on person perception. *Home Economics Research Journal, 10*, 265–270.

Miller, K. A. (1999). Standing out from the crowd. In M. L. Damhorst, K. A. Miller, & S. O. Michelman (Eds.), *The meanings of dress* (p. 212). New York: Fairchild Publications.

Moore, S., & Boldero, J. (1991). Psychosocial development and friendship functions in adolescence. *Sex Roles, 25*(9/10), 521–526.

Morrison, G. M., Furlong, M. J., & Morrison, R. L. (1994). School violence to school safety: Reframing the issue for school psychologists. *School Psychology Review, 23*(2), 236–256.

Mullis, R. L., Rathge, R., & Mullis, A. K. (2003). Predictors of academic performance during early adolescence: A contextual view. *International Journal of Behavioral Development, 27*(6), 541–548.

Mumford High School Dress Code. (1988, September). *Harper's*, 19–20.

Murphy, M. L. (1997). *Public school uniforms: A case study of one school's experience.* Unpublished dissertation, University of Washington.

Murray, R. K. (1996). Effects of school uniforms on student perceptions of school climate and student behavior. *Dissertation Abstracts International, 58*(08), 3011. (University Microfilms No. 9806684).

Murray, R. K. (1997). The impact of school uniforms on school climate. *National Association of Secondary School Principals Bulletin, 81*(593), 106–112.

NAESP. (2000). Backgrounder on Public School Uniforms. Retrieved February 5, 2004, from www.naesp.org/ContentLoad.do?contentId = 929, in an e-mail correspondence from D. Brunsma (November 29, 2004).

National Center for Educational Statistics (NCES). (1994). *NELS 88 (National educational longitudinal study). First follow-up: Student component data file user's manual.* Washington, DC: U.S. Department of Education.

National Center for Educational Statistics (NCES). (1995). *The condition of education 1995.* Washington, DC: U.S. Department of Education.

National Center for Educational Statistics (NCES). (1998). Appendix A: School practices and policies related to discipline. *Indicators of Crime and Safety* (pp. 98–251). Retrieved August 31, 2005, from http://nces.ed.gov/pubs98/safety/appendixA.asp.

National Center for Educational Statistics (NCES). (2004). *Data files and electronic codebook, early childhood longitudinal study, kindergarten class of 1998–99, kindergarten to third grade public use data file.* Washington, DC: U.S. Department of Education.

National School Safety Center. (1996). *News Journal.*

Neilson, W. A., Knott, T. A., & Carhart, P. W. (Eds.). (1958). *Webster's new international dictionary of the English language* (2nd ed.). Springfield, MA: G. & C. Merriam.

Nelson, T. Y. (1997). If clothes make the person, do uniforms make the student?: Constitutional free speech rights and student uniforms in public schools. *West's Education Law Reporter,* 1–27.

Newmann, F. M., Rutter, R. A., & Smith, M. S. (1989). Organizational factors that affect school sense of efficacy, community, and expectations. *Sociology of Education, 62*(4), 221–238.

O'Donnell, J., Hawkins, J. D., & Abbott, R. D. (1995). Predicting serious delinquency and substance use among aggressive boys. *Journal of Consulting and Clinical Psychology, 63,* 529–537.

Office of Educational Research and Improvement (1990). Restructuring schools for young adolescents. *Issues in education.* Washington, DC: U.S. Dept. of Education. (ERIC Document Reproduction Service No. ED 322 649).

Ogletree, E., & Garrett, W. (1981). *Legal issues in education: A review of research.* (ERIC Document Reproduction Service No. ED 213 772).

O'Neal, G. S. (1998). African-American aesthetic of dress: Current manifestations. *Clothing and Textiles Research Journal, 16*(4), 167–175.

Osterman, K. F. (2000). Students' need for belonging in the school community. *Review of Educational Research, 70*(3), 323–367.

Owens, R. G. (1987). *Organizational behavior in education* (3rd ed.). Englewood Cliffs, NJ: Prentice Hall.

Paliokas, K., Futrell, M. & Rist, R. (1996, May). Trying uniforms on for size. *The American School Board Journal,* 32–35.

Paliokas, K. L., & Rist, R. C. (1996, April 3). School uniforms: Do they reduce violence—or just make us feel better? *Education Week, 15*(28), 52.

Pate, S. S. (1998). *The influence of mandatory school uniform policy in two Florida school districts.* Unpublished dissertation, Florida State University.

Pennsylvania Dept. of Education. (1998). *Annual report on school violence and weapon possession. Report period: July 1, 1996–June 30, 1997.* Retrieved August 26, 2005, from http://www.pde.state.pa.us/svcs_students/cwp/view.asp?A=141&Q=60819.

Pennsylvania Dept. of Education. (2000). *Summary of assessment results for mathematics and reading.* Harrisburg, PA: Author.

Pickles, P. L. (2000). Mandating school uniforms at all grades. *The School Administrator,* Focus Web Edition. Retrieved August 31, 2005, from http://www.findarticles.com/p/articles/mi_m0JSD/is_11_57/ai_77236972.

Polachek, K. (1994, July 5). Uniforms help solve many school problems. *Long Beach Press-Telegram,* p. D5.

Polakow, V. (Ed.). (2000). *The public assault on America's children: Poverty, violence and juvenile injustice.* New York and London: Teachers College Press.

Portner, J. (1996, February 14). Dressing for success. *Education Week, 15*(1), 12–13.

Portner, J. (1998, January 21). California district points to uniforms for plunging crime rate. *Education Week,* 17.

Posner, M. (1996). Perception versus reality: School uniforms and the "halo effect." *The Harvard Education Letter, 12*(3).

Reno to visit in support of school uniforms. (1995, December 11). *Los Angeles Times,* p. B2.

Reynolds, B. A. (2004). *An analysis of the evidence produced by quantitative research on the effects of school uniforms on student discipline and academic achievement.* Unpublished dissertation, Brigham Young University.

Riechman, D. (1996, March 2). Public schools try uniforms to focus students, restore order. *The Associated Press,* 2.

Roach-Higgins, M. E., Eicher, J. B., & Johnson, K. K. P. (Eds.). (1995). *Dress and identity.* New York: Fairchild Publications.

Roberts, F. (1989, April). Do school uniforms enforce discipline? *Parents*, 50–60.

Roberts, W., Hom, A., & Battistich, V. (1995, April 18–22). *Assessing students' and teachers' sense of the school as a caring community*. Paper presented at the Annual Meeting of the American Educational Research Association, San Francisco.

Rocky Mountain Behavioral Science Institute, Inc. (1999). *Drug and alcohol use among Mount Carmel Area School District students*. Retrieved August 31, 2005, from http://rmbsi.com.

Rocky Mountain Behavioral Science Institute, Inc. (2000). *Drug and alcohol use among Mount Carmel Area School District students*. Retrieved August 31, 2005, from http://rmbsi.com.

Roeser, R. W., Midgley, C., & Urdan, T. C. (1996). Perceptions of the school psychological environment and early adolescents' psychological and behavioral functioning in school: The mediating role of goals and belonging. *Journal of Educational Psychology, 88*, 408–422.

Rohner, R., & Pettengill, S. (1985). Perceived parental acceptance-rejection and parental control among Korean adolescents. *Child Development, 56*, 524–528.

Saint Paul Public Schools. (2004). Retrieved January 31, 2005, from http://www.spps.org/.

Samuels, K. S. (2003). *The relationship of school uniforms to students' achievement, attendance, discipline referrals and perceptions: An analysis of one urban school district*. Unpublished dissertation, University of Alabama, Birmingham.

Sardella, S. (1995, January 15). Uniformity: Schools adopt dress codes to eliminate distractions. *Boston Herald*, p. A6.

Sarke, D. M. (1998). Coed naked constitutional law: The benefits and harms of uniform dress requirements in American public schools. *Boston University Law Review, 78*.

Sass, L. (1988, November). A style of one's own. *Health*, 24–26.

SB 1269. (1994a, July 7). Assembly roll call. Retrieved August 31, 2005, from http://www.assembly.ca.gov/acs/acsframeset2text.htm.

SB 1269. (1994b, June 30). Current bill status. Retrieved August 31, 2005, from http://www.assembly.ca.gov/acs/acsframeset2text.htm.

SB 1269. (1994c). School uniforms, California State Senate, *Support and legislative co-authors list*.

SB 1269. (1994d, April 18). Senate roll call. Retrieved August 31, 2005, from http://www.assembly.ca.gov/acs/acsframeset2text.htm.

Scherer, M. (1991, December). School snapshot: Focus on African-American culture. *Educational Leadership, 49*(4), 17–19.

Sergiovanni, T. J. (1994). *Building community in schools.* San Francisco: Jossey-Bass.

Shapiro, W. (1996, March 10). Editorial. *USA Today Online.*

Shaw, C. R., and McKay, H. (1942). *Juvenile delinquency in urban areas.* Chicago: University of Chicago Press.

Siegel, L. (1995, August 22). Drop dress-code demands. *USA Today,* p. 2A.

Siegel, L. (1996, March 1). *Point of view: School uniforms.* American Civil Liberties Union. Retrieved July 17, 1996, from www.aclu.org/congress/uniform.

Silverio, J. H. (2000). *Uniforms in public schools: A sign of the times?* Unpublished dissertation, University of Massachussetts, Boston.

Snyder, L. L. (1976). *Encyclopedia of the Third Reich.* New York: McGraw-Hill, Inc.

Solomon, D., Watson, M., Battistich, V., & Schaps, E. (1996). Creating classrooms that students experience as communities. *American Journal of Community Psychology, 24*(6), 719–748.

Soltner, E. F. (1997). *The factors of a voluntary school uniform policy.* Unpublished dissertation, Virginia State Polytechnic Institute and State University.

Song, M.J., Smetana, J., & Kim, S. Y. (1987). Korean children's conceptions of moral and conventional transgressions. *Developmental Psychology, 23*(4), 577–582.

Sparks, R. K. (1983). Before you bring back school dress codes, recognize that the courts frown upon attempts to restrict students' rights. *The American School Board Journal, 170*(5), 24–25.

Stanley, M. S. (1996). School uniforms and safety. *Education and Urban Society, 28*(4), 424–435.

Sterngold, J. (2000, June 28). Taking a new look at school uniforms. *New York Times,* p. A23.

Stevenson, Z., & Chunn, E. (1991). Uniform policy/dress codes: School staff and parent perceptions of need and impact. Washington, DC: District of Columbia Public Schools. (ERIC Document Reproduction Service No. ED 331 933).

Stone, G. P. (1962). Appearance and the self. In A. M. Rose (Ed.), *Human behavior and the social processes: An interactionist approach* (pp. 86–118). New York: Houghton Mifflin.

Stover, D. (1990). The dress mess. *American School Board Journal, 177*(6), 26–29.

Stryker, S. (1980). *Symbolic interactionist: A social structural version.* Menlo Park, CA: Benjamin Cummings.

Suarez, A. (1997, August 8). Calling for uniformity in school dress codes. *The Panama City News Herald,* p. C4.

Synott, J., & Symes, C. (1995). The genealogy of the school: An iconography of badges and mottoes. *British Journal of Sociology of Education, 16*(2), 139–152.

Tamar, L. (1997, September 25). Dress for success: Public school uniforms. *New York Times*, A1.

Tanioka, I., & Glaser, D. (1991). School uniforms, routine activities, and the social control of delinquency in Japan. *Youth & Society, 23*(1), 50–75.

Tawa, R. (1993, October 3). A new fashion statement clothes: San Gabriel Valley public schools are allowing uniforms. *Los Angeles Times*, p. J1.

Texas Education Code. (1995). *Subtitle c. Local organization and governance. Chapter 11. School districts. Subchapter a. General provisions. 11.162, school uniforms.* Retrieved August 26, 2005, from http://www.capitol.state.tx.us/cgi-bin/cqcgi.

Tillman, T. (1999). *Polk County school uniform compliance data.* Retrieved February 2004, from www.gate.net/~rwms/UniformComplianceData/html.

Tinker v. Des Moines Independent Community School District. (1969). 89 S. Ct. 733.

Trump, K. (1993, July). Tell teen gangs: School's out. *American School Board Journal, 180*(7) 39–42.

Trump, K. S. (1996). Gangs and school safety. In Allan Hoffman (Ed.), *Schools, violence and society* (pp. 45–58). Westport, CT: Praeger.

A uniform solution to school violence. (1996, November 6). *CQ Researcher*, 224.

USA Today Online. (1996, March 18). Results of national poll.

U.S. Census Bureau. (2000). *Metropolitan area concepts and standards.* Retrieved August 31, 2005, from http://www.census.gov/population/www/estimates/masrp.html.

U.S. Dept. of Education. (1996). *Manual on school uniforms.* Washington, DC: Author.

U.S. Dept. of Justice. (2000). *Street gangs: Current knowledge and strategies.* Washington, DC: Author.

VanMater, L. A. B. (2003). *A Study to describe perceptions of administrators, teachers, students, and parents about the changes in behavior in schools that implemented a school uniform policy.* Unpublished dissertation, University of La Verne.

Virginia State Dept. of Education. (1992). *Model guidelines for the wearing of uniforms in public schools.* (Report of the Department of Education to the Governor and the General Assembly of Virginia. House Document No. 27.) Richmond. (ERIC Document Reproduction Service No. ED 348 760).

Voelkl, K. E. (1996). Measuring students' identification with school. *Educational and Psychological Measurement, 56*(5), 760–770.

Vygotsky, L. S. (1978). *Mind in society: The development of higher psychological processes.* Cambridge, MA: Harvard University Press.

Wagner, H. (1978). *The social psychology of adolescence.* Washington, DC: University Press of America.

Walker, D. (1995). *School violence prevention.* Eugene, OR: ERIC Clearinghouse on Education Management. (ERIC Document Reproduction Service No. ED 379 786).

Walker, J. E., & Shea, T. M. (1988). *Behavior management.* Columbus, OH: Merrill.

Walsh, D., & Cowles, M. (1982). *Developmental discipline.* Birmingham, AL: Religious Education Press.

Wehlage, G. G., Rutter, R. A., Smith, G. A., Lesko, N., & Fernandez, R. (1989). *Reducing the risk: Schools as communities of support.* London: Falmer Press.

Weintraub, D. M. (1994, November 24). Wilson signs law allowing public school uniforms. *Los Angeles Times*, p. A3.

Welsh, W. N. (2000). The effects of school climate on school disorder. *Annals of the American Academy of Political and Social Sciences, 567*, 88–107.

Welsh, W. N., Greene, J. R., & Jenkins, P. H. (1999). School disorder: The influence of individual, institutional, and community factors. *Criminology, 37*, 601–643.

Welsh, W. N., Stokes, R., & Greene, J. R. (2000). A macro-level model of school disorder. *Journal of Research in Crime and Delinquency, 37*(3), 243–283.

Whitaker-Burke, S. (1990, February). A uniform to die for. *Harper's, 39.*

White, K. A. (2000). Do school uniforms fit? *The School Administrator, 57*(Part 2), 36–41.

White, B. L., and Beal, G. D. (1999). Violence in the schools as perceived by pre-service and in-service teachers. *Contemporary Education, 71*(1), 31–38.

Wickliffe, V. (1999). Culture & Consumer Behavior In M. Damhorst, K. Miller, & S. Michelman (Eds.), *The meanings of dress.* New York: Fairchild.

Wilkins, J. (1999). School uniforms: the answer to violence in American schools or a cheap education reform? *The Humanist, 59*(2), 19–22.

Wilson expected to sign school uniform bill. (1994, August 9). *Long Beach Press-Telegram*, p. E6.

Wilson, R. E. (1999). *Perceptions of school administrators regarding variables that impact violence in urban schools districts and implications for school counselors.* Unpublished dissertation, Texas Southern University.

Winters, K. (1996, March 3). Online interview. Office of the Under Secretary, U.S. Dept. of Education.

Woodard, W. M. (1989, January). New rule: Dress like me. *Black Enterprise, 15.*

Yarborough, S. (1996a, February 27). Lakewood High weighs requiring school uniforms. *Long Beach Press-Telegram*, p. A6.

Yarborough, S. (1996b, September 16). Class attendance at record levels. *Long Beach Press-Telegram*, p. B1.

Yarborough, S. (1996c, September 25). Uniform meetings Tuesday. *Long Beach Press-Telegram*, p. A1.

Yarborough, S. (1996d, October 3). Mandatory uniforms possible. *Long Beach Press-Telegram*, pp. A1, A5.

Yarborough, S. (1996e, November 16). High school uniform plan put on hold. *Long Beach Press-Telegram*, pp. A1, A2.

Yarborough, S. (1996f, December 1). High school uniform plan splits LBUSD. *Long Beach Press-Telegram*. pp. A1, A10.

Yarborough, S. (1996g, December 2). Uniform opt-out foreseen. *Long Beach Press-Telegram*, pp. A1, A6.

Yarborough, S. (1997a, February 14). Uniforms headed to high school. *Long Beach Press-Telegram*, pp. A1, A4.

Yarborough, S. (1997b, February 15). Magnet plan catches L.B. school off guard. *Long Beach Press-Telegram*, pp. A1, A8.

Yarborough, S. (1997c, February 19). A classical approach: Change requires uniforms, 4 years of core classes. *Long Beach Press-Telegram*, pp. A1, A4.

Yarborough, S. (1997d, March 20). Parents express views on 'classical' Wilson. *Long Beach Press-Telegram*, p. A10.

Zimmerman, M., & Arunkumar, R. (1994). *Resiliency research: Implication for schools and policy*. Society for Research in Child Development.

Index

achievement: mathematics, 30–32; reading, 26–30; writing, 32–33
ACLU. *See* American Civil Liberties Union
adolescence, 59, 142. *See also* school uniforms, in middle schools; school uniforms, in high schools
aggression, 5. *See also* violence
American Civil Liberties Union, 58, 163, 176n3, 177n14
anecdotes. *See also* evidence, anecdotal
appearance, 59
Arizona, 63
Atondo, Jesse, 162, 181n38
attendance, 24–25, 54, 58, 69, 71, 75, 185

Baltimore, MD, xi, 57, 63
Bandura, Albert, 4, 5
behavior, 5, 34, 54, 57, 117, 119, 128, 129; problem, 67, 152
Behling, Dorothy, 64, 75. *See also* halo effect
belonging, 79, 88, 89, 96, 100, 101, 102–4, 105, 117
Bivens and Green v. Albuquerque Public Schools, 61
Brunsma, David L., 94, 170, 171, 186

California, 63, 153, 161
California School Uniform Law, 153, 158, 161, 163, 166, 174, 176n5
Cherry Hill Elementary School, xi
class. *See* social class
class size, 20–24. *See also* enrollment
Cleveland, OH, 176n3
Clinton, Bill, xii, 51, 77, 119, 151, 156, 175n1, 185
clothing, 57, 90, 91, 93; costs of, 52, 56, 117, 145, 147; designer, 142; student, 5, 6, 62, 142
Cohn, Carl, 51, 72, 75, 151, 154, 162, 163n41, 176n8, 178n19, 178n21, 181n41. *See also* Long Beach Unified School District
Columbine High School, 35
competition, 56, 64, 75, 143. *See also* clothing, designer; status
compliance/noncompliance, 40, 43–44, 45, 59, 61, 63, 117, 130, 131, 158
conformity, 6, 58, 59
constitution(al), 61, 62, 157
control, 60; administrative, 58, 137, 164; social, 60
control variables, 19, 35, 98
costs, legal, 62
crime, 5, 57, 168

10, 34, 35, 57, 63–64, 70, 72, 73; as symbol, 86, 89, 90, 95, 138; definition of, 55, 60–61, 68, 79, 80, 82, 83, 85–87, 94, 95, 98, 110–11; effects on achievement, 63, 117, 125, 142, 152, 167, 170, 185; effectiveness, 10–11, 15, 24, 26, 33, 45, 64, 69, 71–73, 75, 82, 100–1, 125; enforcement of, 43–44, 130; evaluation of, 76, 112, 129; implementation of, 117, 130; in elementary schools, xvii, xviii, 3–11, 13–48, 63, 143; in middle schools, xviii, xix, 51–77, 79–113, 115–34; in high schools, 148, 155–59; parent resistence to, 9, 117, 156, 160; policy formation, 3, 62, 76, 116, 129; research on, xii, xiii; student resistance to, 58, 59, 63, 70, 74, 75, 143, 145, 155, 156, 160; teacher resistance to, 157; voluntary, 63
school uniforms, types of: formal, 70; group-identifying, 79, 81; logo, 87, 91, 94, 96, 97, 101, 102; "mode of dress," 61
Seattle, WA, 175n2
secondary schools. *See* school uniforms, in high schools
security, 79
self-esteem, 57, 75, 76, 88, 145
social class, 101; and school uniforms, 58, 101, 108, 69, 96, 179, 187–88
societal values, 139–40
St. Paul, MN, xix, 115, 120, 131
staff uniforms, 117, 132

Stanley, Sue, xii, 83, 166, 167. *See also* Long Beach Unified School District
status, 5, 79, 80
student, perceptions of uniforms, 145–47; rights, 4, 58, 59, 61, 62, 75
student–teacher ratios, 20–23
substance use, 33–34

teacher(s), 43, 70; experience, 73; perceptions of uniforms, 145, 147; uniforms, 118, 130
Texas, xviii, xix, 52, 65, 72
Tinker v. Des Moines Independent School District, 62
tracking, 58
truancy. *See* attendance

uniforms. *See* school uniforms
uniformity, 80
U.S. Conference of Mayors, 152
U.S. Supreme Court, 6, 63
urban, 5, 7

validity, 188
violence, 3, 7, 9, 10, 38, 62, 64, 152, 167

waivers. *See* opt-out
Washington, DC, 64, 69, 72
weapons, 3, 6, 35, 37–40
Wilson, Pete, 165, 178–79n21, 183n55
Wyman, Phil, 162–65, 181n37, 181n39, 181n40

About the Editor and Contributors

David L. Brunsma is assistant professor of sociology and Black studies at the University of Missouri, Columbia. He has been researching the school uniform movement and the effectiveness of school uniform policies in public schools for almost 8 years now. His most recent book is *The School Uniform Movement and What It Tells Us About American Education: A Symbolic Crusade* (Scarecrow Press, 2004) and represents one of the most definitive statements regarding the history, theory, implementation practices, effectiveness, and unintended consequences of the school uniform movement in the United States. He lives in Columbia, Missouri, with his family and enjoys teaching and composing music.

Marilyn DeLong is professor and associate dean at the University of Minnesota. Dr. DeLong's expertise includes aesthetics and psychological aspects of clothing related to human behavior and design, history, and perception, and observer influence on patterns of perception. Awards include the ITAA Lifetime Achievement in Design and Aesthetics, Buckman Professor of Design Education, and the Award of Excellence from the American Textile Manufacturers Association for Research. Her education includes a PhD from the Ohio State University. Publications include *The Way We Look* (Fairchild, second edition) and numerous refereed research journal articles.

Linda Abel Fosseen is an adjunct instructor of psychology in the North Harris Montgomery Community College District at Tomball College. She grew up in Rhode Island and Massachusetts and received a BA in zoology from Connecticut College in New London. Her early career was in research, both with the Letterman Army Institute of Research (LAIR, Dental Division) in San Francisco, and the RNA research lab of Sheldon Penman at MIT in Cambridge, Massachusetts. After a move to Houston, Texas, she spent over a decade as a full-time school volunteer and educational consultant before returning to graduate school in educational psychology. She received both her MEd and PhD from the University of Houston at University Park. She is married, with a grown daughter, Katherine, and currently resides in Houston with husband John and six pet rabbits.

Eloise Hughes received her doctoral degree in education from the University of Houston in 1996, her MEd from Houston Baptist University in 1993, and her BSE from Abilene Christian University in 1969. Currently, she is a professor of education and director of field experience at Houston Baptist University. Dr. Hughes is a member and chapter president of Kappa Delta Pi, an education honor society; serves on the board of directors of the Consortium of State Organizations for Texas Teacher Education; and is president of the Texas Directors of Field Experience. Dr. Hughes taught secondary English and speech communication in Houston area schools for over 20 years and is now in her 11th year at Houston Baptist University. Her dissertation regarding attendance, discipline, and classroom atmosphere in public schools where uniforms for students were made mandatory was one of the first empirical studies in the nation on this topic. The Department of Education under President Clinton requested a copy of the research and corresponded with Dr. Hughes extensively on the subject of school uniforms. She has been the wife of James W. Hughes for 37 years and is mother to three grown children. Dr. Hughes remains extremely active in teacher education endeavors in the state of Texas.

Yunhee Kim was born and raised in Seoul, Korea. Dr. Yunhee Kim attended middle and high school wearing the compulsory school uniform. This experience led to her interest in uniforms as the topic for her doctoral dissertation. Her education includes a PhD from the University of Minnesota in 1998 and a master's degree from Korea University. Since returning to Korea, she has been an instructor at Hong-Ik University.

Sharon S. Pate, originally from Booneville, Mississippi, received her BS in fashion merchandising from Mississippi University for Women, where she minored in education. She received her MEd in education from Mississippi State University and a PhD in family and child sciences education with an emphasis in clothing and textile sciences at Florida State University. She was employed in retail management for a number of years and taught for 17 years in large public high schools in Ft. Myers and Panama City, Florida. Dr. Pate has taught at colleges and universities around the country including the University of North Texas, Gulf Coast Community College in Panama City, Florida, and Western Illinois University in Macomb, Illinois. At her current position at Illinois State University, Normal, she teaches apparel merchandising and management in the Department of Family and Consumer Sciences.

Bart A. Reynolds is a practitioner who understands the intricacies of public education. He received his bachelor's degree from Southern Utah University, his master's degree from Brigham Young University, and his EdD from Brigham Young University in educational leadership and foundations. Dr. Reynolds has 10 years of experience as a high school biology and chemistry teacher in rural Utah. For the past 10 years he has been principal of elementary, middle, and high schools in the Sevier School District. Dr. Reynolds is currently the director of administrative services in the Sevier School District in Central Utah. When not working he can be found enjoying his mountain retreat, where he Dutch-oven cooks, fishes, hunts, and rides his four-wheelers.

Viktoria Stamison graduated with honors from the Department of Sociology, University of California, Los Angeles, in 1991. She holds a master's degree in public administration from the University of Southern California. In 2003 she received her PhD in political science from the University of Southern California. She taught in the Political Science Department at the University of California, Irvine. Her areas of interest include American politics, education law and policy, and the rights of dependent populations, most notably children and animals. She has recently completed a manuscript on the symbolic politics of the California School Uniform Law.

Winston H. Tucker III grew up in New Jersey and attended public schools from his elementary through high school years. He earned his bachelor of science in education from Indiana University of Pennsylvania (IUP) in 1989. He earned both his master of education in teacher leadership in 1996 and his doctor of education in educational policy and administration in 1999 at the University of Minnesota. He has been employed by the Saint Paul Public Schools in Minnesota since 1989. He has taught American history, geography, economics, and humanities at the middle and high school levels. He served as an assistant principal and is currently principal at Murray Junior High School. He lives with his wife, Sheri, and 2-year-old daughter, Sophie, in Minnesota.